ROUTLEDGE LIBRARY EDITIONS:
EDUCATION

COMMUNIST EDUCATION

COMMUNIST EDUCATION

Edited by
EDMUND J. KING

Volume 6

Routledge
Taylor & Francis Group
LONDON AND NEW YORK

First published in 1963

This edition first published in 2012
by Routledge
2 Park Square, Milton Park, Abingdon, Oxfordshire OX14 4RN

Simultaneously published in the USA and Canada
by Routledge
711 Third Avenue, New York, NY 10017

First issued in paperback 2014

Routledge is an imprint of the Taylor and Francis Group, an informa company

© 1963 Methuen & Co Ltd.

All rights reserved. No part of this book may be reprinted or reproduced or utilised in any form or by any electronic, mechanical, or other means, now known or hereafter invented, including photocopying and recording, or in any information storage or retrieval system, without permission in writing from the publishers.

Trademark notice: Product or corporate names may be trademarks or registered trademarks, and are used only for identification and explanation without intent to infringe.

British Library Cataloguing in Publication Data
A catalogue record for this book is available from the British Library

ISBN 13: 978-0-415-66826-2 (Volume 6)
ISBN 13: 978-0-415-75325-8 (pbk)

Publisher's Note
The publisher has gone to great lengths to ensure the quality of this reprint but points out that some imperfections in the original copies may be apparent.

Disclaimer
The publisher has made every effort to trace copyright holders and would welcome correspondence from those they have been unable to trace.

Communist Education

edited by
EDMUND J. KING

METHUEN & CO LTD
36 ESSEX STREET LONDON WC2

First published in 1963
© *1963 Methuen & Co Ltd.*
Printed in Great Britain
by Cox & Wyman Ltd London,
Fakenham and Reading
Catalogue No. 2/2619/10

Contents

Preface	*page* vii
1 *The Concept of Ideology in Communist Education* DR EDMUND KING	18
2 *Soviet Educational Psychology* DR NEIL O'CONNOR	28
3 *Russian Children at Home and in School* MISS MARY WADDINGTON	55
4 *The Traditional and the Distinctive in Soviet Education* WILLIAM R. FRASER	78
5 *The Role, Status, and Training of Teachers in the U.S.S.R.* MISS A. ELIZABETH ADAMS	97
6 *Selection and Differentiation in Soviet Schools* PROFESSOR JOHN J. FIGUEROA	124

CONTENTS

7 *The Polytechnical Principle*   153
    KENNETH F. SMART

8 *Higher Education*   177
    DR C. L. WRENN

9 *East Germany – Distinctive Features*   200
    DAVID JOHNSTON

10 *Poland – a Statement of Aims and Achievements*   227
    DR BOGDAN SUCHODOLSKI

11 *China*   258
    DR JOSEPH A. LAUWERYS

12 *Common Ground between Communist and Western Education*   284
    DR JOSEPH KATZ

   Index   305

Preface

The contributors to this volume have all recently visited one or more communist countries to study the educational system as a whole or to survey particular points of interest. Each is well equipped academically for effective insights into the object of his special study, not only on general grounds but by virtue of having sustained interest in the chosen topic for a considerable period before visiting communist countries, and having subsequently collated and checked personal observation with evidence from all available sources. Several of the contributors are competent in the indigenous language concerned; and many are well able to converse effectively in other languages widely understood in the countries in question. Correspondence has been maintained for the clarification of particular points.

However, the main purpose of this book is to present as objectively as possible the "inside story" as seen and studied by professional educators. Few of us are professionally occupied in Comparative Education as a special academic field; but nearly all have made full use of comparative techniques, and all are widely enough acquainted with systems and standards in other countries to be able to make true comparisons. Some have visited the countries they deal with twice or oftener over an extended period of time, and so are also able to make internal comparison of trends or interpretations. All have had the advantage of comparing their observations at first hand with other eye-witnesses; and many have been able to welcome into their own universities or research institutes visitors from all the countries here described, and several other communist countries. Therefore, the theme of this volume is treated not as something utterly remote and alien but as an important human experiment personally interpreted and personally communicated.

For this reason, although there was naturally a preliminary sorting-out of interests to provide as effective a coverage as possible, each contributor was left to present his material at his own discretion. The writers' personalities and divergences of opinion or interest show through, as they should. Almost no editorial pruning has been done – and that only in one or two cases of clear reduplication. Even where more than one contributor has touched on a single topic from different angles, it has seemed preferable to leave the material as it stood; the accounts given are complementary rather than repetitive, and thus the general survey has been enriched. The only field relevant to communist education, at least in so far as that has developed in the U.S.S.R. and Europe, that has been formally omitted has been that of the historical antecedents. Unfortunately the contributor to whom this work was assigned fell ill, and was subsequently unable to complete it. However, the other chapters contain sufficient historical indications for the enterprising student of the communist background to piece together.

One point should be made clear – not for academic reasons, but as a concession to human susceptibilities in a torn world: none of the "Western" contributors is in any sense a communist; and of Professor Suchodolski no questions were asked, for obvious reasons. Most of us have been visiting lecturers in great American universities. The purpose of this entire presentation is not to persuade or convince anyone of anything (except of fact); but it is our aim to present proper material for understanding. That is the essence of humanity. It is the prerequisite of all scholarship worthy of the name. It is now more than ever an urgent matter of personal and political responsibility. Without tolerant and to some extent sympathetic reporting, there can be no effective communication; but such sympathy does not imply personal commitment any more than effective diagnosis by a doctor or teacher necessitates his sharing a patient's or pupil's state of health or mind. In much the same way as these specialists, but also with an intense awareness of our common humanity (and sometimes of our mutual need), we have done our utmost to feel and tell what communist education feels like "from inside".

CHAPTER I

The Concept of Ideology in Communist Education

The present chapter will attempt to provide a survey of the concept of ideology in communist systems generally; but it is convenient to concentrate primarily on the formative example of the Soviet Union. Illustrations will also be drawn from other countries' experience, especially to exemplify particular points.

Visitors to any Soviet school find much to remind them of any continental classroom; they also find much that is quite distinctive and striking. What occasions our surprise depends to some extent upon our own background of assumptions and practices. For example, if our school system concentrates on developing intellectual capacity, or on fostering technological readiness, or on strengthening character and integrity, we tend to be surprised at a school system which concentrates on something else, or which combines our objectives in a somewhat different way.

It is therefore important at the outset to recognize what the supporters of a system believe to be its most distinctive features. We should also endeavour to envisage the whole enterprise against a background of educational experiments and aims not only in our own country but over the world at large. These truisms need emphasizing all the more because both private and public education systems during recent centuries have tended to particularize. They have often had a restricted clientèle, or a narrowly conceived purpose, or a role that has been limited by the educational responsibilities of such agencies as churches, homes, or systematic vocational training. It is hard for educators to envisage education as a whole.

Perhaps the most distinctive single feature of communist education is that it does encompass all educational aims and concerns. The shaping of the future through the training of children is a commitment which extends far beyond the classroom and the workshop into society, and indeed into the ways of thinking and perceiving human relationships of every kind.

It is not claimed here that this ambitious programme is in every sense fulfilled. What teachers do, and what the textbooks contain, are often familiar enough. Observers sometimes think they see in the Soviet school system the early stages of a conveyor-belt system designed to deploy into Soviet technological enterprises the skilled personnel they require. Yet many rapidly developing countries seem to do the same. The increasing selectivity of the Soviet school system is no better example of "the career open to talents" than the French system. If we take the famous saying of Lenin, "The whole of education and upbringing shall be directed to their training in communist morals", that might have been acceptable to the Reverend Thomas Arnold (with a few appropriate changes). What is unique in a communist system is the total control of intellectual, technological, and (as far as possible) aesthetic and moral life. It is concentrated in the all-enveloping power of the Party over government, productivity, investment, schooling, extra-curricular activity, advertising, and every scrap of reading or entertainment.

In so far as such control depends upon efficiency and the willingness of others to fulfil requirements, any educational programme might presumably follow the Soviet model; but if it concentrated only on those aspects just referred to, such a comprehensive programme would still not have touched on the essence of communist education. This essence seems to inhere in the Marxist concept of consciousness and ideology.

Marx himself was far from consistent on this score, and the development of his ideas by successors has certainly been chequered in practice, not to say formulation. However, a few general statements can be validly made. Marxists follow their master not only in being extremely conscious of the influence of environment (including society) on consciousness, but in paying close attention to other aspects of consciousness than those normally developed in schools motivated by other philosophies.

It is not just a matter of different world views, different orders of sensibility and conscientiousness, or of a different valuation placed upon various kinds of creativity. Though we do well to heed those words of Marx, "Philosophers have only interpreted the world in various ways; but the real task is to alter it",[1] this and similar quota-

---
[1] Marx, K., *Eleven Theses on Feuerbach*, 1845.

tions scattered throughout the writings of Marx pay attention only to the social purpose of education, and the social framework of our good intentions.

We who are outside the Soviet system have not fastened on to its distinctive features even with such official Marxist statements as the following: "The distinguishing element in the educational process of mankind is the social-productive involvement of man, which alters his environment."[1] Nor do we have the full picture even with such a quotation as: "The problem of philosophy and the problem of developing the consciousness stand in the closest connexion with the problem of transforming social life."[2]

The heart and strength of a Marxist educational programme lie in its combination of influences on seeing, believing, cherishing and willing. School arrangements and social participation are so contrived that, as far as possible, all citizens share positively and constructively in the "dialectical process". This is in part the process of industrialization, social amelioration, and producing and distributing abundance for all; but it is much more a matter of producing a new world for a new kind of man, made by himself as he reconstructs the opportunities of civilization. Almost every school in the Soviet Union and Czechoslovakia, for example, contains many slogans describing education's purpose as the building up of a communist man in a communist world.

From what has already been said it is clear that such ideas as the creation of man by God for a particular purpose, or the perpetual and unchallengeable truthfulness of a particular principle, or indeed the integrity and autonomy of the individual, must logically be rejected.[3] It might therefore seem that Soviet educational ideas and practices must in every way be alien to those cherished in the West. We might suppose that Soviet practices could have little to teach us. But if we were to do so we should lose important opportunities of taking stock of our own position (much more modified in the past century than we usually suspect), and of discerning some inner inconsistencies within the Soviet ideological world itself.

The educational theories or assumptions of the Western world have

[1] Suchodolski, B., *Grundlagen der Marxistischen Erziehungstheorie*, Warsaw, 1961, pp. 408-9.
[2] Suchodolski, ibid., p. 24.
[3] Though some state-supported religious schools persisted in Poland and Hungary in 1962, and tax-supported religious instruction is given in Czechoslovakia (by priests) to children whose parents insist on it.

tended to be dualistic or multifarious. Among the most conspicuous educational claimants we can see the Church, the parents, and the State. The Christian Church has long claimed to be the supreme teaching institution. On the other hand parents have claimed, and been recognized by the Church as possessing, the right to bring up their children according to their choice. Thirdly the French revolutionaries claimed that education was a function of the State, a claim which has been repeated by a number of countries in our own time.

In any case, over and above these basic claims, distinct areas of perception, interest, and enterprise have been recognized in practice. Apart from the obvious distinction between the prerogatives of Caesar and God's prerogatives, deviations have been anticipated in practice because of free will, sin, and all the blandishments of the devil, the world and the flesh. Notoriously, too in some countries, distinct sections of society have been credited with exceptional virtues or vices. For example, they may have had a monopoly of culture, while others have been servile, or congenitally flawed. Truth and educational ideals so perceived, even in human terms, have seemed perpetual, absolute, and quite unaffected by technological and social change.

We shall soon go on to see how these naïve assumptions have undergone piecemeal attack in our own midst; but it is especially within the communist frame of reference that a thoroughgoing attempt has been made recently to reconcile all these isolationist or divergent elements in human soci ty, by planning systematically according to the logic of industrialization as interpreted by "scientific understanding" of the nature of man. The unifying and motivating concept in all this is that of ideology as the communists interpret it.

It is not a static but an *evolutionary* view of human perfections and possibilities. It is indeed "an inevitable historical process", though human beings can "accelerate the process" by learning to see, believe, will, and work aright. Man's greatest self-realization in thought and deed is therefore conditioned by his environment in past and present, and of conditional value by the criteria of the future.[1]

---

[1] Lenin's *The Teachings of Karl Marx* (1920) quotes with approval the following extract from Engels:

"The great basic idea that the world is not to be viewed as a complex of fully fashioned objects, but as a complex of processes, in which apparently stable objects, no less than the images of them inside our heads (our concepts), are undergoing incessant changes, arising here and disappearing there, and which with all apparent accident and in spite of all momentary retrogression, ultimately constitutes a progressive development – this great

Professor Suchodolski, in describing Marx's views on morality, says: "If man stays in the realm of feelings and imagination, he is morally lost; he triumphs, however, as a moral being when this 'subjective uplift' has as its consequence a concrete alteration in the life he leads." Professor Suchodolski goes on to explain that according to Marx's views this purpose of amendment for the future does not enjoy unlimited choice; it is a matter of deciding whether to co-operate in the "inevitable process" of historical evolution, the struggles of the workers, and the improvement of society, or not. This is what distinguishes it from the morality of the *bourgeoisie* and of the ruling class.[1]

Again: "The way towards revolutionary practice, to the revolutionary activity of the proletariat for the destruction of the capitalist order and of the *bourgeoisie's* supremacy, will from now on be the criterion for educational theory and practice. This criterion will give a sense of direction different from those trends of *bourgeois* educational thought which have played a progressive role at particular stages of historical development, but which have entailed reactionary consequences in the struggle of the *bourgeoisie* against the proletariat."[2]

This all sounds very far away, and exclusively connected with a particular political and economic point of view. The foreignness of a communist point of view seems particularly striking when we contrast it with the concept of Natural Law, which has played so great a part in the development of Western civilization. A. P. d'Entrèves in his book *Natural Law* (London, 1951) says that Natural Law, going back to God, derives its authority from the fact that it is confirmed and implemented by revelation. Natural Law, he says, is absolutely binding and overrules all other laws. It precedes them in time "because it came into

[1] Suchodolski, op. cit., p. 252.
[2] Suchodolski, op. cit., p. 410.

---

basic idea has, particularly since the time of Hegel, so deeply penetrated the general consciousness that hardly anyone will now venture to dispute it in its general form. But it is one thing to accept it in words, quite another thing to put it into practice on every occasion and in every field of investigation.

"In the eyes of dialectic philosophy, nothing is established for all time, nothing is absolute or sacred. On everything and in everything it sees the stamp of inevitable decline; nothing can resist it save the unceasing process of formation and destruction, the unending ascent from the lower to the higher – a process of which that philosophy itself is only a simple reflexion within the thinking brain."

Quoted in Professor M. Oakeshott's *Social and Political Doctrines of Contemporary Europe*, London, 1940, pp. 103–4.

existence with the very creation of man as a rational being, nor does it vary in time, but remains unchangeable."[1]

After reviewing the widespread belief that this natural essence of law is attainable by reason, and is a mould for all forms of command and behaviour, D'Entrèves goes on to show how different is the belief in Natural Law from the belief of legal positivists and those who stress the sociological background. He says: "Natural Law theorists would never have admitted that law is merely the expression of the standards of a particular group or society. They believed in absolute values and they conceived of law as a means to achieve them. 'Law is the furtherance of what is good and equitable.' 'There is no law unless it be just.' 'The end of all political association is the preservation of the natural and imprescriptible rights of man.' I have chosen my quotations at random. We are no longer concerned with what divided their authors, we are concerned with what they had in common."[2]

Behind all these judgements passed upon human rights, public laws, and private morality, was the "internal court" of the human conscience, according to those who believed in Natural Law. Though Churchmen always stressed the reinforcement and indeed the prior origin of revelation, rationalists have always believed that the ultimate perennial truths could be discerned by the use of human reason alone. It took man a long time to be able to distinguish morality from law, so as to be able to question law. With this recognition in mind, defenders of Natural Law are not afraid to admit that every system of *laws* corresponds to a particular ideology or sociological background; but then they go on to protest that the *moral* basis that alone justifies laws, and "absolute truth", are private possessions – inalienable possessions. Law can have no competence in the court of conscience.[3]

It was concepts such as these that enabled men to stand out against the unreasonable commands of kings, as Antigone disobeyed Creon. Because of them churches and priestly hierarchies have been challenged; scientific concepts have been vindicated against all traditions, as Bruno and Galileo vindicated them. It was on the basis of an inner conviction that Ramus was emboldened to use Aristotelian logic to refute claims advanced on Aristotle's authority in the Renaissance

---

[1] *Decretum Gratiani*, about 1140, quoted by D'Entrèves, *Natural Law*, p. 34.

[2] D'Entrèves, op. cit. p. 80.

[3] D'Entrèves, Chapter 5, especially p. 88.

University of Paris; and although he did later produce a system of logic of his own invention, his first intellectual rebellion was caused by something other than this system or a prevailing climate of opinion. Discordant and untimely voices, claiming the right of conscience, have expanded and universalized the great manifestoes of liberty.

Less articulate experimenters, with a similar kind of conviction, have pushed the critical inquiries of science beyond what was until recently imagined to be discoverable and indeed thinkable. What they sought was "objective truth" – in no way dependent for its objectivity upon technological advance, social change, or climates of opinion. The world would be an infinitely poorer place if it were not for this conviction.

However, as has so often happened in the course of human history, devices which have been used to overthrow authority have later taken on an unchallenged sacrosanctity of their own. Or at least they have had attributed to them an autonomy and independence which they could not possess. There has survived into our midst the old concept of absolutely uninvolved free wills, absolutely disengaged and free agents, and (so to speak) the divine right of every single mind. Meanwhile, the process of industrialization and the division of labour have failed to reconstitute a meaningful synthesis of our complementary viewpoints, or an overall world view to give value and constructive significance to the separate parts.[1]

One of the great appeals of the communist concept of ideology to many observers in our own countries, and still more to people in the uncommitted nations, is precisely the supposition that communist ideology reconciles for the first time all the progressive claims made by outstanding individuals and enterprising groups in the past, and all in accordance with the new opportunities afforded by industrialization. Manifestly these make it possible for the great majority of mankind, hitherto greatly underprivileged, to claim the educational, social, political, and economic advantages previously enjoyed by the restricted number who formed the ruling class. Yet it should not be supposed that communist theory and practice sprang suddenly into being without forerunners or concomitants. Both in their virtues and in their faults they reflect both. To understand the force of modern notions of ideology, we have to pay attention to some of these

[1] I have dealt with this problem at great length in my forthcoming book *Nations on Wheels*, and to a lesser extent in my *World Perspectives in Education*, Methuen, 1962.

concomitants and antecedents. It is necessary therefore to make a brief excursion into the history of ideas.

In Mannheim's book, *Ideology and Utopia*, the author begins with an instructive account of how the so-called "objectivity" of truths guaranteed by the medieval Church lost its axiomatic force. He illustrates very well the growing realization in our civilization of the environmental involvement of mankind, and of the need for human beings to express and develop their own points of view in particular contexts. A. N. Whitehead provides a similar historical account in his *Adventures of Ideas*.

By contrast, a belief in absolute and perennially valid truths had persisted; for Descartes (1595-1650) and Spinoza (1632-77) tried to prove their philosophical theories as though they were geometrical problems depending on pure reasoning and certain axiomatic principles. They actually set out parts of their work in this almost geometrical form. In a not dissimilar manner, the Stuart monarchy proclaimed the divine right of kings as something beyond argument.

However, one consequence of the Renaissance and the Reformation was a much heavier reliance not only on personal insight, but also on the repeated testing of concepts in the light of their practical outcome or their social and political implications. Convinced of this necessity, John Locke (1632-1704) was marked by a lack of dogmatism. He was contemptuous of metaphysics. Both he and Kant (1724-1804) were concerned with the limits on human knowledge and understanding. In order to protect themselves against authoritarianism, they relied heavily either on *empiricism* in the case of Locke, or on the independent and *personal* (or "legislative") power of reasoning in the case of Kant. It is worth while placing Kant in this company because he is often thought of exclusively in terms of abstract rationalism – the pure use of "reason" – rather than as belonging in any way to a school of thought paying attention to the practical engagement of human intellects and value systems in the world of material reality.

In the field of physical science, above all, the conspicuous contribution of the Renaissance was insistence on observation and experimentation. From the seventeenth century onwards much more painstaking and instrumentally supported evidence was used as the basis for scientific theories; but theories and "universal laws" still attracted a very wide measure of public interest and esteem. Yet as we traverse the eighteenth century, especially in the British Isles, an increasing tendency to notice the environment and to consider its implications and value as a criterion made impatience arise with theorizing as such. David Hume was not only a great empiricist; he was also the first of the great Utilitarians. That is to say, he believed not only in the need to test conclusions against past observed results, but in the need to assess values in terms of their future long-term results for human happiness.

For such people, reason operates within a world which it can perfect. However, Hume and his contemporaries still lived in a largely unindustrialized world, in which it might have been supposed that a way of life without mechanization and on an agrarian basis would be able to guide the development of mankind in accordance with norms familiar from time immemorial.

The sense of a nearly static world, and perennially valid principles, was much more keenly felt in France. Before the Revolution it was almost impossible for thinkers and would-be reformers to engage in any practical programme of political, social, or even technological reorientation. As has often been pointed out, these circumstances made French philosophers and liberals seek predominantly for "universally valid" abstract principles, and to express them in such great manifestoes as the Declaration of the Rights of Man. There is more than a mere element of the same cast of thought in Kant's insistence on the formulation of universally valid rules, and on a careful distinction being made between perpetual "things" (i.e. abstractions) and everyday "appearances" (i.e. real objects).[1]

A quite different attempt – to see abstract truths in historical *progress* towards self-realization in society and through institutions, not to speak of everyday circumstances – is found to a much greater degree in the Idealists such as Hegel (1770–1831), or in Rousseau's concept of the "General Will" (1762). Hegel is perhaps best known for his theory of the "dialectic of history" – the theory that social and historical progress manifests itself by a series of contradictions, each eventually resulting in a synthesis, which in turn becomes contradicted by its successor phase, and so on. This is undoubtedly an evolutionary theory. It is therefore to be placed in contradistinction to the pre-industrial and static theories recently considered.

Romantic thinkers too sought to escape from what seemed to them

---

[1] For a fuller statement of the paradoxical meaning attached to these terms by Kant, see W. H. Walsh's account in the *Year Book of Education* for 1957, pp. 48–9.

the unmanageable horrors of contemporary civilization, by taking flight away from what Blake called "dark satanic mills" into a golden age which had passed and was the more unchallengeable for that. Musicians, poets, and architects vied with one another in producing masterpieces of grace, order, and perpetual "cultural" respectability. Nevertheless, even such work reveals an inner turbulence and exuberance which is seen to better purpose in the Utopian planning of some socialists, or the piecemeal yet more fruitful planning of Utilitarians.

Jeremy Bentham's (1748–1832) impatience with "fictions" is notorious. A catalogue of his proposals for constitutional and legal reform astonishes the modern observer, simply because so many of them have become actualized fact, or nearly so. Likewise, Robert Owen and other reconstructionists were not content merely to theorize. They were very much men of practical affairs who sought not simply to improve working conditions and wages, but to rejuvenate and humanize and industrialize the world as an educational no less than as a social experiment. To that extent, all these reformers seem to have shared the optimistic eighteenth-century French view of the perfectibility of human nature, especially by perfecting social arrangements.

This was the world into which in their different ways Marx, Darwin, and Freud made their entry. In the present chapter it would be out of place to do more than remind readers that these three thinkers all concentrated on historical and contextual influences on the personality, thinking, and evaluation of human beings.

As a biologist, Darwin was supremely conscious of the interplay of environment and hereditary influences, so as to differentiate species and secure continuous readaptation to the challenges and possibilities of an external world. We very often forget, in reading Darwin, his keen realization that living creatures also help to "manufacture" or predispose their environment to suit their present trends. Freud, for his part, was of course preoccupied with sexual experiences and the influence of sexual concern on the later development of the human individual. His social sense was largely restricted to considerations of one instinct, and what we may call family influences. For that reason he is repudiated by Russian psychologists in favour of those who concentrate attention on wide social and economic influences on personality.

Marx stands in a somewhat ambiguous position. As a pupil of Hegel he also seems to think that there are significant and perpetual determining factors, for he complains that the person ignorant of these is the least free of all and is most thoroughly predetermined in his action.[1] Yet characteristically Marx believed that the methods of production and distribution would determine the social structure, the various roles exercised by man, and the culture of his period or class. More than in the overall outlook of period or class, Marx believed in the strongly formative ideologies or "world views" developed in people according to their sectional engagement in what we would now call technological processes.[2]

For these reasons he refused to lay down a set of permanent objectives. Equally he warned his followers against the idea that knowledge could be the same everywhere and of universal validity.[3] He distinguished knowledge which aimed merely at classification from knowledge which was oriented towards action.[4] So far from believing in abstract intellectualism, he did not consider that it could be legitimate in all situations. Politics, for example, could be studied only from a Party standpoint and could be truly taught only in a Party school.[5] Indeed, in Leninist parlance, the term "objective" implies a degree of Party dedication which makes the word synonymous with "partisan". A proof of this is seen in the word used for it in a Czech translation in my presence (*stranický*—from *strana*, the Party).

This is an interpretation which does not surprise us quite so much when we reflect that many millions of people have long held the same ideas about religions. We hear such phrases as "a good Catholic (or Islamic) outlook" used with all the assumption of objectivity. In a less comprehensive or totalitarian way Sir John Wolfenden reflects a similar point of view in his article on the Public Schools in the *Year Book of Education* for 1957, which seems to assume the universal paramountcy and perennial validity of the ideal of the Christian gentleman, and of the schools which most characteristically foster that ideal.

A more thoroughgoing analysis of these ideological teachings in practice is seen in Mannheim's *Ideology and Utopia*, pp. 126 and 127. The material or technological environment surrounding the subject or observer, and involving him, leads him to observe and eventually to reconstruct a new "objective reality", which in turn will lead to a

[1] See Mannheim, K., *Ideology and Utopia*, Harvest Books edition, p. 189.
[2] Mannheim, op. cit., p. 130.
[3] Mannheim, op. cit., p. 167.
[4] Mannheim, op. cit., p. 185.
[5] Mannheim, op. cit., p. 147.

revision of the world. Therefore knowledge and personality are not strictly separable from the social dynamic, either in the influence of the past on them, or in their collective and constructive influences on the future. Thus there can be no question of intellectual views being alone legitimate in all situations.[1]

This interpenetration of personality, culture, and socio-economic reconstruction was a notion that had been cherished by Marx from his youth. For example, in his *The Holy Family and Other Early Philosophical Writings* (Berlin, 1953, p. 21), Marx had said: "It is not enough that thought should lead to realization (or actuality). Actuality must itself lead to thought." Professor Suchodolski[2] interprets this text of Marx and others like it in the following way. According to Marx, "the distinguishing element in the education of the human being is the socio-productive activity of mankind, which alters the environment. This process proceeds historically; it takes on different forms at different stages of development – according to its circumstances, its productive forces, and the social structure." He goes on to specify that according to Marxist criteria good education must essentially lead to revolutionary activity, as is shown by the quotations already given.

Although Marx stresses the need for this revolutionary activity, and for conscious participation in the historical process, he still describes the latter as "inevitable". To this extent he reflects a prevalent, mechanistic nineteenth-century conviction about the inevitability of progress or evolution. Human advance was often considered to be wellnigh independent of willing or contrivance. It was for this reason that men could so often try to discern the "hidden rules" or laws.

As practical a philosopher as Bentham could aspire to be the Newton of the social sciences, almost as though men's orbits and eclipses were directed as mechanistically as the heavenly bodies. Therefore there were inherent limits on direct action. Thus on the one hand in a manifesto of Marx's in 1850 the proletariat in France was encouraged to support the *bourgeoisie* in their seizure of power (though the proletariat should not permit itself to be disarmed, but should look forward to the seizure of power by itself). On what seems to an outsider to be a comparable occasion, however, German socialists were forbidden by Lenin to

[1] ibid., p. 133. See also Professor H. B. Acton's essay on "Dialectical Materialism" in *Education and the Philosophic Mind*, ed. A. V. Judges, London, 1957, for an admirable and succinct account of these views in relation to education.

[2] Suchodolski, op. cit., pp. 408–9.

support a *bourgeois* reform movement. Profitable action evidently depends on a sociological understanding of history and on topically accurate diagnosis, as Marx made clear. He therefore distinguished his particular interpretation of socialist progress from the piecemeal, Fabian-type socialism familiar to us and from the visionary Utopianism of continental socialists.

Marx's didactic insistence on orthodox socialist *interpretation* must be integrally linked with his concept of ideology as an educative force. Ideological conviction is not simply a matter of purposeful activity for the future, or "socially useful labour" in the present; it is a matter also of reinterpreting the past according to rules, so that we can see that it is always on the side of socialist progress. "The past is on our side".... "What is before us is for us." By means of a proper study of dialectical materialism, the certainty of science can be brought into the humane learning, as well as the dutiful willing and the energetic striving, of those determined to establish a communist millennium.

This all helps the Marxist to differentiate between power in the past, seen as an arbitrary personal power or the State-based exploitation of the proletariat, from the "concept of power as a *social* control serving collective aims".[1] At this point we may remark that the influence of Moscow (perhaps Peking in other regions) depends in the satellites quite largely on a reverence for the orthodox line that comes near to servility. Seeking topical correctness, the uncertain controllers of wavering destinies are quick to turn to the new powerhouse of "directives" in a way that is strangely reminiscent of previous regard for "Holy Mother Church". Even in Czechoslovakia – a country fiercely proud of its indigenous cultural idioms – an important Ministry of Education spokesman in 1962 turned up a brochure written in *Russian* when asked a tricky point about impending developments in Czechoslovak "polytechnical" education. The adulation of Russian primacy in this and many other matters depends not on force but on the excessive hallowing of meticulous ideological orthodoxy.

To provide appropriate teaching, and to keep interpretations consonant with present achievements, the well-organized Communist Party as a small managerial *élite* is clearly necessary according to the Marxist point of view, especially as elaborated by Lenin. The Party is the guarantor of the correct understanding of history. It is for this reason that no one may teach history in the Soviet Union unless he is an

[1] Mannheim, *Freedom, Power and Democratic Planning*, p. 52.

accredited member of the Communist Party. In Czechoslovakia all students training to be teachers must be members of the Party youth organization (Č.S.M.), and become members of the teachers' trade union as soon as admitted to college. Likewise a communistic outlook is taught to young children not so much as a matter of catechism or dogma, but through historically interpretive studies, and also through the way in which the concept of physical basis for all human activity is communicated. Within the limits of a teacher's competence, for example, physics is considered to be a cultural as well as a utilitarian or theoretical subject. Still more, studies of geography, climate, economics, and technological development are all nationally directed towards productivity – not only for practical purposes but also as an active interpretation of the present condition and future prospects of mankind. Some objectionable features in this presentation will be considered at the end of this chapter; but there is nothing essentially wrong with attempting a synthesis.

To divert to communist use a Christian phrase, "He that is not with us is against us." Alternative or purely experimental conclusions about the nature of man and his prospects can be permitted only in so far as they are judged by authority to be consonant with the approved interpretation. No books are published, no newspapers printed, no broadcasts take place, that are not fully approved. Care has been taken to ensure that every definition in every book shall be acceptable according to present interpretations. The next edition of the same book may reveal a quite different formulation to suit a new stage of the "inevitable historical process". Anyone aspiring to a position of responsibility, like all those undergoing any form of further or higher education, must have courses in dialectical and historical materialism and pass the necessary examinations. As we have seen in recent years, it is not only churches and other ideological adversaries of communist interpretation that have suffered oppression if not persecution, but also unwelcome definitions within the scientific world itself. The Lysenko controversy is a case in point.

The literary field is under special supervision. The visual arts too are carefully watched for fear of contamination. There is space on everyone's library ticket in the U.S.S.R. to show a whole series of borrowings. Foreign books and broadcasts are particularly guarded against, though some latitude is allowed here for publications which are kept in the original tongue. Presumably they are read and consumed only by those whose preparatory training has been politically enriched and made safe.

The concept of ideology, therefore, it is clear, must not be considered only in the narrow sense of an external picture of life. It is not simply a cognitive imagery as contemplated by many intellectuals (among them occasionally Mannheim). It comes closer to the apostolic fervour of St Paul, when he spoke of emptying himself out so that Christ might come in. It includes the passionate will to believe exemplified by the prayer: "Lord I believe; help Thou my unbelief." At times it seems to an outsider to approach Tertullian's dictum: *Credo quia impossibile* ("I believe, because it is impossible").

Much attention, therefore, is paid not to pure intellectualism alone, but to the careful cultivation of co-operative dispositions ("a positive attitude"), and an emotional submission to the working out of the total plan which may in its results be compared with the pious ejaculation "Thy will be done".[1]

Yet this patient docility, so clearly marked as to remind any visitor to a Soviet school of the atmosphere of many convents or colleges elsewhere, is not the whole story. School posters remind children to work and study as Lenin did. In the psychological sense of the word, they are socialized from earliest infancy, especially after setting foot in the primary school at the age of seven and taking part in the various stages of the youth organizations. We must remember that it is the latter that sometimes have a greater generally educative power than the schools. By implicating and developing to the fullest extent a total commitment of self to the constructive achievement of the dialectical process, in learning and in technology as well as in social activity, the Soviet system has tremendous power of habituation. Through corporate engagement it develops a strong sense of solidarity. Through the rubbing away of awkwardness and oddity, it very often secures a commitment of the will and a sense of conversion comparable with the character-training force of Public Schools in the United Kingdom or religious schools elsewhere.

Inseparable from the total refurbishing of self and society is the deep conviction of overall righteousness, even if dissatisfaction is provoked with certain details. Practical work and aesthetic appreciation are, according to this prescription, ultimately inseparable from *moral rightness*.

[1] See W. H. Walsh, *Year Book of Education*, 1957, pp. 46-48.

The average or weak personality is sure of the protection of the group. The communist school may seem in some ways to aim at the protection and indeed the production of the average. Undoubtedly, a disciplined labour force is the main immediate objective of the school system. The increase in selectivity for various types of school after the age of 15 which characterizes the 1958 reforms seems again to envisage a docile majority led or at least activated by an expert *élite* of politicians, scientists, and production men and women. Nevertheless there can be no denying that on the whole Soviet children seem extremely well cared for and contented. Partly because the ideological concept is so wide in its implications, and also because of the forms in which it is embodied in para-curricular activities, the gifted or enterprising child is able to feel some excitement and venturing into new interests, new areas of self-development, and at the same time a real commitment to various plans for scientific inquiry or increased productivity.

Many references will be made throughout this book to such para-curricular activities as are fostered by the youth organizations (the Octobrists under the age of 10; the Pioneers from 10 to 15; and the Komsomol or Communist League of Youth, from 15 until eligible to enter the Party). At this point attention will be drawn only to their ideological significance, and to their great power of initiating the young people of communist countries by definite stages into the activity and commitment not only of school but of life and work in the widest possible sense. Posters remind them: "We are learning to live and work as communists", and "Socialism today, communism tomorrow".

In the earliest kindergarten years, long before children are old enough for school, very much emphasis is placed on "self-organization" in youthful collectives for approved forms of co-operation. For example, children in the day-nurseries help with tiny brooms and pails to keep their rooms clean, to water the house-plants and wash their leaves, and also to develop in themselves and each other a "socialist sense of responsibility". In the earliest classes at school, the young Octobrists (called "Sparks" – *Jiskre* – in Czechoslovakia) form a definite link with the older pioneers who began by welcoming newcomers to school with flowers and gifts on their very first day, and who keep up a continuous, personalized tutelary relationship throughout (called *shefstvo* in the U.S.S.R.). This is arranged in three stages: guardians in classes 3 and 4 look after children in classes 1 and 2, and so on throughout the 8-year school. The highest importance is attached to this kindly guardianship and invigilation by older children of those slightly junior to them.

Thus socialization and gradual indoctrination are assured in the blandest possible of ways, by utilizing the child's natural wish to conform and be welcomed. Admiration must be felt for the gentle patience with which the occasional nonconformist is treated. No overt steps are immediately taken; and no punishment is inflicted. The recalcitrant one before long usually does what is required by happily following the example of the others. If an inquirer asks a question about those who do not develop "a positive attitude", the answer will probably concern the use of Pioneers. Pioneers, we may be told, must acquire social skill by stages; and these stages depend in part upon success in handling (gently, and by good example) those who do not quite "understand".

Pioneers, spruced up and eager, attend a Pioneer house or corner on an average of two days a week, spending about two hours there. During this time they will almost certainly take part in one of the special activities or clubs (such as those devoted to physical education, dancing, music, nature, tourism, art, "technology", international surveys, and the like); but a "Pioneer parade", such as took place every Saturday in a boarding school visited, can be a more important proceeding. The programme of school life and Pioneer activity for the preceding week was reviewed; and that for the ensuing week was mapped out and discussed. The Pioneers discussed their fellow-members, and non-positive children were reprimanded or advised. Such unsatisfactory brethren were defined as those "whose behaviour does not correspond to the rules of the group".

To make sure of good standards all round, the Pioneer units in a boarding school, for instance, are each graded weekly by the full-time paid Pioneer-tutor, and rewarded with one of three categories of banner. Within and across the unit (*zveno*) arrangement, children bring much influence to bear on each other through personal friendships (which are warmly encouraged), through praise and formal "honour mention" in the wall newspapers or on the school's intercommunication system, or by attracting the attention of such higher bodies as the school's entire Pioneer brigade (*druzhina* – the word means "companionship"). At meetings of parents, the Pioneer leaders will disclose and discuss the behaviour of their comrades. In all this they are assisted not only by special tutors but by the ordinary teachers, and above all by younger teachers and students in teacher-training, who are encouraged to regard the youth service as particularly valuable experience. "The young teacher is the Pioneer's best friend" says a huge poster in a teachers' college.

Thus there is no sense whatever that children live only in a children's world. There is a *continuum* of interest, gradually enlarging horizons until these encompass the whole adult world of socialist endeavour. In the most junior classroom in the Soviet school the wall display includes a red star, whose five points radiate out to the photographs of the most meritorious pupils (not always for scholastic reasons, but definitely not excluding them). Alongside this are scenes from the juvenile progress of Lenin, the "teacher of all nations". These also appear on postage stamps, in the Soviet equivalent of religious pictures (tinged with the same Nirvana-like rosy mist) showing the child Lenin studying, or playing chess with his father. (In 1960 Pioneer house pictures still showed him doing the same with Stalin, and pictures of Khrushchev were almost entirely absent.) The friendly white marble or plaster statue of Lenin stands with open arms before a crimson velvet drape, and surrounded with flowers. Picture after picture shows Lenin suffering the little children to come unto him, and leading them gently by the hand through flowery fields, or showing affection to dumb animals. There is no mistaking this aura; but it is not a cloistered thing. Over the statue and the pictures appear slogans with red letters: "Long live communism – the bright hope for the future of mankind"; and "Children, live like communists!"; and, still more to the point, "Study, study, study as Lenin studied", and "Live, think, and work like communists!"

Though as many as 90 per cent of the children become Pioneers at the appropriate age, admission is far from being a casual matter. It is accompanied by all the selection procedure and back-stage "vetting" associated with admission to some faiths, or to sodalities and confraternities within the Roman Catholic faith. Neophytes are admitted one at a time or in small groups at a special assembly. It is a ceremonious occasion, at which a solemn promise is recited by the Pioneers before investiture. This in turn may be followed by an obeisance to the flag of the brigade. Reminiscent in some ways of Boy Scout procedure, this initiation is nevertheless into an organization which considers "boy-scoutism" irrelevant and frivolous. Good deeds and honour and enterprise by themselves are potentially extrinsic to the purposes of the collective.

Therefore every endeavour is made to secure complete interpenetration of school, youth organization, work-orientation and life-perspective. There is little hope of preferment in the youth organizations unless pupils are diligent in class work, the marks from which are carefully reviewed by the Pioneer groups at regular meetings, and most of all when election time comes. Each lesson may begin with a reminder to study as Lenin studied. The language exercises reiterate such ideological material as: "When was V. I. Lenin born?"; "In what town was V. I. Lenin born?"; "What town were you born in?"; "Who was the founder of Leningrad?"

Yet indoctrination and implied acts of uniformity are far from being the whole story. The excessively standardized curriculum and pace of the schools would be bound to fall short of requirements if it were not for the supplementation and evocation afforded by the youth organizations – to weaker children and infant genius alike. Special help and encouragement are available through "peer" assistance in the school detachment of the Pioneer organization; but to a much greater extent it is provided in the special Pioneer houses. Soviet educators are wont to place particular stress on the usefulness of these places for diversifying children's interests in the various clubs just described. They also make no bones about the "stretching" of really able children through the special instruction provided in the youth organization, the special apparatus and workshops, and the systematic competitions. These *konkursy* may be local, regional, or all-Union. At that level we find the great Olympiads for mathematics, &c. (Sport competitions are "Spartakiads".)

In the matrix of the youth organizations, such prowess is strongly socialized. It carries with it the glow of religious merit, as well as earning the approbation of one's comrades. National and local festivals, with songs and dances and athletic displays, reinforce the total commitment of endeavour. Massed physical exercises and choirs are important collectivizing devices. Posters, stamps, books, films, and broadcasts remind Soviet children that their socialist world-building is a multinational and multilingual enterprise within the Soviet Union, and an international revolution of the human condition beyond that. Hence, international correspondence clubs in the youth organizations are mostly concerned with other "socialist" countries, or with "socialists" elsewhere. Within this traffic, as in the study of literature, the observer may find a preoccupation with what is politically blessed for the time being. "What is the English for *Miru Mir*?" asks an English-club poster. The abundant and gay English-language magazines in one show Pioneer house had been printed in Bucarest. (The Rumanians use our alphabet!) Galsworthy and Dickens are favoured authors, because of their grim social documentation.

Yet we should not dismiss this careful cultivation of ideology as a simple pumping-in of propaganda. At one youth club (*Komsomol*) meeting in Leningrad, youngsters aged 18 to 27 or so seemed better informed about some current English and American literature than most of their visitors from those countries. After considerable discussion (in English) of Saroyan, Steinbeck, Graham Greene and similar socially indicative writers, they asked their guests for their opinions, for example, on "the later as distinct from the earlier phases of Graham Greene". They were puzzled about our unawareness of contemporary Russian writing, wondering whether to attribute it to plain ignorance or to ideological antipathy. They were pleased that we had got as far as Chekhov, not surprised that we knew about Sokolov and Ehrenburg, and openly amused because Pasternak was such a favourite.

It is on the activity side that a special mention should be made of ideological incorporation. I do not refer only or mainly to the "polytechnical principle" and "work experience", which will be dealt with in another chapter, important though these developments are in communicating the cognitive aspect of ideology and in evoking commitment. The juvenile practice of at least two hours' "socially useful labour" every week is continued in "working brigades" as long as the Party managers can contrive. Teams of young men may be seen helping with road reconstruction, drain-laying, and various industrial or agricultural tasks. Doubtless, they are specially invited to participate. More significant, therefore, is the (spontaneous?) formation of brigades from among the tenants of apartments, or even of university and college teaching staff, to keep streets and gardens tidy. No doubt many of them are at least as passive in disposition towards this activity as many of those taking part in civic and religious observance in other countries. Yet the work seems diligently done: the parks are made tidy, the paint is laid on, and the gesture reinforces a most important concept. One Czech lady of my acquaintance gives free German lessons to three advanced students as her "socialist contribution", though she and her family have materially lost much since 1947. "Labour is a matter of honour and duty."

Despite the perpetual striving forward portrayed in public art, and often exemplified in personal example, not everything in a communist country is as rosy or as educationally successful as we are often given to think, of course. A kind of wry optimism, tinged perhaps with cynicism, is shown in the Czech slang expression for a fat abdomen – *socialismus*; but the joke itself shows that the official propaganda point has been taken. However, the undoubted "Y.M.C.A. feeling" and near-religious dedication that evidently suffice for so many fail to be the complete answer and purpose for everyone. So much is evident not only from official complaints about racketeers, failure to reach production targets, and the like; it is also obvious to any visitor to a Soviet city who is accosted in the streets by a number of youths eager to deal illicitly in foreign currency or clothing exchanges. But the relatively trivial character of these offences (according to our standards) perhaps gives us a clue to their proper interpretation. Teachers and other responsible people constantly criticize regulations in minor detail. The admission of foreigners inevitably introduces a living criticism of the Marxist orthodoxy. Yet those responsible for the ideological containment of the Soviet world are showing a sign of strength rather than otherwise in closing an eye to minor ideological irregularities, provided that these can ultimately be reconciled within the correct communist framework.

Similarly the so-called "thaw" in the literary world, and the succession of complaints permitted to appear in Party newspapers about inadequacies of interpretation or conduct are one more sign that no fixed standard can be finally acceptable. It is all part and parcel of the concept of evolutionary justice,[1] evolutionary truth, &c. &c.

Everyone knows that Soviet publishing tends to be didactic and politically purposeful. Theatre, ballet, broadcasting and even statuary must be educative. That the lesson has gone home is evident from the willingness of Soviet citizens to read textbooks where we might read paper-backs or glossy magazines. But teacher-parent associations, trade union meetings, and the most unexpected occasions of a more practical kind are also made as evocative, informative, and acculturating as the Party managers can contrive. Undoubtedly the character-forming influence of socially useful activities, the inducements offered in

[1] Mannheim, *Freedom, Power and Democratic Planning*, p. 218.

co-operative farming and similar collective enterprises, and the reinforcement given by such conspicuous triumphs as the space flights, all help to build a new Soviet personality with a politically correct world outlook.

The tedious insistence on "the collective" does not necessarily grate on Russian ears any more than a similar monotony in American concern for the community and other forms of social engagement does in the United States. But for all its insistence on work, social purpose, and other "links with life", much Soviet educational thinking seems to many Western Europeans to have over-intellectual origins; it also has links with the Tolstoyan sense of Messianism in "the Third Rome", which in turn derives from the Russian Orthodox background. The earliest Soviet educational theorists were conscious of their indebtedness to American life-orientation theories of education, to activity methods, and to the "polytechnical" ideas of such pioneers as Robert Owen. The post-1958 reforms, with their renewed insistence on work perspectives and the "polytechnical" idea, seem to indicate some dissatisfaction with academic trends under the school programme initiated under Stalin.

It is significant that Professor Kairov, President of the Academy of Pedagogical Sciences of the R.S.F.S.R., when invited to give three lectures in London in 1959 on any subject of his choice, offered to speak entirely on problems of moral education. A similar preoccupation has marked the observations of other Soviet educators in recent years. Over-intellectualism and over-practicality have both evidently had similar shortcomings.

Visiting Soviet observers in the United Kingdom have taken a great deal of interest in the processes of habituation and character forming which Britons often associate with the great Public Schools. Clearly it is realized that instruction, training, and vocational and political moulding are still not enough. Something stronger and more positively active is evidently called for, at least among the *élite*. This in part explains the tremendous growth in recent years of boarding schools. They rose from 47 to 2,700 between 1958 and 1961. The number of children attending them was given as 600,000 in 1961 and is expected to reach two and a half million by 1965.

These schools are described as the schools for the future, and "the schools of communism". In them every conceivable device of habituation, emotional link, religious aura, as well as activity and instruction, are used to foster an ideological dedication which is comparable only with the devotion expected in religiously inspired schools outside. Soviet leaders are at pains to point out, however, that their boarding schools are every child's school. That they are popular is shown by the readiness of parents to send their children there, even though fees must be paid for boarding. Boarding school children may spend week-ends or other long periods at home; but both in connexion with these schools and with the ordinary type, abundant provision is made for extended corporate activities on ordinary days and at the week-ends, and above all during the long summer holidays, so as to enfold the children in a totality of protective and evocative occasions.

This incomplete picture is enough to show the vital influence for communist education of the concept of ideology in its complementary and interpenetrating aspects. It interprets the past; it delineates horizons in the present; it helps to evaluate man's status and possibilities; it orientates towards assured achievements in the future; but most of all it attempts to co-ordinate and make mutually helpful the cognitive, conative, aesthetic and affective aspects of personality. Educational systems elsewhere – no matter how well they succeed with one or more particular aspects – frequently fall short of what might be desired for the all-round cultivation of personality, particularly when the expansion of educational opportunity to whole populations places squarely on the official educators the manifold responsibilities previously shared (or neglected) by many different agencies. Those foreign educators who look in on communist systems of education (for successes as well as failures) without relying on this criterion, and without discerning the paramount importance of ideology in it, are seriously hampered in their observation and will almost certainly err in their interpretation.

Having paid due attention to the all-inclusive comprehensiveness of ideological considerations, we must remember some serious drawbacks. In our Western countries we now recognize, for example, that the accounts given of the American War of Independence on opposite sides of the Atlantic are often contradictory, and that neither is absolutely true. A similar statement could be made about the mutual portrayal of each other by antipathetic sects. Such travesties are as nothing compared with the opposing caricatures presented to us in the communist world and the "West". A great deal of the irresponsible lampooning of communist aims and achievements in our own countries is robbed of some of its viciousness because it is based on the ignorance and insecurity of private persons or unofficial groups. Sometimes, to be sure, it is associated on our side with large-scale ideologies such as well-organized religions; but these hardly ever have control over the apparatus of government, and there are other limitations on their comprehensiveness.[1] The huge difference between communist countries and everywhere outside is the effective enthroning of ideological criteria in the central positions of communist power, and above all in communist education. Therefore, whatever appears in the books is the "official line" – the truth for the time being.

It must be admitted at the outset that perhaps the great majority of communist educators are sincerely concerned with the propagation of truth and the furtherance of human improvement in every possible way. No encounter with them can leave any doubt of that, or of their sincere belief that truth is always "on their side". On the other hand, an examination of textbooks – particularly in history and geography, but also in foreign languages – all too frequently shows misrepresentation of the world beyond the frontiers of "socialism". Some inaccuracies can be attributed to genuine error – for the sense of being shut in within a total reorientation of life lends a semblance of unreality to what goes on in what we call "our world". But there is no shirking the conclusion that some misrepresentation is more positive and deliberate than merely inevitable.

Let us look at this more closely. A 1961 Czech textbook called *Zeměpis pro desátý ročník* (Tenth grade geography), despite some very good presentation, divides the whole world into two contrasted "spheres" – the "socialist" areas and the rest. Apart from the geographical farcicality of this concept, there is thoroughly objectionable portrayal in parts, and the whole intention is made clear by the pictures alone. The one picture for Spain shows "primitive methods of agriculture as practised in Spain"; that for Italy "poverty-stricken dwellings near an ancient aqueduct in Rome"; that for West Germany shows police scattering demonstrators who were protesting against a post-war meeting of members of one of Hitler's tank divisions. Of course, the "socialist" world is portrayed as a realm of industrialization, education, and mutual aid. Huge tracts of the earth are not dealt with at all in this year's work, though to be fair they

[1] See my *World Perspectives in Education*, pp. 235 ff.

are equally well defined into non-regional categories in the other years.

A similar travesty is seen in *Anglický od A do Z* (English from A to Z) – a revised and recently re-issued book being used by Czechoslovak university students in 1962, and so widely demanded that it was almost immediately sold out. The original of this work was a pre-revolutionary publication. The present edition combines on one page details of present-day expectations and institutions in Britain with figures of wages &c. that would have been unfavourable a long time ago. (For example: "Together with family allowances from the state their weekly income has never exceeded £4. 10. 0, about half your own income. – Doesn't it make you laugh?") And so it goes on. The whole tone is malicious and many details are absurdly false; but the extracts are written in excellent English and, seeming realistic, are widely credited.[1]

Communist intellectuals are frankly ashamed of excessive partisanship on the part of textbook writers and publishers. They know some facts are false. They also know that purposeful misrepresentation has been, and may still be, widespread. It seems perfectly clear that, believing genuinely that truth is on their side, they would like factual and interpretative errors to be cleared up. Textbooks are constantly being revised, and in many ways are surprisingly up to date. When I once commented in a public statement on the type of misrepresentation just referred to (readers should note that this is possible), no fewer than eight important officials and professors earnestly sought fuller comments in a matter of hours, and asked for help in correcting material. On the other hand, it is uncertain what corrections would secure official acceptance.

There is a serious risk of Platonism in the concept of Party leadership. Plato's *Republic* and *Laws* envisaged the need for the guardians to secure popular compliance by means of "myths" and indeed lies. It is easy to see that ruthlessly determined doctrinaires might be tempted to claim a latter-day "evolutionary infallibility", particularly in the early uncertainties of a revolutionary take-over, when new loyalties and good will must be promptly secured. Yet with growing security, and with confidence in the publicity value of manifest "socialist progress", even diehards must see that any conversion of the uncommitted part of the world will depend upon a reasonably clean record and the

[1] op. cit. p. 132.

avoidance of provable misrepresentation. Moreover, we outsiders should remember that communism has often developed out of institutions and attitudes associated previously with authoritarian churches or politics – the worst of whose features have sometimes survived.

The "absent-minded" momentum of established practice – or, so to speak, the automatism of institutions – may be one reason why most communist spokesmen seem to outsiders to overestimate the importance of mystique (as distinct from practical technique) in their revolutionary progress. After all, in nearly all democratic countries (in the Western sense of the word) many of the practical programmes of communist countries and many of their educational improvements would be welcomed without reference to the new canon of ideological reorientation. The manifest boredom or indifference of many communist-educated students undergoing instruction in Dialectical and Historical Materialism must ultimately bring home this lesson in its native territory. Eventually, perhaps, communist educational practice may shed some features which are attributable to the mere accidents of a Russian or East European matrix. More wide-awake communists may one day come to believe not only that history is on their side but that all humane progress everywhere is on their side too – at least to the extent of their being willing to tolerate its peaceful evolution in an alternative idiom. For this to happen, frequent and friendly contact at the level of personal encounters seems prerequisite. Fortunately these are now easier than they have ever been.

It seems vitally important for us who live outside the communist world to recognize that many of the ingredients that have found favour there are part and parcel of our own traditions. The philosophical assumptions, pedagogical modifications, and social aspirations which have found favour under the red flag are variants of prototypes which have flourished at one time or another in the West – often in a cruder form than we sophisticates now admire. The association of school with life; links between recognition, value, and commitment; a dedicated eagerness to share positively in the construction of a new civilization for all, with all the advantages of industrialized productivity – these are ingredients in today's communist ideology which we might adopt or modify to better purpose in keeping with the experimentation and liberalism which we prize in the West. The tight managerial embrace of the Communist Party and its plans facilitates the administration of a thoroughgoing programme; but if we have some disadvantages in this respect, our own room for creativity and further evolution is a countervailing treasure. But it is a potential treasure only. Its value depends entirely on our making it viable for the future by a corresponding commitment, and an overall view of our global responsibilities.

CHAPTER 2

Soviet Educational Psychology

Orientation

No survey of Russian educational psychology in any comprehensive sense is given in the following pages. This has recently been done by Simon (1957) in more detail than space would permit here. My purpose is rather to review significant sources of Soviet experimentation and to describe trends. A great many experiments have been carried out which have a bearing on child education, just as a great many opinions have been expressed. Some of these theoretical views such as those of Leontiev (1960) have been explored by experimenters; but such work as that of Makarenko (1951) has led to practical, but not to experimentally verified conclusions.

There is no complete uniformity in the theories presented by any body of educational psychologists any more than there could be, for example, in relation to medicine. This is because of the diversity of the subject matter. Thus Pavlovian physiological experiments went a long way to lay a foundation for Soviet psychology, but naturally said little about social psychology. The ideas which were current in physiology and general psychology in the U.S.S.R. since 1917 influenced the development of Soviet educational psychology. However, the influence which these ideas had was more prominent in other, more academic, branches of psychology. In the practical sphere of education, practical needs and political and philosophical ideas also played a part. The influence of ideas from other countries also seems to have played less of a part in Soviet educational psychology than in other branches of the subject in more recent times.

In previous centuries philosophical ideas have been the chief formative forces in education; but in England and the United States in this century a new trend can be discerned. Psychologists of note have begun to influence educational experiments and educational practice. Despite the relatively independent attitude of teachers towards psychologists (compared with, say, that of nurses towards doctors), the position of the psychologists has become one of prestige in the field of education like that of the doctor in medicine. There is no doubt that in Western psychology this position was partly the result, first of Binet's and then of Burt's application of psychological theory or technology to education.

The revolution initiated by Binet was twofold. He considered first how to measure the effects of educational practice and secondly how to estimate the effects of education on pupils of different individual abilities. Neither of these possibilities had been systematically formulated by his educational predecessors. In the event, the exploitation of the concept of individual differences in Europe and America has had certain serious drawbacks. Many authors have for example criticized the theory of educational selection by I.Q.

But the effect of psychologists in the first fifty years of the twentieth century has been deep and extensive in the educational world in the West. The concept of intelligence developed quickly into 'g', and was formalized as the Intelligence Quotient. It rapidly became the arbiter in the 30's and 40's of scholastic ability, leading to streaming and 11-plus selection. Like the too simplified concept of human genetics current in the first decade of this century in England and America, this too simplified idea of scholastic ability arose from an enthusiastic acceptance of this new I.Q. tool. Its application in effect seemed to justify the existing tripartite system of education, a remarkable coincidence of theory and existing practice.

In the Soviet Union, on the other hand, the triumph of the application of Binet's views in educational psychology was short-lived. In the two lines of development of Western and Soviet educational psychology we can compare the aspirations of the two cultures and their philosophies. In both the U.S.S.R. and (for example) England, psychological ideas become transformed in educational psychology into instruments of policy. It was not Binet who decided on a policy of selection at 11 years of age. In the same way few Russian physiological or psychological findings could have been held responsible for the theory of the general educability of all children. However, this idea had strong force in the Soviet Union after 1936.

In what follows therefore some effort will be made to trace both philosophical and psychological forces in Soviet educational psychology. Readers should remember, however, that for practical reasons other branches of Soviet psychology may have a quite different recent history.

In tracing in Russian educational psychology the relationship between philosophical ideals and their realization in experiment and in classroom practice, many gaps appear. This is inevitable because no system of ideas is universally comprehensive. Most theories apply only to the slice of experience on which they are based, often precariously.

Part of the problem of the differences between axioms, and the similarities of their appropriate practices, is the fact (unwelcome to many of whatever opinion) that axioms are sometimes capable of several different interpretations. It is scarcely necessary to exemplify this statement, but one relevant instance which will serve as an introduction is that axiom of epistemology stated by Lenin in *Materialism and Empirio-Criticism* (1927) – namely the theory of reflexion. "Thought," he states, "is the function of the brain; ... perception ... the images of the external world, are effects of the external world, are effects of external objects on our sense organs." This theory of reflexion, a basic principle of materialistic monism, is a statement of faith – one which I in common with many scientists happen to accept, but which none the less requires detailed exposition. How does it come about that we interpret (reflect) the external world in the way we do? Lenin himself points out that even Karl Pearson, an empirio-critic and subjective idealist, none the less accepted the idea that the brain was the organ of thought. This in itself makes clear the difficulties and inconsistencies that can arise from apparently simple and clear axioms. Why does it come about that both materialistic monists and dialecticians, like Lenin and Engels, can accept the same view of thought as Pearson, an idealist, a political conservative and a Darwinian geneticist? Clearly such things happen because no man's ideas are quite logically systematic. No theory embraces all instances or situations, not even idealism or materialism. Issues of principle are apt to merge and disappear as concepts develop. So Lenin quotes the idealist Pearson: "Consciousness has no meaning beyond nervous systems akin to our own."

Thus does Russia's leading dialectical materialist acknowledge a point which was occasionally overlooked subsequently by Marxists, that adherence to the trappings of an epistemology are no guarantee of a "correct" reflexion of reality, which may none the less be hit upon by a non-Marxist. The same proposition applied to Christians or Mohammedans would give rise to no surprise. Nor should Marxists think that because Marx made a thorough, precise and fundamental re-analysis of economics and history, Engels or Lenin could do the same for physics or education without themselves becoming experts in the field.

The axioms therefore which have been laid down as a basis for learning theory are statements of socially or humanly desirable ideals. They need interpretation in detail by experts. The statement of these same axioms has often been the opening page of psychological statements concerning learning. As once stated by Ananiev (1950), Professor of Educational Psychology in Leningrad, these principles say that mental processes are properties of the brain, that such processes, consciousness notably, reflect the external world, and for this reason vary with historical changes. Finally consciousness is formed and developed in practice. This all too brief summary of these principles must serve to describe views which have profoundly influenced discussions in Russia. They continue to do so, but in ways which need to be seen historically. There have naturally been several "periods" in Russian psychological development as London (1951) showed. It is in examining work done during these periods that we can come to appreciate the significance of current studies. It is possible to subdivide the study of Soviet educational psychology into several historical periods and describe trends in each. This is done in the next section.

Studies and trends 1917-60

One important source from which the following section has been drawn is an article by Bogoyavlenski and Menchinskaya (1960). That article, in itself more extensive than this chapter, probably covers most important experimentational and philosophical trends in the periods concerned. It seems in part to neglect some of the special work from Ananiev's laboratories, says little of Georgian work and reports few studies from the Ukraine. However, it reads very much like a thorough statement of aims, trends, and experiments in the leading Soviet institutes.

Bogoyavlenski and Menchinskaya divide the years since 1917 into three, 1917-36, 1937-50 and 1951-60. The reasons for these divisions are fairly clear. We mentioned Binet in connexion with English education. In Russia Binet's views were interpreted on the English and

American pattern until 1936. After that they were not used. Between 1937 and 1950 very considerable efforts were made to develop a dialectical-materialist psychology.

First period 1917–36

The background against which this movement began can be seen from Bogoyavlenski and Menchinskaya's article. Before the revolution psychologists like A. P. Nechaev (1909) saw in psychology the basis of a rational educational theory. At this stage pedagogics, as in Binet's eyes, was seen as a futile and irrational pursuit lacking the careful checks of the scientific method. It might be saved and reformed by scientific psychology. But the results of research, as so often happens, did not justify the hopes of these investigators. Many of the studies of this period have a familiar ring even today. Studies were made of performance as influenced by age and personality, and interests were examined in school children with instruments similar to the Thematic Apperception Test.

Despite the fact that these studies were based on a critique of pedagogics, the psychologists, for example M. M. Rubenstein (1913), tried to relate them to practical conditions in schools.

After the Soviet October Revolution the expression of the difficulties which in some sense are at the centre of educational psychology continued. A debate between P. P. Blonski and the better-known L. S. Vigotski is described by Bogoyavlenski and Menchinskaya. In the book *Educational Psychology* (1926) Vigotski objected to Blonski's assertion that educational psychology on the one hand takes from theoretical psychology things which are of interest to educationalists, and on the other hand "discusses the educational requirements put forward by life from the point of view of their conformity to the laws of mental life". Against this Vigotski argues that it is useless labour to transfer to educational psychology ready-made chapters of general psychology: nor does he accept the second part of Blonski's thesis just quoted. He points out that "it is impossible to allow life, without the intermediary of any science, to put forward educational requirements. This is theoretical pedagogy".

For L. S. Vigotski turning educational psychology into an independent science by no means meant that it should swallow up pedagogics. In refusing to accept the second part of Blonski's thesis, Vigotski also argued that such an expert role could not be taken by psychology. This is once more emphasized in his reflexions on the need to work out in planned research questions of educational psychology as an independent branch of science. The attempts at workers' education and the ideas of the revolution were naturally prominent after 1918.

Bogoyavlenski and Menchinskaya's account continues as follows:

However several years passed before psychologists began research on the process of applying knowledge to practice and began to solve the various problems involved.

The demand for educational psychology – for its subject matter and problematics – outstripped by far the actual opportunities for carrying out research in new directions.

And even in L. S. Vigotski's book on educational psychology which appeared in 1926 (and can without doubt be considered a definite landmark in creating the principles of educational psychology) there were still no new factual data obtained from experiments in the field of educational psychology.

The lack of the necessary research data on the psychological activity of children, gained under conditions of actual education and teaching, made it extraordinarily easy to find psychological "proofs" for different and sometimes contradictory educational points of view. Concepts from general psychology about thinking as the solution to a problem, about the role of perplexity in giving rise to thinking, were put forward as psychological justification for different methods proposed, as for example the Dalton plan. Psychologists easily found a theoretical basis for the "look and say" method of teaching reading, by calling on the viewpoint in general psychology about the "whole" nature of children's perceptions. Not infrequently different psychologists would justify contradictory educational viewpoints, using established psychological principles. In textbooks of educational psychology for this period, for example, we often find mention of vision, in its broad sense, as an indispensable aid to teaching, the authors basing this on the concreteness inherent in children's thinking; but in other textbooks, on the contrary, there is talk of the harm done by visual methods, reference being made to different principles of thinking, namely, that thinking originates when there are difficulties and obstacles, whereas visual methods lead to the expulsion of thinking difficulties for children (such, in particular, was the view of L. S. Vigotski in his book on educational psychology).

Such arbitrariness in the psychological basis of different educational principles was inevitable at this stage of the development of psychology, inasmuch as at that time psychological facts were established and altered *outside concrete conditions* (author's italics) and there were still no studies of the mental processes of children, carried out under conditions of real activity in the process of education and teaching.

This early period with its many attempts at psychologizing seems to have been a long continued flirtation with psychologically based concepts. However, unlike the situation in Western Europe and America, this association did not continue. As is now well known, it was sharply terminated in 1936.

Second period 1937–50

The break resulting from the 1936 Decree of the Central Committee of the C.P.S.U. was apparent in advance. Vigotski and others had already attempted to introduce a practical approach into psychological experimentation and had tried to draw psychology and pedagogics somewhat closer together. In addition such workers as Blonski (1935), began to draw attention to the problem of the complex interaction of different mental processes in, for example, thinking and problem solving. He notes that the use of different combinations of processes depends on different stages of children's development and also on the relative difficulty of problems.

To justify this statement Blonski quotes a whole series of different experiments (maze tests, an experiment in which the subject has to find something, learning texts by heart). The data obtained showed that different methods of solving a problem occurred not only in different subjects (depending on their age and intellectual development) but also in the same subject (depending on the degree of difficulty of the problem he had to solve). This conclusion of Blonski's was not of central significance – it was made, as it were, in passing – but in later stages of the development of educational psychology it acquired very great significance.

Although Vigotski died in 1934 his influence continued throughout the period under discussion. As early as 1936 his views on concept development were well known in the Soviet Union and in England. They continue to influence Soviet psychologists today in the person of Luria and in his studies of the internalization of concepts. The recognition of the importance of the acquisition of speech and its effects on concepts was one way in which Vigotski helped educational psychology. Despite certain over-simplifications, he also introduced into educational psychology a recognition of the importance of speech in aiding abstraction.

This period then opens with a series of investigations which attempt to provide scientific answers to questions of educational psychology. But, as Bogoyavlenski and Menchinskaya say,

> the movement was extremely slow and the development of psychology as a science was in that period extraordinarily delayed by uncritical borrowing of the theories of *bourgeois* psychologists, broadly propagated by the pedagogues. In published work it is not always possible to distinguish between live psychological investigations and pseudo-scientific pedagogical judgements and facts. The efforts of many psychologists were directed at working out tests supposed to distinguish pupils' degrees of mental ability and to "measure" their scholastic success.
>
> The Central Pedagogical Laboratory, which was then in Moscow, tried to analyse the cases of lack of scholastic progress, by carrying out "researches" (author's quotes) on a broad scale, the substance of which lay in determining the coefficient of correlation between pupils' success in school on the one hand, and on the other hand the amount of living space they occupied, and the amount of meat they consumed. They substituted this kind of "research" for the scientific teaching of children. The pedagogues held sway in the schools, and their activity flowed on, estranged from teachers and from scholastic affairs. Psychologists did not oppose this harmful practice by another practice, based on scientific knowledge about the child.

The position changed after the Central Committee's decree of 4th July 1936, on "Pedological Distortions in the Commissariat of Education"[1]. This decree which passed judgement on the theory and

[1] As this chapter is being printed, there is a current report that some intelligence tests have again been in use (perhaps experimentally) in the Soviet Union since 1st September, 1962. On general grounds it seems unlikely that they will be used for selection, although such an experiment is being conducted in Warsaw in connexion with the police force.

practice of education, exercised a decisive influence on the development of psychological science and above all on the development of that branch which is concerned with schools, i.e. educational psychology. After the decree of the Central Committee psychologists undertook a radical re-examination of the basic principles of the science and began to work to overcome the anti-Marxist, false statements that had taken deep root in psychology.

They directed special attention towards overthrowing the chief "law" (author's quotes) of the pedagogues, according to which the development of children is fatally determined by two factors – heredity and "unalterable environment" (author's quotes). To do this it was necessary to study changes in the mentality of pupils under the influence of a changing educational process; to trace, in particular, how methods of teaching and the content of the material studied are reflected in the psychological characteristics of the assimilation of the material taught; and what is the significance of the pupils' own activity in the process of assimilation. It became sharply apparent that a critical reconsideration was needed of the concept of age, of those rigid, unchanging age-standards which came to us with the principles of *bourgeois* testology, the use of which essentially kills the very idea of development.

The age-characteristics of children were established in close connexion with conditions of upbringing and teaching, with the concrete stage of teaching reached, with the experience acquired by the child in the course of his life. The view that psychic processes are not only displayed but also formed in activity (a view put forward by S. L. Rubenstein in 1934 and later elaborated by him in his *Foundations of Psychology* (1946)) occupied a central position in psychological theory. It acted as a stimulus to the development of research into psychological processes in changing conditions of activity, into the development and establishment of such processes. This helped to achieve a more clear distinction of the particular subject matter and aims of educational psychology, as apart from the general body of psychology. The subject matter was the pedagogically determined scholastic activity of pupils, and the aim was the discovery of the psychological principles underlying this.

This conception of the aims of research made it necessary to study psychological activity not only as a manifestation of abstract psychological functions but as the activity of a human being, an active agent, living in defined social-historical conditions and guided by socially conditioned aims and purposes. Activity was thus studied as a single dynamic process. The cornerstone thus being the study of activity as a process, psychology thereby promoted the view that *genetic* methods of investigation were of great significance, as they permitted this question to be studied *in the practical conditions of teaching*.

This transition from study of individual functions to study of concrete activity opened to educational psychology broad perspectives for using the results of experiments in the *practice of school teaching*.

The position of psychology was at this stage radically changed. It was made to depend on educational experience and practice. Psychologists were obliged to consider new ways of studying learning processes in children. The test method was rejected and a genetic form of study introduced – in other words the examination of children's learning at different stages of their growth, but also at different stages of teaching. With these aims, a new form of "realistic" experiment was developed, the so-called "teaching experiment", in which the psychologist himself formulated the essential knowledge, skills or habits, combining together in his own experience study and influence.

Bogoyavlenski and Menchinskaya continue:

From the years 1936–7, experimental work in the psychology of teaching acquired in our country a great impetus. In the centre of research was the process of teaching children, in all its forms: studies were made of the process by which children understood different scholastic material; the assimilation of concepts and the mastery of cognitive operations in the process of studying the basis of sciences; problem solving; the development of habits and skills; mistakes made by pupils were studied with a view to discovering their psychological nature; psychological hypotheses of more effective assimilation were examined; pupils' motives were studied, and the role of appraisal in the process of assimilation; and so on. Such research was conducted on a still broader scale from 1944, after the formation of the Academy of Pedagogical Sciences.

In addition "subject specific" studies were begun although a little more slowly. This latter point might be glossed over except that it seems to form a new stage in Soviet psychology of education. It had both its good points and its bad. It introduced a note of concreteness into what had tended to be a somewhat philosophical approach to learning theory. But it did not tend to develop generalizations of wider application. However, arising out of these studies and related to teaching practice came one of the lines of emphasis which marks a key point of difference between Soviet and Western educational psychology. It was maintained that the establishment of stages, steps or levels in the mastery of knowledge depends not only on the age, degree of scholastic preparation and development of the child but also on the degree of completeness of the methods of teaching and also on the content of the scholastic material to be learned.

This treatment of the question of degree of development is in sharp contrast to the concept of development which was shared by the pedagogues, by which the stages of mental development replace one another according to laws of age and maturity, and independent of the content of the material to be learned. This question is dealt with in articles by A. N. Leontiev (1937 and 1941). The kind of view expressed in these works was still a strong influence in the 1950s.

Part of the reason for the emphasis on teaching as an aid in developing stages of assimilation in a child was the Soviet emphasis on consciousness, referred to in an earlier section. This led them to reject all Behaviourist theories and to attack Thorndike (translated into Russian in 1932)[1] as did Schwarz (1937). The direction of educational psychology in the U.S.S.R. in the period just reviewed was towards a detailed analysis of the reasons for fast and slow learning in different pupils at different stages of assimilation of some particular subject.

The last ten years 1951–61

The last ten years in Soviet general psychology have seen a very considerable expansion of techniques and approaches. It is perhaps going too far to say that there has been a basic modification of ideas. This is not so, but many techniques not previously widely understood or used have now been tried and developed. For example, factor analytic and mean difference techniques are now more widely accepted; cybernetics, regarded previously as not characteristic of Marxist psychology, is now acceptable; and social psychology, although not highly devel-

[1] It is not clear which of Thorndike's books was translated.

oped, is being discussed. Many kinds of psychology are now accepted as worthy of investigation, whereas a foreigner reading Soviet psychology before this period would have noticed the widespread dominance of Pavlovian physiological psychology.

Educational psychology does not reflect this expansion of interests in the same way. As can be judged from the previous section, many practical and theoretical decisions had been made in relation to education, and Soviet views represented a reaction not only against Western (*bourgeois*) theory but Western practice (selection and inherited intelligence etc.) as well. To convey the general picture of present attitudes in the psychology of learning, therefore, one could do worse than discuss the work of Leontiev, who represents important trends in the Academy of Pedagogical Sciences in Moscow today.

The theory underlying much of the psychology of learning arises from the direction of a group of psychologists, of whom Leontiev and Luria are two. Others are carrying out similar work; but Leontiev has himself set forth the views on learning which might be supposed to characterize the investigations going on in his laboratories in central Moscow. The articles from which the following statements have been selected are entitled "On the formation of abilities" and "Learning as a problem in psychology". The first appeared in 1950 and the second in 1957, both in *Voprosy Psikhologii*. They are summarized in Leontiev's article in *Problems of Psychology* (1961). It is sensible to deal first with the article concerning learning. Leontiev addresses himself to the problem of the adaptation of animals to new conditions, the basic and essential learning situation. This essentially simple situation Leontiev sees as a direct connexion between the organism and the environment. At some point however a further complexity is introduced when one external event becomes temporarily connected with another and in this respect has meaning for the observer. The first event has become a signal for the second and in this sense, means it. It has become an orienting signal. This, says Leontiev, is the mechanism of the organism's orientation to the environment, its mechanism of the reflexion of the environment and its sense of its own place in this environment. This signalling function of events is sometimes referred to by the author as an orienting and sometimes as a conditioned reflex. Both aspects of learning through conditioned reflexes have been stressed in recent Soviet work, although of course the orienting function of some signals in their non-conditioned state has received more recent emphasis.

Leontiev draws attention to the need to trace the physiological bases of these temporal connexions. At the same time he makes it clear that Pavlov's experiments were concerned with classical and not operant conditioning, and in addition were conducted under highly artificial (laboratory) conditions so far as the normal environment of the dogs was concerned. However, he also stresses the difference between Pavlov's neurologically based learning theory and Western behaviouristic theories of learning. Examples of attention to this difference are the intra-sensory and intra-modal researches of Soviet laboratories, which were until recently unknown in American research. Similarly the perceptual findings of Russian work began, they state, with an analysis of such concepts as Gestalt psychologists first noted, and then proceeded to explain them. In this respect Leontiev's observations might also be used to describe work now going on in Canada in Hebb's department, and at Reading in England, on the general topic of mechanisms of perception.

Another important part of the testing of Pavlovian findings in natural conditions which is also different from Western work consists in the treatment of the organization of the adaptation of motor acts to environmental stimuli. The modification of motor acts by the process of operations is a feature of learning peculiar to higher animals. Conscious manipulation of the environment results in an entirely new learning process which cannot be subsumed under any simple S–R formula. This kind of learning arises from the manipulation of the environment through labour. This conception of labour is similar in some ways to the Western idea of operant conditioning, but is more fully developed as a philosophical theory. In some respects also it is the foundation of work on stereognostic perception of objects at Leningrad.

Another important part of the work discussed by Leontiev concerns the relationship of the two signal systems, first and second, and the effect of the development of the second on human learning. This leads to the fundamental change in learning which distinguishes men from animals, namely man's dependence on social conditions and social learning rather than, as for animals, on adaptation to the natural environment. The interaction of the two signal systems makes possible the transformation of individual experience by contact with the experience of society encapsulated in words. Leontiev describes how important words are for signalizing qualities in objects, and how children learn this signalizing quality from adults. By associating qualities with objects children also learn generalization. Yet it is not the word itself, or alone, which results in generalization but both the word and the experience of, or orientation towards, the qualities of the objects. The mental action of the student or child forms the basis for this abstract kind of learning.

Leontiev here and Luria in other connexions both continually emphasize the importance of the process of the internalization of actions as the basis for learning. Leontiev suggests that this can be seen (as Piaget sees it) as a gradual modification of thought concerning objects into logical operations. However, interiorization is more complex, involving three components. These are extension of generalization, contraction of operations and strengthening of the independence of the operation from circumstances. The meaning of the first is obvious; the second refers to that objective simplification of operations like assuming that eight counters in one pile together with four in another form a pile of twelve. The strengthening of the independence of an operation concerns the child's ability to carry it out when no adult is present to guide and correct him. Each of these operations can be learned to a different level of competence or conscious mastery. It is in the process of learning, thinks Leontiev, that new mental actions and reasoning operations are formed.

It might be thought that Leontiev's views are confined to learning processes, but he has also turned his attention to the problem of individual differences and their bases in abilities, whether biologically based or of socio-historical aetiology. It has naturally been assumed by some English psychologists that because testing and selection for schools was abandoned in the U.S.S.R. in 1936 Soviet psychologists had also given up the idea of individual differences. This is not the case. Leontiev admits the existence of, for example, differences in speed of conditioning or resistance to the inhibiting effect of negative stimuli. Teplov's sub-division of types of nervous system obviously also provides a physiological foundation for differences in particular abilities. But Teplov's dispositions are not abilities. Abilities – even innate ones – says Leontiev, are dependent on external conditions as well as on dispositions. Leontiev illustrates this by referring to the speed with which trained animals solve laboratory problems in comparison with animals which have not had this experience. It is implied that training can re-organize the pattern of individual differences found in any sample of people. Even fundamental nervous type can be changed by a particular régime of experience. Thus even basic abilities have environmental as well as constitutional origins. The tremendous importance of technical and social change is thus introduced. Not biological adaptation but a satisfactory social milieu determines the psychology of man.

However, this is to discuss only basic abilities. These in themselves are featureless and not specific to the material learned. Thus language, the perception of geometrical forms, etc., are not given but must be learned. They can be learned in no wise except from contact with society. This is the characteristically human aspect of learning. For the child this means learning from the adult.

At this stage Leontiev makes a point which is of great importance for Russian learning theory and which has at least one parallel in American experimentation. This is the suggestion that any one human skill may have as its base a number of combinations of basic dispositions. Woodrow (1946) in a long series of studies has shown that this is inevitably true over a long series of tests of one task. As skill increases new abilities come in and some others drop out. However, Leontiev here suggests that an individual may succeed at, say, algebra with one set of capacities, and have as his equal someone whose skill is based on quite other capacities in a different combination but in the same subject.

To illustrate the importance of the social development of abilities Leontiev uses an illustration connected with lack of pitch discrimination. First he showed its prevalence among people who use atonal language (most European languages) and then its non-existence among languages based on pitch, like Chinese. He then shows that tone deafness could be eliminated in Europeans by appropriate training. He uses this example to make the point that "abilities" need certain conditions to be fulfilled. If the conditions are not present, such abilities may be absent.

The matching of the pitch of sound can be used to illustrate an entirely different point frequently made by Soviet psychologists. This is the possibility of using one sense to aid another. In this case the visual representation of the pitch of a note was made available on a cathode ray tube.

The implications of this sort of finding for educational practice are clear enough. Instead of streaming,[1] anti-streaming. Thus if a child has a deficiency, try to overcome this deficiency in some skill by employing other combinations of abilities. Leontiev says:

[1] In U.S. terminology, homogeneous grouping according to ability.

Must we, however, undertake merely the study of this process of general development of human abilities? I think not. The next problem is to master the processes of the active formation and education of abilities.... It is possible to discuss, in this sense, the prospect of creating pedagogical abilities, based firmly on exact scientifico-psychological data ... to lay the foundation for a pedagogy of this nature is primarily a psychological problem.

Further aspects of recent research

Previous sections have laid down the broad lines of recent research, but further points can be illustrated from current reported research. In referring to these I will draw from a recent article by Zaporozhetz and Zinchenko (1960), and on a discussion held with Zaporozhetz in Moscow in 1959. I shall also draw on further material of the extensive survey of Bogoyavlenski and Menchinskaya. In taking up the work reported by Zaporozhetz and Zinchenko, we shall cover work recently carried out in the Ukraine but shall leave out of account Ananiev's work in Leningrad and the work of Prangishvili and Natadze in Georgia. The relevance of the Leningrad work will be assessed in a short paragraph describing experiments by Lomov and others, and that of the Georgian work by brief descriptions of two of Natadze's articles.

Zaporozhetz and Zinchenko (1960) recently discussed scientific papers from the Institute of Psychology of the Ukraine at Kiev. Among the studies which they mention are those about memory for numbers in children by Kostiuk (1954) and the ways in which perception may be viewed as a function of the relatively complex interaction of visual and motor function as in studies by Vovchik-Blakitnaya (1960). This work and that of El'kin (1960) in space and time perception show the relationship of motor, visual and verbal functions in the active manipulation of the environment, and the generalization of particular experience through words to other situations. Zaporozhetz and Zinchenko record the experiments of Milerian (1957) on attention, and follow his description of stages in attention in the child: from involuntary attention, to voluntary attention evoked by words, to organized directed attention at between 5 and 7 years of age.

Zinchenko himself specialized in memory function. His extensive work has appeared in an article already published (1960), and was largely concerned with the features of involuntary and voluntary memory.

Raevskii (1960) in other studies of memory attempted to show that first memories are related to the beginnings of speech. Many studies concerning the origin of the perception of objects, and of the development of such concepts as numbers, are briefly described; and other studies by various authors concerning thinking in school children are mentioned. An interesting investigation of the development of generalization is attributed to Skripchenko (1957). Processes of generalization, he says, become more and more complex proceeding by the following stages:

1. Visual-practical
2. Visual-verbal
3. Imaginary-verbal
4. Comprehended speech.

Similar studies have been carried out with problem-solving.

Kostiuk's (1954) work is again mentioned in connexion with understanding. This author sees it as a thought process attempting to discover links and relations in objects. It is inferred that the processes of understanding will vary according to the nature of the material to be understood. Many other studies are mentioned in this short article, which aims at giving a review only of work carried out in the Ukrainian S.S.R.

Since it was published Zaporozhetz and Zinchenko have carried out work in Moscow and Leningrad respectively; and Zaporozhetz is working in the Laboratory of Child Psychology in the Moscow Institute of Psychology. In 1959 he described his work to me as including the kind of studies reviewed below.

He said that experiments were being conducted in the estimation of sensory levels in young children, and the raising or lowering of these levels by vocalization. They were also concerned with the study of the manipulation of objects and the effect of such handling on the way in which objects were seen. Children were asked by Lenitskaya, for example, to represent the pitch of a tone by a hand movement, first with the eyes open, then (as in the experiments of Neverovich) with them shut. In this way discrimination thresholds are improved. Zaporozhetz also spoke about the study of eye movements in perception. These were thought to reduce gradually as perception became more sophisticated. This work had been carried out by Ushlakova. Similarly studies of orienting activity were carried out by Bogaslavskaya using natural situations to explore the orienting activity of children at such different stages of their development as those in which touch and later visual exploration predominate.

Most of these studies were with young pre-school children. There were, however, in the Ukraine several studies of group behaviour and the effects of discipline. Many more studies of classroom practice in subject method have since been reported, and some of these will be discussed below.

The further trends which are apparent in these studies over and above those presented in previous sections can be supplemented by reference to Bogoyavlenski and Menchinskaya. However, in evaluating this work it is apparent that many of the results presented cannot be assessed without further examination of the material referred to. This would be equally true of work of this kind in any country and the reasons for it are well known to research workers. A further complication is that in this report these authors are not concerned with work in the West. As a result it is difficult to know whether or not they consider their results original. Many of the statements they make are like research results described in English and American journals, except that their quoted sources are quite different. As a result it is often difficult to estimate the extent to which Pavlovian theory, for example, has inspired or directed a piece of research which may state as its conclusion that, in order for two similar things to be clearly differentiated, they must be presented side by side. Differential inhibition, a Pavlovian concept, was given as a source in one such study. It is a phrase with a precise and clear meaning in terms of classical conditions, but to associate this process with difference learning at a complex level may beg many questions.

To round off this review of recent studies we can examine four separate topics. These are comprehension and concept formation, problem-solving, skill and habit acquisition, motivation and individual differences.

Turning first to comprehension: one Soviet view is that this is general, i.e. its stages from simple and limited to detailed understanding follow the same course irrespective of subject matter. As a result we are dealing with a general psychological law based on "physiological laws of generalization and differentiation established by I. P. Pavlov".

But in discussing the general question of comprehension a different and interesting point is made. This concerns the impact of the visual character of the displayed material. The more the child is at first attracted by the obvious visual content of the material, the less easy it is for him to appreciate its general cognitive meaning. This is of course a reflexion of the well understood fact that comprehension is based on experience, and lack of a system of ideas will mean that ideas in a display are not readily appreciated. Thus, according to the stage of development, visual material can be either a hindrance or a help. This general conclusion has been set out by Leontiev (1947).

In studying comprehension and assimilation, space is given by Bogoyavlenski and Menchinskaya (1960) to the work of P. A. Shevarev (1941). He talks of two kinds of association, the association of two concrete instances and general association. All association is seen as part of reflex theory and as analysis and re-synthesis. But the ability to assimilate associations is dependent in part on the ability to use them and apply them. An active state of the brain is essential. Expressed in this way the idea is attributed to Pavlov. Lack of correct analysis and synthesis is the reason for backwardness. Lack of experience of course contributes. Weak abstracting ability can thus have a number of causes. Finally, on the question of comprehension it must be said that considerable differences in children's levels are found. Only a few show an inability to pick out the essential signs in concept material. Generalizations can take place on different levels; and it is worth quoting a brief extract from *The Psychology of Teaching* to emphasize the different levels of generalization described. In dealing with backward children it is common to find solutions which appear to be based on principle, but whose principle of solution cannot be verbalized. Bogoyavlenski and Menchinskaya say:

> In contrast to formal dialectic logic, the process of cognition is a blend of the sensory, rational and practical. Sensory cognition, being acquired in objective activity of man, is capable of reflecting correctly signs which are general for different objects, even when this general feature cannot be generalized on the verbal-logical plane. Such cases are called in psychology pictorial generalizations. Such generalizations provide a possibility of correctly generalized actions with a limited circle of objects, without recognition of the principle underlying these correct actions.

This leads to a discussion of the association between words and images in learning. It is suggested, following Troshin (1915) and Zhukov (1959), that a kind of generalization *in concreto* takes place. Naturally such a form of generalization is incomplete and insecure in so far as it rests on a dissociation of the first and second signal systems; but it does occur, as anyone who has worked with imbeciles will easily admit. Another instance is, of course, the acquisition of speech itself. This in a curious way takes place as it were independently of the second signalling system. A general idea can be readily formed by pictures; but a more general notion can arise only from a comprehension of function, inevitably expressible only in words.

The application of generalizations in practice has been less well investigated in the U.S.S.R., but such investigations as exist, like those of Fleshner (1958) and Zikova (1956), suggest that the application of abstract principles and concepts depends on the manner in which the concepts were acquired. And, finally, on concepts it is suggested that they depend for their appreciation on their integration into a hierarchical system.

The other directly cognitive aspect of direct educational psychology which has received a good deal of attention is problem-solving, which is regarded as a basic function in school work. Appropriate set is emphasized in the solution of these problems; and rigid or crystallized, as distinct from flexible, approaches are referred to as characteristic of children with the sequelae of various inflammatory conditions. Studies showing this are those of Menchinskaya (1954), Andreyeva (1951), and Bubnova (1955). Proper and appropriate analysis and synthesis excludes the mechanical application of habitual forms of solution. Various inappropriate strategies are listed by Fleshner (1958) such as trying habitual solutions and giving up on first failure; or a long series of trials which is none the less purposeless; or, for example, a third group, members of which make a thorough and comprehensive analysis of the problem. Jakobson (1956) showed that the lower levels of solution were characterized by an ignoring of the verbal instructions. The two main findings, therefore, in problem-solving would appear to be the development of proper analytic-synthetic methods, and secondly the importance of the role of speech.

The formation of habits on which many workers, including Ananiev (1955), have carried out experiments is considered important. One observation made in connexion with habit formation seems to be of great importance. This is the simple but shrewd observation that repetition leads to the perfection of the behaviour and not to the strengthening of the initial action. This phenomenon noted also by some Western psychologists is of course of considerable importance in the development of motor acts. The shortening of processes of thought and action was noted by Vigotski (1926) and Shevarev (1941), and is presumed to be based on a consciously formulated rule of behaviour. This basic reasoning underlies all operational steps, but after habituation is called upon only in rare cases of difficulty. Habituation therefore in the view of Soviet educational psychologists involves deverbalization and the shortening of processes. They take the view that the process by which the structure of intellectual habits and abilities is formed is governed by the same laws as those which govern motor habits. This view closely follows Pavlov's idea that the laws of nervous activity are the same for the first as for the second signal system.

In the same way, when we turn to motivation in school learning, Pavlov's precepts are again respected. He stressed the importance of an active state of the cerebral cortex in learning. Coincidental connexions, conditioned reflexes, cannot occur otherwise. Social-orienting stimuli are therefore given emphasis. Games and projects, as L. S. Slavina (1951) has shown, can be used to change the motivation of disinterested pupils. This aspect of Soviet educational psychology closely resembles views expressed by educationists in England and America. However, such views allow for considerable variation in statement. For example one author notes that a positive attitude to learning by no means guarantees a good speed or level of acquisition. This observation obviously has something to do with individual differences. Other aspects of motivation, previous experience and interests have been examined by Soviet psychologists. Their views, apart from the references to conditioned reflex theory, might correspond closely with our own.

On the subject of individual differences, of course, Soviet views are at variance with American and English opinions. The research can be classified by saying that some investigators list all children's characteristics irrespective of age and synthesize them to suggest clusters of features. Others look for defined features of thought and classify children accordingly. The approaches are regarded as complementary. The first is seen as personality study, the second as the study of thinking processes. S. L. Leites (1956) has attempted to describe some aspects of the connexion between these two approaches in so far as he has studied the daily life activities of children with different types of nervous systems. In such work as this, we see in some respects the full circle of Soviet educational psychology's investigations. By refusing to place complete reliance on inborn individual differences as explaining scholastic skills and lack of skills, it has developed a positive approach to the interaction of teaching and learning. In this way it can now afford to return to the problem of individual differences and admit them without implying in any way that this need mean a difference in achievements which is basically unalterable. The exact limits of individual differences within which such a view may reasonably be held remains to be established. As the bases of Teplov's (1961) work on individual differences were mentioned above they are not developed again here.

An evaluation

Amid such a mass of work, by no means all of which has been even mentioned, certain basic principles emerge. Soviet educational psychology is clearly directed towards maximizing the effectiveness of education. It would be fair to say that this is true of any professional educational psychologist anywhere. However, there is also no doubt that in England (for example) the emphasis arising from a long line of human genetics research, including the genetics of intelligence, has put a premium on ability differences. This trend in research probably reflects social structure. Until recently the Soviet psychologists' position on abilities has been obscure, but recent translations of Leontiev and Teplov's works have made it more clear. In view of this clarification we can now present a relatively complete picture of Russian educational psychology.

It might be reasonable to say that the major fields of research in both the West and the U.S.S.R. are similar. For example, educational stages in comprehension, concept formation and problem-solving, the acquisition of skills and habits, memory, motivation and individual differences, are subjects studied in both East and West. In America, for example, motivation has probably been more widely studied than anywhere else. In England there has been a greater and longer term emphasis on intellectual differences, and in some American universities, notably Chicago, this has also been true. However, within limits both East and West have had the same aims, namely to increase the effectiveness of educational techniques. There has been, however, a very different social milieu behind the two, and this has led to much greater educational opportunities in the Soviet Union than in England. In addition, some of the assumptions based on the concepts of inherited intelligence have been rejected officially in Russia, whereas they are only now being gradually eliminated in England by trial and error. The psychologists' information in the two countries is, however, similar in its general findings, although of course very different in detail. One might say that in both countries the basic physiological nature of individual differences is admitted, but in England such differences are regarded as major factors, whereas in the Soviet Union they are seen only as foundations on which buildings of many different kinds can be constructed.

This is perhaps the key difference between the two psychologies, but two other differences warrant notice. These are respectively the differences which Soviet psychologists have with Piaget concerning stages of growth and also their relatively greater reliance on Pavlovian theory.

The question of stages of growth is an important one and has so far not been adequately stated in English. If in fact, for example, growth stages can be accelerated by education and retarded by the lack of it, this would be a strikingly different situation from that generally accepted in the West. Small advances or retardations are of course accepted by many Western psychologists, but big differences could be of great significance. Unfortunately no decisive material on such questions has yet appeared.

It is when consideration is given to school practice that the wide social differences between a class and a classless society begin to appear. In the U.S.S.R., given a relatively intact nervous system, potential equality of scholastic achievement is assumed. Strenuous efforts are also made to aid teachers to achieve such relative parity, and psychologists participate in such activities. In England no such assumption is made, and headmasters are still frequently wedded to the notion of innate differences. Psychologists also accept individual differences in patterns of abilities as relatively unchangeable. However, these matters of opinion, whilst weighting practice heavily in one direction or another and influencing research, are also frequently modified by research findings. It is thus impossible to maintain any longer in England that selection techniques are an adequate basis for useful selection at the age at which they are used. At the same time the possibility of equalizing achievement by appropriate techniques is far from being demonstrated in any completely satisfactory way in the U.S.S.R.

How then should Soviet educational psychology be evaluated? Its technical competence and range are two possible criteria. From these points of view it would seem to be good by Western standards, although naturally variable. It is less sophisticated in its use of techniques than English psychology but is catching up rapidly. Like many European schools it is much more fertile in its analysis of mental function than English educational psychology can be said to have been in the last fifteen years. Much the same thing could be said for the development of studies concerning the use of language by the severely subnormal. In this field Luria's development of Pavlov's suggestions is original and very interesting. No appreciation of it is given here because his studies are readily available in English in several recent books such as those edited by Joan Simon (1959), Tizard (1961) and O'Connor (1961).

In the same way many ideas developed by Zaporoshetz and Zichenko concerning the voluntary control of movement break new ground. The same thing could be said of the work of Ananiev, Vekker, Lomov *et al.* on spatial cognition. This review has given a very summary exposition of an immense field. In many ways it is misleading; but if it serves the purpose of interesting Western educational psychologists perhaps their interest will lead to a further examination of this field. Soviet educational psychology occasionally appears to lack method, but it is often extremely ingenious and generally profound.

It may turn out, as has happened in some other fields, that a closer examination will bring to light more detailed and critical work. If this proves true, whether the Russian views are correct or incorrect, the Soviet Union will have greatly enriched our ideas on school behaviour, concept formation, motivation and individual differences. It is to be hoped therefore that someone will soon make a complete and thorough book-length analysis of Soviet educational psychology.

BOOKS

ANANIEV, B. G. (1950) *Basic Tasks of Soviet Psychological Science.* All-Union Soc. Dissemn. Polit. & Sci. Knowledge, S.C.R. Psych. 5, Trans. B. H. Kirman.

ANANIEV, B. G. (1955) Analysis of pupils' difficulties in learning to read and write. *Izvestia APN RSFSR*, 50.

ANDREYEVA, E. K. (1951) Disturbance in the formation of associations in cases of inflammation of the frontal lobes. *Dissertation*. M., In-t. Psikhologii.

BLONSKI, P. P. (1935) *Memory and Thought*. M., Cotsektiz.

BOGOYAVLENSKI, D. N. and MENCHINSKAYA, N. A. (1960) Psychology of Learning, in *Psikhologicheskaya Nauka v S.S.S.R.*, II, 286–336.

BUBNOVA, B. K. (1955) The solving of arithmetical problems by patients with inflammation of the brain. *Izvestia APN RSFSR*, Vip. 71.

EL'KIN, D. G. (1960) Research Institute of Psychology of the Ukrainian S.S.R. Scientific Papers, Vol. VIII, referred to in *Voprosy Psikhologii*, No. 1, 165–72. (See also Zaporozhets and Zinchenko.)

FLESHNER, E. (1958) The acquisition and application by school pupils of certain concepts in physics. From *The Psychology of Applying Knowledge to the Solving of Scholastic Problems*. Pod. Red. N. A. Menchinskaya, APN RSFSR

JAKOBSON, P. M. (1956) A psychological study of building activity by pupils of the 7th class. *Voprosi Psikhologii*, No. 3.

KOSTIUK, G. S. (1954) *The Psychology of Reasoning*. Ministerstvo osviti URSR, Institute of Psychology, Naukovi Zapiski Institutu Psikhologii URSR. Kiev.

LEITES, N. S. (1956) Test showing the psychological characteristics of temperament, from *Typological Characteristics of the Higher Nervous Activity of Man*, APN RSFSR.

LENIN, V. I. (1927) *Materialism and Empirio-Criticism*, Vol. XIII, Collected Works, Martin Lawrence, London.

LEONTIEV, A. N. (1937) Psychology and education, *Sovietskaya Pedagogika*, No. 2.

LEONTIEV, A. N. (1947) The conscious nature of learning. *Izvestia APN RSFSR* Vip. 7.

LEONTIEV, A. N. (1960) The formation of abilities. *Problems of Psychology*, Nos. 1 and 2, 1–11.

LEONTIEV, A. N. (1961) Learning as a problem in psychology, in *Recent Soviet Psychology*, N. O'Connor (Ed.), Translated from *Voprosy Psikhologii*, No. 1, 1957, 3–17.

LONDON, I. D. (1951) Psychology in the U.S.S.R. *Amer. J. Psychol.*, 64, 422–428.

LURIA, A. R. (1961) *The Role of Speech in the Regulation of Normal & Abnormal Behaviour*. J. Tizard (Ed.), Pergamon Press: London.

LURIA, A. R. & YUDOVICH, F. YA. (1959) *Speech and the Development of*

Mental Processes in the Child. Joan Simon (Ed.), Staples Press: London.

MAKARENKO, A. S. (1951) *The Road to Life*. Foreign Languages Publishing House: Moscow.

MENCHINSKAYA, N. A. (1950) Political unmasking of Edward Thorndike. *Sovietskaya Pedagogika*, No. 12.

MENCHINSKAYA, N. A. (1954) The relationship between word and image in the process of acquiring knowledge. *Dokladi na soveshchanii po voprosi psikhologii*, APN RSFSR.

MENCHINSKAYA, N. A. (1955) *The Psychology of Teaching Arithmetic*. M. Uchpedgiz.

MILERIAN, E. A. (1957) The formation of skills by the application of knowledge in practice with older scholars. *Tezusui dokladov na sovbeshchanii po voprosam psikhologii truda*, APN RSFSR.

NECHAEV, A. P. (1909) Current experimental psychology in its relationship to questions of school education. Izd. 2, T. 1. Pb.

O'CONNOR, N. (Ed.) (1961) *Recent Soviet Psychology*. Pergamon Press: London.

RAEVSKII, A. N. (1960) Research Institute of Psychology of the Ukrainian. S.S.R. Scientific Papers. Vols. IV & VII referred to in *Voprosy Psikhologii*, No. 1, 165–172. (See also Zaporozhets and Zinchenko.)

RUBINSTEIN, M. M. (1913) Outline of educational psychology as related to general psychology. *Zadruge*.

RUBINSTEIN, S. L. (1946) Osnovui psikholog. M. Uchpedgiz. izd 1–1940; izd 2–1946.

SCHWARZ, L. M. (1937) Critical analysis of the psychological concepts of Thorndike. *Sovietskaya Pedagogika*, No. 2.

SHEVAREV, P. A. (1941) The nature of habit in algebra. *Uchenie Zapizki Instituta Psikhologii*, T.2.

SIMON, B. (Ed.) (1957) *Psychology in the Soviet Union*. Routledge and Kegan Paul: London.

SKRIPCHENKO, A. B. (1957) Characteristics of generalization in pupils in 1st-2nd Class. *Meitcoialnui soveshchania po psikhologii*, APN, RSFSR.

SLAVINA, L. S. (1951) Improving the performance of a group of retarded children in the first class. *Izvestia APN RSFSR*, Vip 36.

TEPLOV, B. M. (1961) Typological Properties of the Nervous System and their Psychological Manifestations. In *Recent Soviet Psychology*. N. O'Connor (Ed.), Translated from *Voprosy Psikhologii*, No. 5, 1951, 108–130.

TROSHIN, G. Y. (1915) Comparative psychology of normal and abnormal children. *The Psychology of Learning Grammar and Spelling.* T.1. Protsessi umstvenoi Zhixni Pg.

VIGOTSKI, L. S. (1926) Educational Psychology. M. Izd-vo, *Rabotnik Prosviescheniya.*

VOVCHIK-BLAKITNAYA, M. V. (1960) Research Institute of Psychology of the Ukrainian S.S.R., Scientific Papers Vol. VI. Referred to in *Voprosy Psikhologii,* No. 1, 165–172. (See also Zaporozhets and Zinchenko.)

WOODROW, H. (1946) The ability to learn. *Psychol Rev.,* 53, 147–158.

ZAPOROZHETS, A. V. & ZINCHENKO, V. P. (1960) Scientific Papers of the Institute of Psychology of the Ukrainian S.S.R. Problems of Psychology, Nos. 1 & 2, 94–102.

ZHUKOV, S. F. (1959) Learning verbs as parts of speech. Sb. *Voprosy psikhologii usvoienia grammatiki i orfografii,* APN RSFSR.

ZIKOVA, V. I. (1956) Psychological analysis of applied geometry and solving problems with a concrete, real-life content. From *The Psychology of Applying Knowledge to the Solving of Scholastic Problems.* Pod Red. N. A. Menchinskaya, Ucheniye Zapiski LGU, Vip 9, L. No. 214.

ZINCHENKO, V. P. (1960) Research Institute of Psychology of the Ukrainian S.S.R. Scientific Papers, Vols. I, II, III, IV, VI & VIII, referred to in *Voprosy Psikhologii,* No. 1, 165–72. (See also Zaporozhets and Zinchenko.)

CHAPTER 3

Russian Children at Home and in School

The bringing up of children is no easy matter under any conditions in any country, because there is no perfect balance between the full development of each human individual and the demands of the society around him. It is properly the responsibility of us all – the general public as well as the home, the school and, traditionally, the church – to see that each child has the best opportunities that can be provided. The sharing of these responsibilities is the foundation on which each nation's child-rearing is based.

In the West, a child is the responsibility of his parents unless the State can prove that this is detrimental to his welfare. Only with such proof can parents' decisions be overruled. In Russia the State assumes primary responsibility for children and the parents are the individualized channel through which a child's upbringing takes place. The State decides the pattern towards which its future citizens are to be reared and the type of personality and character to be produced: the parents' rights are those delegated to them and are not primary.

Parents are responsible financially for the support of their children whether they are at home, at boarding school or removed from their care to a State institution.

After the Revolution family ties were weakened as far as possible, but in the 1930's this policy was reversed. Whether this was because the family was no longer a threat, whether the authorities decided that family ties were too strong to break, whether it seemed better to acknowledge the family as the primary group to be federated into larger units, or whether it was the rise in juvenile delinquency that was convincing, the fact remains that since then the closeness of families has been acknowledged. Research No. 27 on juvenile delinquency, quoted by J. N. Hazard,[1] states that the great majority of juvenile delinquents were at home very little and had both parents working. Divorce became more difficult to obtain.

[1] J. H. Hazard, *Law and Social Change in the U.S.S.R.*, London Institute of World Affairs, Stevens & Son, 1953.

In parallel, after the Revolution, adoption was regarded as a means of exploiting children, and the mass institutional upbringing of children was expected to increase apace, but nowadays (in 1962) adoption and fostering are both encouraged and an intermediate status called "dependence" is established. By this a child is cared for and supported, but does not change his name.

Apart from the care of his health, a young baby is mainly the responsibility of his immediate family; but on the whole Russian babies are born into larger groups than British or American babies are. This is due partly to the closer living conditions, which make it natural for friends and neighbours to play a bigger part in family life, but also to the fact that aunts, uncles and cousins often live with the family. A Russian baby often grows up in a quite large community and is used, from the beginning, to being handled by a number of people. Men are not afraid of appearing effeminate and will help with young children in any capacity. Their role is kind and supporting, and they are not, as in some cultures, regarded as the disciplining sex.

Among the surrounding adults Babushka is of outstanding importance. Usually she is the paternal grandmother, but on occasion can be any older female relative. In contemporary Russia the mother is finally responsible for the upbringing of her child, but traditionally the grandmother is a very important influence. After all, she is still head of the household, old or numerous though her daughters and daughters-in-law may be. In a close community someone must have the final sanction in domestic matters, however able and important in their own spheres the next generation may be. This is true, of course, of many cultures, and has a remnant in European and American jokes about mothers-in-law. The high proportion of working mothers in Russia means that in any case vast numbers of young children spend their weekdays in the care of their grandmothers. This reverence for the elderly, although admirable in itself, can slow down the acceptance of new ideas on child-rearing. In some families it can mean that an idea can take two generations to be carried out. This happens if a girl in school is taught some new principle, but, unable to apply it because of Babushka, can make her learning effective only with her grandchildren.

Swaddling is probably the most traditional Russian custom in question. Obviously no generalization can be accurate among different districts or people of different levels of education in a huge country like the Soviet Union; but, as one continues to read and to inquire, certain opinions emerge again and again. Swaddling does not seem to be generally regarded as a desirable custom either by the authors of child care manuals or by consultants in maternity clinics, but at the same time it seems to be generally practised. There are many practical reasons for this, beyond its centuries-old following. Peasants working in the field cannot carry their babies with them as they work, whether it is on a big combine harvester or hoeing on foot. If they leave them with their coats in a corner of the field, they have to take precautions to keep them safe. Swaddled, they are kept away from damp earth, chilly winds and, to a certain extent, rain and snow; they cannot throw off their covers or roll over and so catch cold; they cannot wriggle out of their warm wraps; they cannot crawl into danger or touch anything that will harm them. At the same time they cannot experiment with their arms and legs or put their toes into their mouths. How far this delays their development is unknown, but it seems probable that their muscular co-ordination soon catches up with that of children who have never been swaddled, once they are unbound.

Whether their emotional development suffers, no one knows, although close binding of this sort is not in accordance with Western teaching. Emotional results are always difficult to establish, while Russian arguments in favour of swaddling are clear and direct. Some Russians, and they are not always the older generation, argue that tight binding guarantees a straight back and ensures that the baby will not have bow legs. Others feel that tight binding gives the baby a sense of peace and security. Yet others feel that in bitter winter conditions, babies can only be taken into the fresh air if swaddled. Several times, when parents were asked why they swaddled, they replied that they did not have any faith in the practice, as they were taught in school; but that on this occasion they felt it was necessary because this particular child was especially strong and might wriggle off the bed; or, because this particular winter was especially cold, the child might get pneumonia; or a mother might say that she would never swaddle her children, but her mother-in-law insisted on it. In any case the time for which swaddling continues seems to be lessening. John Rickman mentions eight or nine months as usual in 1918, but many mothers nowadays mention two or three. Geoffrey Gorer[1] also suggests that the

---

[1] Gorer, Geoffrey, and Rickman, John, *The People of Great Russia*, London, The Cresset Press, 1949.

expressiveness of many Russians' eyes may be due to swaddling. Immobile all day, a child can use only his eyes, and it seems reasonable to suggest that constant practice will give highly developed muscles. Young children at play can give the impression that they turn their eyes towards an object where Western children turn their heads, but this is only conjecture. The movements of kindergarten children playing ball in a wintry playground are certainly different from those of Western children in similar circumstances. They turn round on their feet, their bodies all in one piece, to follow the flight of a ball or beanbag, but this may be because they have to wear so much heavy clothing in the cold climate.

Again in the matter of methods of rearing, obviously no one rule applies to so huge a country; but we do know that child-rearing was generally permissive in Russia until the Revolution, except among the intelligentsia who were much stricter with their children. Nowadays a good deal of strictness seems to be recommended. Russian national characteristics which the Soviet Government are anxious to change are unpunctuality, waste, and a lack of neat orderliness. How far this has been an ingrained part of their teaching which permeates their approach to child-rearing and how far they believe that the earlier the children are trained to these habits, the better they will learn them, is not easy to assess. Probably both. Clinics and welfare centres often recommend feeding exactly to time, whether the baby is awake or asleep, and not feeding a child who wakes up hungry ahead of schedule. When her baby cries, a mother is often recommended to check whether anything is seriously wrong, and, if it is not, to leave him to cry. At any rate in some clinics and centres mothers are advised to begin cleanliness training earlier than is now generally recommended in Western countries. This is in accordance with general psychological theory. The Russians seem to believe that through suggestion and unremitting training, a child can gain the habit of controlling his physical functions. Most British and American specialists in child care agree that this can be done (with exceptions), but that when purely bodily habits are established, control tends to break down when the child begins to think and notice what happens. Many Westerners feel that it is better not to worry a very young baby, but to begin training when he can co-operate. There seems to be no doubt that there is a good deal of enuresis among Russian children, lasting sometimes into the early school years.

Corporal punishment of any sort is illegal in Russia – no adult may strike a child in any circumstances – but parents can occasionally be seen to slap their children, for instance on a long journey in a crowded railway carriage. One official, when asked, said that he had never had to hit any of his three girls, but that he had felt obliged to use corporal punishment twice with his son. On one occasion the boy was having a temper tantrum and on the other he did not stop throwing stones when he was told to do so.

At one time in Russia all children with infectious diseases went to hospital. If there is someone in the home who has not had the disease, they still must do so, but as housing conditions improve, some children are now nursed at home. Apparently if the parents can keep the child isolated, promise that no one will call, and put a sheet dipped in disinfectant over the door, the child may stay at home. Parcels of food and toys may be sent to children in hospital, but visiting is allowed only once a week, on Sundays. This is contrary to the practice in Western countries where a sick child is thought to be in special need of the love and reassurance of his mother's presence, and frequent visiting is encouraged. If a child is dangerously ill, parents in Russia may visit during the week, but not otherwise. In some hospitals cubicles are provided for nursing mothers and their babies. Some trade unions run centralized hospitals for members and their children (for instance for tuberculosis), and these may be thousands of miles away from the children's homes. In these circumstances there is no contact between children and the type of parent who does not write letters.

As already mentioned, for some time after the Revolution the close bond between parents and their children was suspect in case it interfered with the close integration of children into the collective. Probably the bond was too strong for an impersonal state to break, and it was, therefore, accepted and incorporated into the new emerging system; but it may be, too, as Western people have found, that unless a child forms a happy relationship first with one person, and then gradually expands his affection to his immediate family and then wider and wider, he cannot at first form a generalized relationship and remains a personality without real and rooted affections and without loyalty. For some years now parents have been expected to form a stable home background for their children. As Yesipov and Goncharov[1] put this: "The feeling of love for father and mother is the first noble feeling

[1] Yesipov, D. P., and Goncharov, N. K., *Pedagogy*, Moscow, 1946.

which arises naturally in a young child and which plays a central role in the life of the individual." There is no doubt that the immediate family have not such close emotional ties as they have in the West, partly because their family units are so much bigger.

Nurseries, both day and resident, may be provided by group enterprises such as collective farms or factories for the children of their women workers who are under three and have no one at home to look after them. It is very difficult to judge how far the need for places is met, as the nurseries are not all open to any children in the locality, some taking only the children of mothers employed by one institution, and being run by that institution under the supervision of the Ministry of Health. As the main concern is the health of the babies, each nursery is under a doctor, and the need for adequate sleep, suitable food and plenty of fresh air is stressed; but the assistant staff are encouraged to talk to them and sing and show them tender care. It is not necessary to wean a baby before he or she comes to the nursery, because nursing mothers are allowed to come to feed their children, and feeding times count as working hours. The tremendous rise in the standard of parental care is clear when the recommendations for parental education issued to the nurseries in the thirties are compared with those issued now.

About twenty per cent of the children between the ages of three and seven years attended kindergarten in 1960, and this proportion is increasing. In 1958 2,280,000 places were available; but during the Seven Year Plan 1959–65 these are to be expanded to 4,200,000. Availability of places varies greatly from district to district and even within one area, because there are two kinds of kindergarten; but the selection of children varies little. First priority is given to those who have both parents working, or one parent working and one dead, and to children of unmarried mothers, if there is no grandmother, aunt or other responsible adult living with them. This proviso reduces the waiting-list in Russia far more than it does in the West where large, composite family establishments are unusual. Vacancies are then offered to the most needy of those on the waiting list, that is to parents who have an income of less than a hundred roubles[1] a month, or who have many dependants or very large families. How far this provision meets the wishes of parents is difficult to judge partly because some kindergartens are provided by big State enterprises such as collective

[1] Figures for roubles here quoted are at the 1962 rate.

farms and large factories. These can judge the number of places required by the number of their employees and provide accordingly. At least some of them are able to offer a place at once to a child of any employee. On the other hand some State kindergartens which serve the general community have long waiting-lists. It remains to be seen whether the increase by almost 50 per cent in the number of places by 1965 will satisfy the demand and abolish the waiting-lists.

Kindergarten education is supervised by the Ministry of Education and the State pays the teachers' salaries. Parents pay fees, which range from purely nominal to realistic charges, according to their means. Buildings, furniture and equipment are provided by the sponsoring organization.

The educational aims of the kindergarten are specifically stated to be "to prepare for school". Little stress is laid on the importance of play or self-directed activities; much stress is laid on skills needed "to watch, to listen, to carry out instructions and to behave in a disciplined manner". For example, many table games and puzzles are provided, but little creative material. To quote one official handbook, "The system of education in the Soviet kindergartens aims at developing the child physically, mentally, morally and aesthetically. The children here are taught to speak correctly in their native language; they are given object lessons in wild life and the life that surrounds them; they are taught games, singing, dancing, drawing, modelling and work habits."

Staffing is generous – one adult to four children – but this ratio includes cooks and caretakers, and it has to be borne in mind that the kindergartens are open twenty-four hours a day. Day children can arrive at any time between 7 and 9 a.m., and go home any time between 4 and 7 p.m. This means two shifts each day, six days a week, of teachers, assistants and maids. Those children whose parents are on night shift sleep at the kindergarten, which means that night nurses must be employed; and a few children are weekly boarders. One kindergarten of a hundred children had a staff of twenty-five adults, consisting of two teachers, two assistants and a maid for each of the four groups, a headmistress, a music teacher, a secretary, a cook, a caretaker, two nurses and two night staff. Another of two hundred and fifty children and fifty-four adults had a director, an assistant director, twenty teachers, fifteen nursery assistants, a music teacher, a nurse, a doctor, a cook, a caretaker, a secretary and eleven domestic and night staff. Teachers in future will be trained at the Pedagogical Institutes and

Secondary Pedagogical Schools; but many of the present staff were trained from the ages of 14 to 17 in special secondary schools.

Two teachers and two assistants are allocated to each group of twenty-five children, and work in six-hour shifts. Sometimes a teacher is always responsible for the same age-group, and receives new children each year. In some kindergartens there are groups for each age, while in others there are separate groups for the threes, who are the new entrants and the 6-year-olds, who are regarded as a transitional class getting ready for school, while the fours and fives are grouped together. There seems to be no "family grouping" where children of every age are in every group, as sometimes practised in England.

Accommodation varies from kindergarten to kindergarten. The most generous provision is a "flat" for each group of twenty-five children, consisting of a playroom, a dining-room, a dormitory and washrooms. As in most countries, the dining-room is often omitted, and the children have their meals in their playroom. In some kindergartens space is too much needed to allow for separate dormitories, and the children sleep and eat in their playrooms. During busy periods, such as harvesting on the farms, temporary nurseries and kindergartens are sometimes opened.

As in all countries, the parents and staff come to know each other well. Meetings are arranged; and the welfare of the children, their health, growth, development and care are discussed.

The children themselves are happy and friendly and there is an atmosphere of warm kindliness and patient and loving care, although there is much more stress on uniformity than there generally is in Western countries. Conformity to the idealized pattern of the "good boy", who is quiet and obedient and always remembers to do what he has been told, is heavily stressed. Art is a craft to be learned; the best artists are those children who can copy the teacher's drawing, for instance of a feather, without smearing or blotting, or can give an exact replica of a dainty pattern in a small space. There do not seem to be large sheets of paper and thick brushes for children whose small muscles develop later than the big ones and are difficult to co-ordinate. Fine brushwork is taught from the age of three years, as a useful training for the fingers so that they will be the more skilful with the pen in due course. There is no question of regarding art as one of the means by which a child can co-ordinate his intellectual faculties and come to terms with life by expressing what he has observed.

The same purposeful training for life rather than the opportunity for experimentation provides the criterion on which play material is chosen. There is, therefore, a proliferation of mechanical toys, which are regarded as the foundation of science training, and of table apparatus which is designed to train the senses. Most Westerners feel that this kind of material, (which, devised by adults, can be used only in one way and requires no thought in its usage) is not the best material for exercising intelligence, ingenuity and initiative. Children often love these mechanical toys when they first receive them, but quickly tire of their rigidity and lack of adaptability. So often they then misuse them by trying to make them do something which they were not designed to do, and they then break. Alternatively, children try to find out how they work, open them up, break the mainspring by overwinding, snap the elastic band or dislocate the cogs with an investigating finger, and ruin a toy which should be specially cherished because of its expense.

In the Soviet Union mechanical toys are often regarded as a wonderful means of increasing a child's knowledge, enriching his experience and introducing him to mechanized modern life. In Western countries they are frequently bought for children by adults (and the presence of children is sometimes an excuse for adults to enjoy working this type of toy); but the educational experts feel that these toys are limiting to a child's ability to create, and that, although they are legitimate amusement, they inhibit rather than increase his thought and his imagination. Much sense-training apparatus is also provided with the hope that practice in manipulation will later bear fruit in increased academic skills. This type of table apparatus is no longer in favour in Britain or America, where it is regarded as time-wasting because it may train nimble fingers possibly on occasion, but without involving the exercise of the intelligence in planning or reasoning, or requiring any social or emotional response.

Dolls and bricks are provided; but their use seems to be regarded mainly as an attempt to train in miniature for adult life, and as a childish attempt to copy the grown-ups. During a number of discussions on young children's play no Russian teacher suggested that play with these two materials was often the beginning of his social life with his equals. At home he is with his parents and other adults who are in charge of him, a hierarchy of older children who have some authority over him, and younger children whom he is supposed to help; but in his play at the kindergarten, generally with dolls and with bricks, he is making his first relationships with his peers. Doll and brick play in Russia, therefore, tend to be isolated occupations, and not something of vital consequence in social development; there is little of the colourful multi-faceted home play in the Wendy House that is so characteristic of British, Commonwealth and American nursery schools.

It is possible that dressing-up clothes may be provided in some Soviet kindergartens, but they never seem to be mentioned in any written or verbal description; so it is unlikely that they are regarded as important. Most Western educators rank them high among the play materials that are most valuable to children under 7; they offer to children such opportunities of taking on other people's personalities with their clothes and so seeing their point of view. Children can often shed their shyness behind a façade of another personality; in fact most of the value of role-playing in contemporary social psychology can be exemplified in the dressing-up of young children.

It is very interesting that the occupations regarded by the West as particularly valuable in the social development of young children – house play, big building and dressing-up – are given little stress in Soviet kindergartens.

Plants, aquaria and pets seem to be introduced wherever possible. Indoor plants, often arranged along the windowsill, are especially valued because of the long, bitter Russian winter. Teaching is direct and didactic. Learning is not incidental or left to personal interest.

Obviously in such a huge country no generalization is possible about books; but they seem to be used for instruction and amusement, and not so much as an opportunity for vicarious experience and emotional release. The characters in stories that are popular with young children the world over are black or white; both children and adults are very, very good and are rewarded, or are very, very bad and punished. Children do not understand and therefore do not like characters in their stories that are partly good and partly bad. Before the age of eight years it is unusual for them to enjoy delineation of character. Even by these standards many of the books in Russian kindergartens obtrude their moral teaching, and do not rely on deduction and implication.

Paddling pools and sandpits are regarded as desirable wherever garden space and weather conditions permit, and so is plenty of outdoor play, at least until 9 a.m. breakfast, and sometimes later in the day too.

Basic raw materials are provided for play in some Soviet kindergartens; but they are not regarded as essential, because some have none. In Russia water, earth, sand, clay and wood seem to be regarded as healthy play materials giving plenty of good physical exercise. In the West they are generally regarded as basic raw materials, the handling of which in early life is essential in an artificial, mechanized world. Soviet teachers tend to concentrate on the provision of mechanized toys where teachers in the West believe in the provision of water to dabble in, pour, filter and spray, or sand to trickle through the fingers, draw in, puddle, dig, mould and shape. It may easily be that the majority of Russian children have had the basic materials to play with for centuries and adults are delighted to be able to provide them with contemporary toys that "work", whereas Western children have had sophisticated toys for a long time and, although relatives still give them, and children still enjoy receiving them, educators feel that they are not enough and that children should also have the opportunity to experiment and create.

In the socialist countries, as elsewhere, play is valued as the chief educational factor in the life of young children; but on the Russian side it is regarded primarily as a preparation for school life, whereas in the West it is felt to be essential for the development of personality, for social adjustment and for the release of emotional tension. The Russian values which play is designed to serve seem to be functional, and concerned with personal success, whereas those of the West are, comparatively, humane and aesthetic.

We should therefore expect, and we find, long periods of uninterrupted play in the best British and American institutions, and shorter periods in a carefully balanced programme with plenty of change of occupation in the Soviet Union. The children in the first two years in the Russian kindergarten are often referred to as "the juniors", and these children, aged 3 to 5 years, could in England be in a day nursery, a nursery school or a nursery class. In both countries the programme is closely parallel, made up at it is of play, although play with rather different materials, rather lengthy meals and a sleep in the afternoon. In the Soviet Union, however, there is one definite period of instruction of fifteen to twenty minutes some time between 9.30 a.m. and 11 a.m., and the afternoon period from 3.15 to 4 p.m. may be used specifically for physical education.

There is, however, a world of difference when the syllabus is consulted. British nursery schools do not set standards of attainment which every child should reach and no one exceed. Children are expected to develop at their own maximum rate with every help that a teacher and a good material environment can provide; number teaching is incidental, perhaps while the children are laying tables or lacing their shoes; language teaching is not taken as a formal lesson, but by encouraging the children and adults to talk; nature is studied as the occasion arises; handwork is a matter of choice. Children are found to develop best if encouraged to pursue their own interests in a stimulating environment. Most good nursery schools have abolished the Morning Ring when only one child can speak at a time and all the rest have to sit and listen. Music is often optional and children join in if they wish, but are not called away if they are busily concentrating on something else.

In the Soviet Union the 3-year-olds have a definite syllabus to cover. In number they learn the difference between one and many, and to count up to three; in handwork they have specific teaching in painting and drawing (40 periods), clay (30 periods) and paper appliqué (10 periods). Deana Levin[1] gives an interesting and detailed account of the 250-word syllabus on art for 3-year-olds. To save space just the smallest section, that on appliqué, is quoted in full:

> Using coloured geometrical shapes already cut out of paper to make patterns. Learning the names square, circle. Learning the names of two colours. Matching these colours. Sticking the patterns on a plain piece of paper. By the end of the year learning the name triangle, edge, corner, middle.

Nothing could be much further from the contemporary Western approach to child art.

As already mentioned, one lesson of fifteen to twenty minutes each day is recommended for the 3-year-olds; and as the number of lessons each year is suggested – forty for number, eighty for art and handwork, and twenty-one folk tales, six classical stories and nineteen Soviet stories – it seems that the general arrangement of lessons each week is: one each for number, art, handwork, story, music, and one for language including nature study. The firm direction from authority and lack of independence of the individual kindergarten may be partly due to the need to establish minimum standards. Many of the staff finished their training at the age of seventeen years, although every effort is made to provide refresher courses for them.

[1] Levin, Deana, *Soviet Education To-day*, London, Staples Press, 1959.

In general, Soviet 3-year-olds are more tightly controlled by the adult and are expected to conform to a planned pattern. The very limited choice offered, if any, requires little initiative and imposes little strain. The kindliness of the adult brings security; and the definite ideals of obedience and the acquisition of knowledge are easy to understand and within the compass of the majority. This kindliness in the adult is one of the few factors in common with British nursery schools. In Britain the teachers, who are paid on the same scale as all other teachers, and who, at the *minimum* for many years past, have not been able to qualify before the age of twenty, impose the least control that is compatible with public safety and the welfare of all. The wide choice of occupation means that the child must learn to choose, to make decisions, to take the initiative and to persist in a self-imposed task. Thus much more is required of the children, and high standards of teaching to ensure each child's maximum development are essential. A discipline that is protective and supportive requires much more of the adult than one that is authoritative. Condensed into one sentence, the Russian kindergarten prepares for school, whereas the Western nursery offers a child the opportunity to explore the world in circumstances which are protective.

At the age of seven (that is the top group in the Soviet kindergarten, the top class in the British infant school and the second grade in the American elementary school) education has approximated more closely in the different countries; yet it is also much more difficult to compare because Russian education is standardized, while the practices of schools both in Britain and America diverge widely.

In the Soviet kindergarten the 5- to 7-year-old children are often referred to as "the seniors". These are the years that all British children spend in the infant school or kindergarten,[1] whereas only a proportion attend in Russia. Under the American system attendance is optional for the 5-year-olds and usually compulsory for the sixes. It is ironic that in Russia and America, where the attendance of 5-year-olds is optional, the numbers steadily rise, whereas in Britain, where attendance has been compulsory since 1870, there is a campaign, although as yet not particularly popular, to make attendance voluntary or for half a day only.

---

[1] In American terminology these British "kindergartens" should be described as regular first and second grades. They do not correspond to an American kindergarten, which is equivalent to a British nursery school.

The programme for the 6- to 7-year-olds in the U.S.S.R. is in many ways similar to that of the 3-year-olds. The children play, if possible in the open air, until everyone has arrived and then have breakfast at 9 a.m. Two thirty-five minute formal lessons follow. After that the children play out of doors or go for a walk or short expedition until 12.30 p.m. lunch which is followed by rest until 3 p.m. From 3.15 to 4 p.m. there is usually a gym lesson and then tea. Children may go home any time between 4 and 7 p.m. Supper is provided for those who remain at 7.30 p.m.

Bed-time is later in the Soviet Union than it is in Britain – 8 p.m. for children aged 3 to 5 years, and 9 p.m. for those of 5 to 7; but all the children have a long afternoon rest, which makes the total time spent in bed about the same in both countries. In Britain an afternoon rest is unusual in the infant school and even the 4-year-olds often are allowed, if they cannot sleep, to get up and look at books or follow some quiet occupation that does not disturb the others. This difference in the time of the day given to sleep may easily be a reflexion of the housing shortage against which the Russians are struggling. If there is no separate bedroom for the young child, it is very difficult to get him to sleep in the noise and bustle and interest of older people's evening occupations.

Blocks, table games, puzzles, dolls, mechanical toys and books are again the most common occupations, and there is a dearth of raw materials or creative work; but good periods of free play with a choice of toy are still provided. This last year in the kindergarten is regarded as transitional to school and the number syllabus includes counting at least to ten, number bonds to ten, addition and subtraction of small numbers and simple problems. The children learn their letters but do not put them together to form words. The art and handwork syllabus is quite specific, and is a continuation of the teaching of skills that were begun with the 3-year-olds. It includes painting and drawing ("Drawing objects correctly from observation . . . Using half-tones . . ."), using clay, appliqué ("Continue practice of cutting out by eye, folding paper to make symmetrical patterns . . .") and model making ("Toys made from paper and cardboard . . . Doubling a piece of paper . . . Finding the centre of a square . . ."). Little stress is placed on self-directed activities.

In addition to the permanent kindergartens, camps are provided for vast numbers of children under school age. There seems to be much more freedom to play with natural materials in the summer kindergartens organized in the country. The children live here during the three summer months and parents may visit on Sundays. Some factories provide transport for parents every third Sunday and for the Parents' Committee every week, so that they can report back to the others between their visits. The long separation is probably not as damaging to these young children as it would be in a culture where the mother-child relationship is closer.

The investigation of the best age for beginning the basic skills is one into which interesting research is at present in progress. In the middle of the fifties some children, who were not attending kindergarten, were admitted to school in the last few months before their attendance became compulsory for a short period each day and given half-hour lessons in reading, writing and arithmetic with a fifteen-minute break between each. This was also tried in parallel with children of the same age in kindergartens. The teaching was less formal than is usual in Soviet schools, but more advanced and systematic than that in the kindergartens. The experiment was a great success. In any case some parents have always taught their children to read before they were 7 and came to school. This causes controversy, as the teachers are trained for class teaching and everyone must be kept in step. The concept of readiness by which each child matures physically, intellectually and socially at a different rate, and should be taught systematically as soon as his powers are developed enough for him to succeed, is not acceptable in the U.S.S.R. At the same time it is important to remember that the problem has not really arisen there yet. While the age of entry is 7, it is uncommon to find many members of the school entrants who are not ready to begin reading. This principle needs much more consideration in Great Britain where the reception class is only 5 years old.

Many teachers would like the children to start school earlier and quote the success of the reading experiment as evidence in favour of this, but 7 has been the age of school entry for many years (it was 8 before the war) and in any case many schools are already working on a two-shift system and could not possibly accommodate any more children.

There is friction between the school and kindergarten teachers about the scholastic level to be expected from 7-year-olds, as there is in Britain between infant and junior teachers. The teachers who receive the children feel that they have been inadequately prepared and the teachers who send them up feel that too much is expected. Children forget a great deal during the summer holidays, so that when the receiving teacher feels that she can quickly teach them a great deal, she is sometimes only reviving what the sending teacher has efficiently taught. However, in Britain the two types of teacher are paid on the same scale and are given the same amount of training, so the argument is between equals; whereas in Russia the kindergarten teachers are paid less, and, at any rate until recently, have generally been given less training. In the race of competitive examinations the most intelligent tend to go to university and then teach the older children, the next layer to go to the pedagogical institutes and teach the middle range of ages. Kindergarten teaching gives a lower intellectual status as well as less pay. To a certain extent this happens in Britain; but all teachers there are paid on the same scale according to their qualifications, and those graduates who particularly like young children teach them without losing status or pay.

At the Institute of Psychology much interesting research is in progress, not so much into the stages of a child's development, but into the stages of his acquisition of knowledge. Many of the results found in Moscow agree with Piaget's findings; but the Russians feel that what he discovered was the result of methods of teaching, whereas they are finding the chain of thought which makes up a child's logic. There is also some interesting work going on concerning the complicated connexions between maturation and psychological development.

As there are no private schools in the Soviet Union there is no question of choice of education, although in those regions where Russian is not the native language, there may be the alternative between schooling in the local language or in Russian. Even those schools that offer a foreign language from the age of eight are neighbourhood schools which serve a defined catchment area.

Although there is a very little, if any, choice of school, there is a wonderful welcome for every child. When the great day arrives, the newspapers print the nation's good wishes; the head teacher welcomes the newcomers and their parents; the children themselves, wearing their ceremonial white pinafores, carry flowers to their new teacher; and the grown boys and girls in the top class give each entrant a present. There is great expectancy among these 7-year-olds as they assemble in their new school uniform with the new school textbooks provided by their parents. Each child is welcomed and issued with a school pass with the twenty-one school rules printed on it. The good wishes in the newspapers, the present from the older children, the wearing of school uniform and the issue of his pass are a form of initiation ceremony and make a child feel that he now belongs to a community which is enthusiastic for his welfare. He also knows from the beginning that he is expected to work hard, make steady progress along clearly defined lines, and keep stated rules. Most visitors are impressed by the extent to which the Russians are "committed" to education as a means of national advancement.[1] School attendance is regarded as a privilege of which a child should be proud.

The local authority has previously given to the head teacher the names of all children in his or her area who have turned 7 during the previous twelve months; so the numbers are known in advance, and a check is made on the enrolment of all children. If there are too many for one class, the children are usually allocated as they arrive to one class until it is full and then another is started. Sometimes the children are divided according to the area in which they live to facilitate the teacher's home visiting; sometimes, if parents specifically ask, they can choose the teacher. Great faith is placed in sorting children by chronological age although it has never been proved to have any beneficial effect. Why a child born in August should have affinities with a child born a month previously in July and go up the school with him, but not have any affinity with a child born a month later in September, who has to wait for another year before he goes to school, is difficult to say. If faith is implicit in streaming by the calendar, it is curious that, in those schools where there are enough children for two parallel groups, the classes are not divided into those children of seven to seven-and-a-half, and those from seven-and-a-half to eight years.

The teachers of the first year grumble a good deal because some of the children have been taught to read at home, some have learnt their letters at kindergarten, and some have had no instruction of any sort. This offers a wonderful opportunity for group teaching; but Russian teachers believe in class teaching, so they find the different levels of attainment difficult to deal with. Those children who can read have to learn their letters again, and those who have not started are rushed through the sounding of their letters until they can pronounce meaningless syllables in three months. After the first three months the

---

[1] *Soviet Commitment to Education*, Report of the First Official U.S. Education Mission to the U.S.S.R., Bulletin 1959, No. 16, U.S. Department of Health, Education & Welfare.

first-year teacher hopes to have the children all at the same level marching forward in step. It is not surprising that so many teachers complain of the naughtiness of clever children. Some of the teachers of young children go so far as to correlate intelligence with mischievousness and to regard them as two aspects of the same thing. No allowance seems to be made for the fact that some of these children are eleven months older than others or that some are more mature or that others have had wider experience. Occasionally a child who is only a few weeks short of seven years is admitted. The children's attainment is certainly measured and compared with that of other years; but no attempt is made to measure their progress or to see whether they know any more at the end of their first term than they did when they entered school.

It is also interesting that these children, most of whom have not been to kindergarten, are expected to coagulate so quickly into a collective of thirty to forty children without going through the stage of forming small groups which gradually combine, especially as, for many of them, it is their first experience of adapting to their peers. However, the aim is not to form self-selecting groups, but to see that every child is a participant in the collective in which he finds himself so that his conduct, feelings and aspirations are incorporated in it. This is not meant to make children anonymous members without personality. The class is not, at its best, a crowd of children, but a responsible collective in which each child can find fulfilment and self-determination through acceptable channels. Teachers do not aim at breaking a child's will but at persuading him to take over the class's wishes as his own. Young children's work and play groups in the West are smaller in size, self-selecting and child-centred, whereas in Russia the unit is the whole class, has adult-imposed standards and is firmly led by the teacher. By participating in a collective with stated aims a child learns to take over communist morality as his own. By observing the rules and belonging a child finds security. In its extreme form the collective gives each child his character and his role. From his entry into school each child's moral growth is planned by making him increasingly aware of the claims of the community, by convincing him that more and more difficult things are expected of him, and by gradually changing the need for present satisfactions to acceptance of the prospect of postponed pleasures. Gorky taught that the greatest respect which could be shown to any person was by asking and expecting a great deal of him.

Russian educators draw a distinction between the words "friend" and "comrade", feeling that friendship can be all-absorbing, emotional and negative rather than positive in its contribution to the community, whereas a "comrade" is helpful to all and is willing to give much to the community. Makarenko claimed that any youth collective that started with a nucleus of less than seven members would inevitably deteriorate into "an isolated group of friends and bosom friends".

Again the class is not interested in the forwarding of individual interests but rather in making each child its faithful representative. Makarenko felt that personality can only be realized within a community, so there can be no personal happiness outside the happiness of the community.

Presumably in all countries the aim is to allow external discipline to become self-discipline, but stress can be placed differently. The aim everywhere is to secure the active participation of every child up to the limit of his capacity. In the Soviet Union the children themselves are given a list of printed rules on the first day of school, and the teacher gives authoritative directives to the class. At this stage the children are to take responsibility for small, practical matters, such as their duties as monitors; but the main means of discipline is precept and example. Russian children are left in no doubt as to the type of ideal man they are to copy. Western educators are often at a disadvantage here, because in their effort to develop the children's innate abilities and not to force them into a mould they offer a wide variety of heroes and heroines as models. This means that Western children have to take the responsibility of choosing what type of person they hope to be and how far they are willing to make the effort to be such a person, where Russian children have a constant ideal put before them and every kind of encouragement to carry this ideal into practice. There is also the possibility that some individualist will take objection to the model set and deliberately go in the opposite direction. Western children often cannot do this, because their education is aimed to develop them themselves and not to mould them into a pattern.

In Soviet schools there is much emphasis on memory and recapitulation. Most lessons include the checking of work by question and answer with the distribution of marks, each child first raising his hand, then standing when chosen to answer, and remaining standing until told to sit. The amount of factual knowledge to be stored and recapitulated on request is great. Children themselves have little share in building up this knowledge inductively by practical work or by wide reading. Discovery and experiment play little, if any, part. The pace is geared to the average so that the able are bored and the slow are breathless with effort. The teacher gives her class a firm framework within which to co-operate and the children are docile and self-effacing. The teacher directs; the pupils react to her stimulus without showing initiative; and there is little interchange between child and child.

The teacher teaches every subject and stays with the same children for the first four years of their education. Very few, if any, children transfer to another group, so that the class will become a closely-knit collective. The principle behind this is that, by this means, children develop their personalities within the group, taking over the collective's purpose as their own, whereas children who move in temporary or changing groups develop their personalities for themselves. The class is regarded as a society in embryo, and the aim as being to involve each child in shared experience; but is this true? A class is not selected by the children as their future society will be, either among friends of their own choice or in their own selected occupation; it is structured into departmentalized sections of time, each devoted to an organized purpose; and it is closely directed by an unchosen leader, the teacher. Also all members of the community in a class are of the same age and doing the same thing on the same level, whereas later in life the children will probably be working in a group of mixed ages, maturity, skill and experience, where each plays a different part in order to forward the common purpose.

Streaming[1] is condemned as inhuman, not only because Soviet psychologists deny that there are inborn intellectual differences except those due to brain damage – there are only differences of experience and interest – but because of the value of comradeship among widely diverse individuals. The progress of each is the responsibility of all, although official class meetings and the election of class officers are not begun until the fifth year of school. However, although many British and American educators, like the Russians, do not believe in streaming, it is by no means proved that the juxtaposition of different types of children makes them friendly towards or even tolerant of each other. Horace Mann[2] drew attention to the fallacy of believing that "because we group children together we have trained them to accept each other

---

[1] i.e. homogeneous grouping according to ability.
[2] Mann, Horace, How real are friendships of gifted and typical children in a programme of partial segregation? *Exceptional Children*, 23, pp. 199–201, Feb. 1957.

for what they are". In some Rudolf Steiner schools where sanguine must sit with melancholic, and choleric with phlegmatic, much irritation and impatience, not sympathy and tolerance, are sometimes shown.

The power of the collective has great significance in character training because it sets hourly, daily, weekly, monthly and yearly targets, and so always provides a goal immediately ahead. Satisfaction and shame are enhanced because they apply to the collective as well as to the individual, and the standards demanded are internalized. The collective supervises and criticizes to the point of discussing every mark and action. Conformity not only supplies a secure framework for school life but brings comradeship and shared interest. Misbehaviour, the concrete expression of nonconformity, leaves a child open to public reprimand from his fellows as well as from his teachers.

People who work with children everywhere believe the cause of delinquency to be an exceptional individual's inability to meet the social demands made upon him. Now that the effects of war, *bourgeois* training, poverty and lack of opportunity can no longer be blamed, the Russian authorities often blame the parents' faulty upbringing and especially spoiling. They regard delinquency as learned behaviour which can be corrected by re-training and example. The child's emotional needs are given little weight; the stress is always on conformity to society, and never on any failure of society to satisfy his basic needs.

Most British and American educators give more weight to emotional factors, particularly to early child-parent relationships and the ways in which a child gradually takes over adult values and patterns of response. They feel that, if a child through unsatisfying human relationships fails to take the normal steps of adaptation to life around him, he is left with primitive patterns of behaviour which are suitable for younger children. He remains a child with special needs still to be met, and any situation to which he cannot adapt may be the occasion for either delinquency or neuroticism. The Western approach to cure emphasizes the need to supply what was not given at the time, and every encouragement to the child to take hold of life again and develop to the limit of his abilities from there. The decision is made by the child, helped and supported by the adult. By the Russian method the adult decides on the best training and imposes it on the child, seeking his co-operation, but giving him no initiative. If a child under twelve steals, his parents are fined for giving him faulty training. Parents may also be fined if their children are rude, break the traffic regulations, ride on the back of a bus or walk on the grass. There are no probation officers, although a child may be released to his parents "on their word". Russian professional workers agree that having both parents working, or a widowed mother, or dissension within the home, can hamper good upbringing, but only on the practical level of neglect, and not on the level of emotional deprivation. The Russians have great faith in the boarding school as a cure for delinquency; British and American educators feel that emotional links between parents and children should be untangled and enriched, and only broken as a last resort.

Maladjustment is not an acknowledged category in Russia. If a child does not conform to the normal standards of behaviour, the other members of the class are asked to see that he does. Shaming an individual in front of his group is one of the most used forms of punishment. His teacher will do her best by encouragement and scolding. Next the parents will be sent for. If all these fail, the parent-teacher association, the house committee (if the child lives in a block of flats), and the trade union to which his father and mother belong will all bring pressure to bear on the parents. In extreme cases a child may be expelled from school. Alt[1] quotes a leading Russian psychiatrist as saying that "for many individuals a change of habitual mode of life and occupation means great difficulties and may give rise to a neurotic state" and goes on to mention the difficulties of school entrants in learning to sit still and not talk to each other. Enuresis is often mentioned as a problem in the first year or two of school life. Speech difficulties are also common.

If all the efforts of the school fail, the child is regarded as sick, and the educational problem becomes a physical one. Psychoses in children are regarded as the result of poliomyelitis, encephalitis, meningitis or brain damage. Pavlov regarded steady, gradual retraining of the nerve cells as the road to cure. Curiously enough the health visitor, who has no special training for her work, investigates the home, parents, housing, the financial position and school work, and recommends a disciplinary school, a colony or a mental hospital; though treatment does not seem to take her investigation into account, but generally takes the form of vitamins, diet, rest, remedial exercises, tranquillizers, stimulating drugs or sleep therapy, but not electric shock (Alt, ibid.) for children.

Many points of interest arise from the consideration of children's upbringing in the Soviet Union. Does swaddling have any permanent

[1] Alt, Herschel and Edith, *Russia's Children*, New York, Bookman Associates, 1959.

effect? Is the intensive training and stimulation of babies and toddlers, and the intensive coaching of school children in the acquisition of factual knowledge successful, or is it connected with the high incidence of enuresis and speech difficulties? These two problems cannot be hidden, but others are less obvious and may exist unacknowledged. Does the massive quantity of facts to be stored in the memory inhibit children's initiative? It may be that children can memorize in this way for most of the day and also develop their creative abilities. At the same time self-expression and speech difficulty are obviously linked, and this is one of the two biggest problems among children against which Soviet educators are struggling. Is this also connected with the Russian approach to fantasy? Imagination exists, but only as a spur to reality and not in its own right; feelings represent weakness and lack of control. Strength lies in harnessing imagination and feeling to practical tasks.

Then we have to consider whether the rearing of children in nurseries for long hours, if not the whole day or even week, affects their development. Are very young children able to standardize their human relationships and their approach to life if the authorities who handle them, both mother and teacher, are systematic? Can they have satisfying emotional experience on a less intense level than a mother-child relationship?

The provision of a model to copy gives Russian children a purpose and a clear aim. Can the diversified development of a child's abilities to the full in the service of the community provide an objective near enough to be an inspiration?

In the West patriotism has become unfashionable, and children are taught that the good of mankind is more important than the good of one nation. But the good of mankind is a distant objective which is difficult for children to visualize. If we are not, like the Russians, to use patriotism, what principle can we use to inspire children to make sacrifices, and to take positive action beyond the concern for their personal affairs?

CHAPTER 4

The Traditional and the Distinctive in Soviet Education

In trying to assess the distinctively Soviet contribution to educational thought and practice, let us look at the schools of the U.S.S.R. and see whether it is possible to distinguish traditional Russian and European features from those which are peculiar to communist schools. Several of the latter spring to mind, the terms by which they are known being commonly associated with Soviet education: the upbringing of the new man, the acquisition of a specialism at school, the integration of the school output with economic planning, polytechnical education, the absence of streaming in school classes, the unified labour school.

The idea of a planned educational system was itself no innovation in Russia. Catherine the Great took her plan from Diderot; and Alexander I's remodelled system resembled Condorcet's design. The detail and the widespread implementation of the communists' plans were probably something new, though Hans[1] claims that the rapidly developing schools of the pre-revolutionary Duma could have made the nation literate in another decade and that the planning of the enlightened tsars was based on a "ladder" system so liberal in its intentions that its implementation in the period 1906–16 seemed to presage the triumph of a democratic tradition in Russia.

Going beyond mere liberal reform communists have at times both introduced distinctively socialist features such as the unified labour school and have encouraged "progressive" practices such as the Dalton Plan, study based on a "complex" of nature, labour and society, and liaison between the school and agricultural or industrial enterprises. Innovations borrowed from Dewey and Decroly were justified in the early post-revolutionary period because of the place they gave to work, to manual activity, and to the relationship between schooling and

[1] N. Hans, "Education in Soviet Russia", *Year Book of Education*, 1933, London, Evans Bros., p. 746.

productive trades. Features which can be traced to Kerschensteiner and to Robert Owen were justified by reference to the well-known passage in Marx;[1] that is to say, to a communist tradition or canon. But even as we begin to discern the dogmatic framework of thought introduced by the communists in order to support and circumscribe educational thought, we recognize also the perpetuation in a new guise of traditional Russian axiomatic philosophy. With a bow to Kant and Pestalozzi, "the true founder of social pedagogy", Pinkevitch[2] goes on to say: "To a Marxian therefore social pedagogy is only the first important step which must be followed by a genuine proletarian or socialistic theory of education." Following his "correct" train of thought, Pinkevitch can then clarify the difference between Dewey's view of labour and that of the communist school, where the centre of activity is "not merely active and socially useful work, but production as a whole".[3]

Time and again Soviet educational policy has been changed to fit more adequately some line of thought declared to be in the true tradition of Marxism–Leninism. Orthodoxy and autocracy combine with national interest to form a trio of criteria very reminiscent of Count Uvarov's three fundamentals of conservative policy. In educational terms these are translated into the political, cultural and vocational aims of the Soviet school.[4] Russian national tradition, respected Marxist precept, and contemporary communist innovation are then hard to disentangle. Even the vocational schools of Peter the Great could be claimed as ancestors of those which were established after the dismissal of Lunacharski in 1929, when the "labour school" replaced the "activity school" and the word "work" was interpreted as "production" rather than as the creative basic activity, "congenial and free", which Lunacharski had envisaged.[5] With the support of Krupskaya, Blonski and Pinkevitch, he had aimed to teach children a distinctively proletarian outlook. In the unified labour school he had sought to provide free instruction, initiation into work, and an

[1] K. Marx, *Capital*, London, Allen and Unwin, 1928, pp. 521–522.
[2] A. Pinkevitch, *The New Education in the Soviet Republic*, New York, John Day, 1928, p. 33.
[3] ibid., p. 200.
[4] *The Changing Soviet School*, ed. Bereday et al., London, Constable, 1960, p. 13.
[5] L. Volpicelli, *L'Evolution de la Pédagogie Soviétique*, Paris, Delachaux et Niestlé, 1954, p. 27.

atmosphere of mutual respect between pupil and teacher.[1] A unified profession, such as had existed before 1880, and the best possible economic circumstances for teachers had been among his aims. Marks, examinations and punishments were abolished.

No wonder that the progressive educationists of Europe and America voiced approval of these breaks with tradition (their own as well as Russia's), or that Krupskaya and Blonski protested[2] when the school programmes designed to "stabilize" the schools re-introduced in 1927 examinations for students proposing to go on to higher studies, and demanded a sound knowledge of subjects from pupils passing out of elementary into higher schools.

It was a brusque adjustment to economic pressures which ended the period of innovations. The fulfilment of the Five Year Plan depended on the speedy training of specialists.[3] Schools and factories were linked in mutual aid. Classes and courses were improvized. Syllabuses were again designed as systematic sequences of knowledge. General education fitting pupils for further study was pushed out into those schools which gave nine, or in a growing number of cases, ten years of instruction; and through this new growth was transmitted the traditional academic function. In 1934, by order of Stalin and Molotov, the "intermediate school" replaced the "labour school", and its function as an instrument of the State and the Party was made clear.[4] As an institution for selecting the talented, the school also improved its efficiency: annual examinations were re-introduced, the authority of the teacher over the pupils and of the school vis-à-vis the Komsomol was re-established, and the characteristics of the "passive" school became dominant. In 1935 the Party restored the five-mark grading system.[5] Work in brigades and cells fell into disfavour. The pupil's individual responsibility for his own work was stressed and is still upheld by the system of daybooks for recording his performance in homework and classwork.

The schools now make quite traditional European demands upon their pupils. Lenin's exhortation to study, study, study, is frequently displayed and is backed by the moral pressure exerted on sluggish pupils by talks from teachers and Pioneer leaders, by interviews between teachers and parents, by the weekly grades recorded in class and

[1] ibid., p. 18. [2] ibid., p. 99.
[3] ibid., p. 125. [4] ibid., p. 161.
[5] *The Changing Soviet School*, p. 72.

read by parents at the week-end, and by honours lists on the school notice boards. Much of the current discussion about the effects of polytechnization reveals anxiety lest the academic sequence of study in mathematics or physics be disturbed by the need to give classwork that will tie in with what the pupils are about to do in the workshop or factory. The full development of the ten-year school for all, which was the aim until December 1958, can only have been abandoned reluctantly and under pressure from a strong complex of forces. Among these the strongest two may well have been the desire to prevent the growth of a disgruntled, academically minded group of candidates for higher education for whom no adequate outlet existed, and the urge to provide manpower for the swift expansion of industry. Full-time general secondary education for eleven years is available to the talented, and common schooling for all is being extended from seven to eight years; so a considerable degree of egalitarianism has been found to be compatible with more stringent selection of the talents to which the administrative and professional careers are opened by higher education. Divers para-scholastic "cultural" activities continue to provide variety outside the traditional curriculum of subject instruction. These are pursued in palatial quarters belonging to the Pioneers, and combine the delights of chess circles and inventors' clubs with the "upbringing" effected by "educators".

A third source of influence and instruction will be the factory personnel supervising the training of school children. It is not then surprising that the increase in the numbers of boarding schools being built is justified on the ground that socialist upbringing of the young can be achieved more cohesively there than in day schools. All the elements of the educative society, except the family, can be combined in one closely controlled operation. In country districts boarding schools may also help to overcome the unfortunately clear distinction between provision made for town-dwellers and the inadequacy of rural education. Even as late as July 1960, Mr E. I. Afanasenko, the R.S.F.S.R. Minister of Education, reported that "we still have shortcomings in the seven-year general education system, as a result of which a good part of the youth have not received a full seven-year education", and referred specifically to the Altai Territory and to the Tiumen in Astrakhan. We may note in passing that the contrast is no longer expressed in terms of tsarist neglect and communist progress. The present difficulties arise from the stresses of innovation within the communist system, from the tensions associated with planning how to use resourses which are stretched by the pace of reconstruction, modernization and expansion. The development of rural regions is encouraged by campaigns for the opening up of virgin lands, for heroic pioneering recompensed by high wages, adventure, the approval of society – and the prospect of honourable return after three years, preferably to a large town where careers are built.

The demand for a teaching appointment in Moscow is so great that priorities are established and preference is given, for example, to those who have an aged and dependent parent in the city, or whose spouse already has a job there. The attraction of a metropolis gives rise in turn to aggravated housing problems, and it is interesting to note how boarding schools are advocated because they help to solve this social problem also. Two architects, writing in "Science and Life" and quoted in *Soviet News* (March 22, 1961) write:

"Boarding schools, kindergartens and creches will make our life easier in many ways ... Under the collective method of upbringing in boarding schools and kindergartens, where they will stay for the whole week with the exception of holidays and week-ends, the children, experiencing the beneficial influence of their own contemporaries, will be brought up from an early age in a collectivist spirit. The extreme individualism and egoism which are frequently characteristic of spoiled children brought up in small families will be eradicated.

"The construction of new club premises, gymnasiums, swimming pools, libraries and rooms for music and the other arts, where people will be able to satisfy very varied tastes and interests, will eliminate the need for very large personal libraries and other premises for individual work at home.

"In this way new and better forms of public amenities will eliminate the need for flats with a large number of rooms."

In sum, the State has intervened to encourage this assembly of forces and their physical integration in one institution. The traditional communal interest in standards of behaviour has been maintained and at the same time transformed into more effectively directed pressure upon, or upbringing of, the young. A difficult housing problem is eased. And it is recognized that the formerly large diffuse kinship system which operated as a family has contracted to the nucleus we now call "family" in any modernized, mobile, industrial society. Control has passed and is passing from the stray relatives and neighbours to the instructor and the educator.

It is tempting to regard this stiffening of classroom control and the exclusion of experimental methods as the necessary concomitants of centralization and the authoritarian State. Kandel proffers this thesis. "The current trends in educational theory cannot be carried out successfully under a centralized system of administration."[1] And regretting the incomplete realization of post-war reforms in France, Roger Gal has suggested[2] that this may be due in part to the rigid centralized administration which inhibits tentative experiment. While it is true that in the U.S.S.R. innovations must be sanctioned by central authority, this does not prevent the use of certain schools or areas as testing grounds for pilot projects. Bereday and his colleagues see the conflict as one existing between rigid planning and the provision of mass education, the former plotting the course of progress, and the latter defying restriction.[3] Referring to the reforms introduced in 1958 they write: "It was virtually certain that a concentration on exclusive academic study would throw out of balance an orderly supply of highly trained manual workers, just as it is certain that the present planned trend towards training for manual work will endanger traditional academic standards. When the dynamics of an expanding system require flexibility, planned national (and hence bureaucratized) policy will be looked to in vain as a remedy."

This incompatibility was not admitted by Hans twenty years ago, who interpreted the Soviet system as "a new system of education, which unites the structure of a democratic ladder system with the substance of a privilege class system."[4] Certainly it can hardly be the planning itself which endangers traditional standards after 1958; for the exigencies of a planned economy may be said to have revived them in 1934. Nor are distinctively Soviet innovations frustrated by centralization. The re-introduction of polytechnical features in 1958 followed experimental work done in over fifty schools.[5] To designate such schools and areas is not difficult in an authoritarian State. Even after the

[1] I. L. Kandel, *The New Era in Education*, Harrap, 1955, p. 118.
[2] *Education Nationale*, Paris, April 9, 1959.
[3] *The Changing Soviet School*, p. 19.
[4] N. Hans, *History of Russian Educational Policy*, London, King and Sons, 1931, p. 7.
[5] F. Korolev, *Education in the U.S.S.R.*, Soviet News Booklet No. 24, London, n.d., p. 31.

reform was agreed and enacted, a certain degree of flexibility in practice was assured by the legislation, for article 30 of the Act stipulates that students engaged in the study of complex theoretical subjects and receiving extensive laboratory training shall not have their full-time study interrupted by "work in production" during the first two years. Gold and silver medallists are entitled to priority places in higher educational establishments.[1] And the entrance rules referring to these institutions in 1960 stipulate that "not less than 20 per cent of all vacancies will be reserved for young people without the required work record of two years."[2]

Introducing the proposals to reform Soviet education in September 1958, Khrushchev said: "Our general education schools suffer from the fact that we have taken over very much from the pre-revolutionary gymnasiums, whose purpose was to give their pupils a certain amount of abstract knowledge, sufficient to receive the matriculation certificate ... We still have a sharp distinction drawn between manual work and mental work, and there remains a situation, inherited from the past, in which preference is given to a certain section of young people who, as it were, must without fail be enrolled in higher educational establishments, and not go into factories or collective farms."[3] The exemptions quoted above will tend to perpetuate this traditional academic stream and their selection by competitive examination. The production of excellent results in the sciences and mathematics demands that the stream be allowed to flow uninterruptedly. At the same time, communist tradition, traced back to Lenin, Engels, Marx, Chernyshevsky, Owen, Fourier and Campanella, is invoked to justify a reform which solves a social problem set by 1,250,000 secondary-school-leavers of whom only 450,000 could find places in universities and institutes in 1957.

Perhaps the shortage of technical manpower which the reforms also aim to alleviate will tend to make the dynamic from the centre less inflexible in its operation. Workers must be enthused rather than driven. Economic councils and factories are being allowed more authority to take decisions. This parallel is even being urged by some scientists as part of the case for the decentralization of the academies of science and of research work. The planners who plot the course of

[1] *Soviet News*, November 16, 1959.
[2] *Soviet News*, April 12, 1960.
[3] *Soviet News*, August 10, 1959.

progress are not always, however, at odds with the masses whom they direct. The drive from the centre is partly communist in its nature, but it is also justified by the size of the country, and it is explicable in historical terms. It might be defended too on psychological grounds as a force that successfully uses hope in the future as an agent for transmuting lethargy into productivity. The dynamic liberates initiative and provides an exhilarating sense of purpose. For these reasons it does not seem to the Russians to be a strange, new or foreign imposition. There is some analogy here with the highly centralized government which the French claim is a defence of their State against disruptive tendencies, a guarantee of liberties against autocratic sections of the nation, and a necessary control over an excessively individualistic citizenry.

The two traditions seen by Hans are both still operative. What is distinctive and peculiar to the Soviet system is the readiness to make a brusque alteration in policy as soon as the Party quotes statistics that reveal economic or social problems. This is one of the senses in which the school system is geared to the national economy and the over-all plan. In implementing the general directives so as to write "productive work" into the schools' curricula and make them distinctively communist, the authorities have run into difficulties that are both theoretical and practical. E. F. Korolev, writing in *Sovetskaya Pedagogika*,[1] complains of the stress still put on verbal methods; of the "incorrect" ratio of general, polytechnical and vocational studies in secondary schools; and of an inadequate definition of "manifold development" in young people. "This definition does not contain that which distinguishes Marxist teaching about the manifold development of personality fundamentally in principle from the *bourgeois* educational theories in this problem, namely the instruction on combining training with productive work." Using terms that recall the watchwords of the 1920's he asserts: "The mistaken, one-sided understanding of the teacher's guiding role led to the point that methods began to be cultivated both in theory and in practice which eliminate the activity, initiative and self-expression of the school children." He traces the tradition of labour education back to Pestalozzi, Rousseau, Locke, Comenius, Bellers, Rabelais and Thomas More. The new, distinctive element introduced in 1958 is, according to Korolev, that in the second stage of

[1] *Sovetskaya Pedagogika*, No. 10, 1959, translated in *Soviet Education*, New York, International Arts and Sciences Press.

secondary education general polytechnical and vocational studies are combined organically on the basis of the combination of teaching with productive work. Korolev is here expressing a forecast, or perhaps interpreting a trend; for the law of 1958 does in fact provide for the division of the second cycle of secondary education into courses given in different sorts of establishment. The unified labour secondary school beyond the age of fifteen still lies in the future.

The Russian Minister of Education, E. I. Afanasenko, reporting in July 1960 to the All-Russian Teachers' Congress,[1] stressed the same "new" outlook: "The new school does not have and cannot have a single subject which does not prepare the pupils for life and labour. The fundamental difference between the eight-year and seven-year school is that, besides giving a good grounding in the fundamentals of science and polytechnical knowledge, the former also consistently applied a system of educating pupils through work which, starting with the lower grades, must prepare them both psychologically, and in practice for socially useful, productive labour. In the same report he issues the now familiar caveat, lest the weight of innovation swing the pendulum too far away from the traditional academic schools. "Some heads have come to pay less attention to instruction in general educational subjects, especially the humanities, as a result of which the standard of the school-children's knowledge has declined, the number of excellent pupils has dropped, while the number of just passing marks has grown. On the other hand, some schools have over-indulged in labour education, regardless of the actual capabilities and powers of their pupils. The excessive burden is making the pupils dislike labour and is giving the parents legitimate grounds for dissatisfaction. We cannot tolerate at all any repetition of such mistakes, which discredit the very idea of the school reform."

The discretion of local authorities and head teachers is also called for in linking the eight-year schools with production. This operation has led to some planned decentralization – whether it could be called greater flexibility is doubtful. "The school network in each of the autonomous republics and regions must be planned in such a manner that it can train cadres for the trades and professions needed by the respective administrative economic districts, while preserving the pupils' right to a free choice of their occupations when finished with the eighth grade at school, and giving each of them a real possibility of

[1] *Sovetskaya Rossiya*, July 7, 1960, translated in *Soviet Education*.

finishing secondary school... This must be done in co-operation with the regional, area and republic planning commissions, the economic councils, and the boards and departments of the Executive Committees. All the more so since the choice of the occupations in which the pupils in the secondary and industrial schools are to be trained has been vested in the Councils of Ministers of the autonomous republics and the Executive Committees of the local Soviets by a law of the Supreme Soviet of the R.S.F.R."

As in dealing with content, so also with regard to method Afanasenko tries to keep the balance between accepted practice and reform. He quotes, approvingly, Krupskaya's call for initiative and creativity in awakening the child's interest; upholds the current system of marking and grading; but warns that "we cannot permit 30 to 40 per cent of the lesson to be spent on it"; reiterates the need for homework, and suggests that its character could profitably be brought more into line with productive activity. The refurbishing of method has been more practically discussed by M. Kirilov[1] who analyses and criticizes the conventional lesson of a respected teacher whose notes were carefully prepared, whose allotment of minutes to each point was carefully calculated, and whose lesson was clearly set out in parts: repetition of previous material, interrogation, and study of new material. It was all very correct, with the pupils "participating actively" when they recalled something they had read in the textbook passage set for homework. But the lesson lacked fire, and the pupils had their books closed and were ready to depart before the bell went. It was a "Procrustean bed of categorical and one-sided provisions", felt to be too restrictive by those who would teach a love of literature rather than an examination technique.

That the bed should not be too narrow is also the recurrent theme of speeches made over the years by Kalinin.[2] "Many people are under the false impression that the development, the shaping of human beings consists in young people occupying themselves with their Komsomol duties. But these Komsomol duties consist mainly of mastering the ABC of politics, studying Marxism – in a word, social problems. It seems to me that such a narrow view of problems concerning the formation of human beings is a wrong one... That is why, I think,

---

[1] *Narodnoye Obrazovanie*, No. 9, 1959, translated in *Soviet Education*.
[2] M. I. Kalinin, *On Communist Education*, Moscow, Foreign Languages Publishing House, 1950, *passim*.

the Komsomol organization should help not only to give the younger generation the rudiments of political knowledge but also see to it that their political knowledge is based on those branches of general education and knowledge that are considered the necessary attributes of more or less every developed person" (1926). So the distinctive communist education was to have its sound traditional base.

In 1939 Kalinin combined the elements even more inextricably: "We want our schools to give a communist education . . . What do we mean by education? We mean influencing the physical and moral attributes of the pupil . . . moulding him as a human being. Communist principles, taken in their elementary form, are the principles of highly educated, honest, advanced people; they are love for one's Socialist motherland, friendship, comradeship, humanity, honesty, love for Socialist labour, and a great many other universally understood lofty qualities. Communist education . . . is the struggle for a higher level of labour productivity." The juxtaposition of these last two sentences strikes jarringly. But traditionalist educators in Western Europe would accept many of Kalinin's terms; perhaps only A. S. Neill and W. B. Curry and a few others would refuse the godlike task of "moulding" the young human. And even higher productivity is not so exclusively communist an aim now as it was in 1939.

At any given moment the relative emphasis on general education or on vocational training, the latter justifiable by reference to Lenin and to Peter the Great, the former justifiable by reference to Lenin and to Lunacharsky, will depend on the country's need for specialist technicians or future technologists. The thread of tradition leading back to Peter I or even to Catherine II is weak. An Academy, certain great schools and some cypher schools were, it is true, founded by Peter. And Catherine thought in rational (French) terms of the establishment of a nation-wide system of schools that would educate citizens. But the communists' outlook is much more wholehearted and its policy is more vigorous than that of either of the tsars. Soviet educationists have made repeated and obstinate attempts to establish a working relationship between schooling and production, and between schooling and social upbringing. The distinction is partly one of greater numbers, of more efficient civic machinery, and of more widespread implementation, but it passes from a distinction of degree to one of kind when we contemplate the impact of ideological thought upon so vast and well-controlled a system of institutions.

Changes introduced into so big an organization must be resolutely made, and are bound to appear ruthless; and they must be powered by so strong a dynamic that past inadequacies tend to be condemned as bad and the innovations praised as salutary. The terms have a missionary ring. In so large a territory with so many languages and cultures the scope for varied and conflicting interpretations of traditions and of present needs is vast, and the country can only be held together by government and education if central pronouncements about policy and values are declared to be universally valid and are enthusiastically proclaimed. Determination to overcome the obstacles of distance and misinterpretation may account in part for "the Russian inability to temporize; everything must be adjudged as either good or bad".[1] It may also help to account for the Russians' reputation for rigidity, dogmatism, orthodoxy and autocracy as opposed to pragmatic, tentative, decentralized liberalism. If this argument is acceptable, then the communists can be seen as carrying out by recognizably Russian tactics the aspirations of the reforming tsars.

But not all of these attributes are exclusively Russian or Western. Size and pragmatism, for example, are characteristics which one observer finds common to both the U.S.S.R. and the U.S.A.[2] "The likenesses in the education systems of the two nations show the influence of their surging industrialization within wide boundaries, and a pragmatic orientation of schools. The differences are due in part to the Soviets' preservation of many Continental concepts such as separate educational streams." Anderson is referring in this last comment to the division of courses following the seven-year school. Bereday and his colleagues make a similar observation.[3] "It is significant to note that Soviet educational planners in their discussions with American visitors exhibited more interest in the English tripartite system, which divides 11-year-olds into academic (grammar), technical, and modern (general) 'streams', than in the American comprehensive school, which postpones specialization until 15 and insists on its taking place under a common roof."

It would, however, be misleading to interpret the communist decision to provide general education with some guidance towards a

---

[1] Alexander Hertzen (1812–70) quoted by W. E. Johnson, *Russia's Educational Heritage*, Carnegie, 1950, p. 230.

[2] C. Arnold Anderson, *School Review*, Chicago, Spring 1959.

[3] *The Changing Soviet School*, p. 17.

"speciality" in the unified eight-year school and then to divide the various schools, as a compromise between Western European and American practices. The Soviet school system, including their development of boarding schools, is not the result of decisions about the acceptability of school systems seen in other countries but of a distinctively Russian complex of economic and social and ideological pressures. The decision to alter the articulation of various stages of schooling, to alter the balance of authority in the schools, or the amount of vocational training in the curriculum, or the prestige of the Komsomol vis-à-vis the headmaster, or the emphasis on individual work and competitive rewards, or the structure of the school system is made by the Central Committee of the Communist Party in the light of their interpretation of these pressures. Over-riding all other traditions, or drawing them into its service, is the movement towards the building of communist society. Method, curriculum, political upbringing, and the structure of the school system are all eventually tested against this criterion.

Mead and Calas report comparable developments in the child-rearing ideals of Soviet theoreticians.[1] After a post-revolutionary period in which the older family patterns were rejected and Western progressive practices were imitated, the family was reinstated and parents were re-established as models of behaviour and sources of authority. Parents share in the task of shaping the "moral countenance" of the child. Parental love is given or withdrawn, as is the approval of the teacher and the child's classmates, as a form of discipline. Children are taught to avoid vanity and conceit, "the vice so often pilloried in old Russian literature". In place of the former diffuse system of authority vested in many dissimilar figures, we now discern "a solid ring of individuals, old and young, at home, in school, in youth organizations, in the work collectives, the party, the State, all of whom are expected to express the same values, at all times in all places. ... Today the literature suggests that the Soviet Union is moving towards a type of education which resembles (but, as we shall see, also differs from) the older Russian form of many authority figures operating upon an individual sense of general guilt or unworthiness. The authority of the parents has been re-emphasized after the attempts to reduce it during the first fifteen years of the régime ... Furthermore, parents are seen as

[1] M. Mead and E. Calas, *Childhood in Contemporary Cultures*, ed. Mead and Wolfenstein, University of Chicago Press, 1955, p. 179 ff.

only one part of a completely harmonized attempt to bring up the young in the way they should go.... Instead of the old inconsistencies between standards and sanctions presented by many individuals in the environment, one set of standards is to be presented."[1] A. S. Makarenko puts this succinctly when he suggests that the defaulting parent should ask himself: "Have I, in my family life, acted like a Bolshevik?"[2] The decisive factor in successful family upbringing, he says,[3] lies in the constant, active and conscious fulfilment by the parents of their civic duty towards Soviet society. He too stresses parents' authority, which they derive from living the "full, conscious, moral life of a citizen of the Soviet Land".[2]

The urge to act systematically and to be tidy and punctual, which visitors to the Soviet Union will recognize as an important attribute of the "cultured" citizen, is well expressed by Makarenko in the following passage:

> The old intellectual "Russian" impetuousness was able to combine, it would seem, two incompatible things. On the one hand, thinking intellectuals could always come out with the most radical and rational ideas often exceeding the bounds of plain reality, while at the same time they always exhibited a passionate love of slovenliness and disorder. Perhaps they had a special taste that could discern in this disorder a gleam of something higher, something that touched them deeply – a precious gleam of freedom. In the Bohemian muddle of their everyday life they were able to see some high aesthetic meaning. In this love there was something of anarchism, of Dostoyevski, of Christianity. But the fact is that in this slipshod "leftish" way of living there is nothing except historical poverty and nakedness. Some people even today, at the bottom of their hearts, still despise punctuality and orderly movement, a mode of living that pays proper attention to details.
>
> "A slovenly attitude to life cannot fit with the style of Soviet life. With all the means at our disposal we should exorcise that belated Bohemian spirit which only by a great misunderstanding is considered by certain comrades a token of poetic taste. In scrupulous accuracy, in collectedness, in strict and even severe consistency, in

[1] ibid., p. 198.
[2] A. S. Makarenko, *A Book for Parents*, Moscow, Foreign Languages Publishing House, n.d., p. 17.
[3] ibid., p. 24.   [1] ibid., p. 181.

the thoroughness and thoughtfulness of a human action there is more beauty and poetry than in any 'poetic disorder'."[1]

The reference to Dostoyevski is interesting. Visitors to the U.S.S.R. have heard it said that "even in Russia" (i.e. before 1917) he was reckoned to be a man with a sick conscience. His melancholy and despair are held to have been excessive, pessimistic, and negative, and are therefore regretted as being a less edifying aspect of his work. Writers, it is said, should struggle to overcome their gloom. This attitude fits well with other themes we have encountered in this chapter. All the engineering and architectural feats which are shown to foreign and provincial visitors in Russian cities underline the thesis that achievement results from positive drive. They also remind the people how much more productive are mastery and enthusiasm than resignation and brooding. A channel is provided for people's energies: and with release and canalization have come speed and power for industrialization and modernization. It is to this operation that the schools contribute.

Such prescriptions are characteristic of the society which has had to save itself by conscious effort and by nationally recognized and fully operative government, and which is concerned to maintain itself by the civic virtues of orderliness and loyalty. What served to advance and stabilize dominant societies of the past can be incorporated into present policies; authority of teacher and parent, hard work, study, mastery of subject disciplines, and so on. What serves to distinguish the new order from previous orthodoxies, autocracies and nationalisms, is perpetuated by myth and legend built up into the new distinctive tradition and transmitted by a well-recognized process: "Still others, especially the school practitioners of cultural pedagogics, find the educative power of a culture to be founded in the immanent spiritual content of each of the culture's goods, a content which was originally alive in the creator of that cultural lore and now, split away from him, lives on it as a latent power. So when the docile subject approaches this cultural heritage, reads the poem, sings the song, studies the philosophical system, or contemplates the painting, the immanent latent energy in them comes to life and is transformed into kinetic energy which works upon natures that are receptive to it."[2] In Soviet terms

[1] ibid., p. 302.
[2] F. Schneider, *Triebkräfte der Pädagogik der Völker*, Otto Müller Verlag, Salzburg, 1947, p. 160.

the lore and culture involved in such a process are national songs and dances, heroic odes to the Party, paintings of Lenin and of the current Chairman of the Council of Ministers, plays and films about revolutionary heroes, and so on.

In the classrooms of other countries there may hang a crucifix, or the national flag, or a portrait of the Queen, or one of the Lord Mayor; or, as in some schools in Vienna, both the crucifix and the Lord Mayor may be honoured. But the U.S.S.R. is still building its revolutionary tradition with zeal, not just out of habit or courtesy. Other schools have parents' associations, but in the U.S.S.R. they are expected to work with the teacher, not to hire and fire her. Other schools have links with local industrialists, but not links forged by the local economic planning councils. Others have a democratic ladder system of comprehensive schools designed to serve a social purpose; but few pursue that purpose so determinedly – and then legislate so that beyond a certain point the precious twenty in each hundred scholars can contract out of an educational process deemed in principle to be salutary for all. Makarenko's precepts are still revered; but his own practice was not always consistent with them. He himself records with delight that one of his successes in redeeming a juvenile delinquent began when he forgot his principles and threw a chair at the lad. The combination of apparently irreconcileable elements struck Sir Eric Ashby in the 1940s as an enduring Russian feature in the Soviet scene, and he quotes the prosecutor Kirillovich from *The Brothers Karamazov* in support of his analysis: "We are broad natures ... able to accommodate every possible contradiction ... we are broad like Mother Russia herself; we find room for everything, we reconcile ourselves to everything."[1]

This "breadth" has probably been reduced as the standards of behaviour and judgement prescribed for the Party members have filtered down through the schools to the masses, and by the canalization of energies and emotions referred to above. Enthusiasm and optimism and revolutionary zeal are not always tolerant virtues. Even Makarenko, with his emphasis on individuality and variety, was not very quickly accepted as canonical. And by him, as by Kalinin whom we quoted earlier in this chapter, full individual development is prized for its greater contribution to the collective. (This is not so very far from some Western concepts about "education for service to the

[1] E. Ashby, *Scientist in Russia*, Pelican Books, 1947.

community", but the difference in the placing of the emphasis is usually noticeable.) We often call this a communist characteristic; but here again, to attach labels is too simple; for historically there is a link with the communal society of the *mir*, whereas English history since the Reformation shows rather the atomization of old social and religious structures and the growth of individual enterprise and conscience. Even Makarenko's self-questioning "have I acted like a Bolshevik?" is not to be equated with the analytical, unattached inquiring mind of the English liberal Protestant or the French free-thinker. The aim of Makarenko's question is to facilitate return to the fold, not independence from the flock. Moreover the use of a communist criterion for right and wrong leads to a vision of values in simple black and white. Mastery of oneself, of nature and perhaps also of the teachable masses is not compatible with forgiving oneself, or with tolerating the faults of one's neighbours and competitors.

So too the criteria which sound universal tend, in the enthusiast's mouth, to become national. This is still discernible when Frenchmen speak of their Revolutionary ideals and of the universal march of humanity towards enlightenment and brotherhood, with France in the van. It was not fortuitous that Khrushchev, visiting the French fair in Moscow in September 1961, remarked that the French seemed to have somewhat forgotten their Revolutionary motto and that the U.S.S.R. had taken up the banner. So the teaching of communist ethics and of universal values coincides in the schools, and the struggle for socialism is equated with progress towards world peace. All missionary and revolutionary movements use universal terms, and many of them claim world allegiance; but the distinctively communist combination of convinced rectitude with complete power is alarming. The autocracy of the tsars was limited in a way that totalitarian government is not.

Nor does the "broad Russian nature" so far express itself scholastically in the sorts of analytical sociological studies that tend in Europe and America to weaken our convictions about the inevitability of our culture, about its superiority and its durability, about its providential nature, and about the irrefutability of our beliefs. Communist interpretation of social and psychological data is still done by reference to the canon. Taxed with this similarity to the Roman Catholic Church a Moscow University professor remarked to the writer: "Why not? Look what a power the Church is still." As in other matters we have discussed here, this sense of mission can be traced historically to a

Russian belief in themselves as a chosen people. So too were the Franks. But in the eighteenth century the French *bourgeoisie* expressed its dissatisfaction in freemasonry, in circles of free-thinkers and in the verbal rejection of authority on the grounds of much-discussed general principles; whereas in twentieth-century Russia the revolutionaries took over the autocratic apparatus and developed it making sure that no middle class or intelligentsia as we understand the term will be allowed to challenge the ideological élite by building an alternative channel. Those matriculated students emerging from the ten-year school with pretensions to a status that had no occupational justification have been diverted into labour productivity as soon as they began to constitute a social problem. The teaching given in school and the organization of the educational system re-direct the traditional elements of Russian breadth, Russian messianism, Russian individuality into a channel that is distinctively communist.

This is not to imply that tolerance has suddenly become intolerance. The tendency to suspect foreigners and to see international differences in simple terms can also be recognized as a lasting Russian characteristic. Alongside this feature, "breadth" exists in friendliness and in hospitality,[1] in personal conversation and in humour, and perhaps in their enjoyment of persons' temperaments and quirks. (It has been suggested that the English tolerate ideas fairly easily so long as their propounders conform in custom and habit to English practice.) Breadth of viewpoint also exists within the canonical framework, that is so long as fundamentals and aims are not questioned. Existing tensions are not now between pre-revolutionary and post-revolutionary ideas or cultures.[2] Nor are they between traditional practice and communist innovation: we have seen that in making a system that is distinctively new, the communists have successfully incorporated and re-directed attitudes and habits that are recognizably Russian. The tensions arise rather from the pace of competitive modernization which requires revolutionary zeal, brusque adaptation of school practices and organization to each recurrent demand for manpower, self-discipline, self-mastery, and the postponement of consumers' enjoyments.

The teachers' journals reflect ferment, inconsistency, error and correction as the Marxist precept meets established practice. Profusion

---

[1] W. Miller, *Russians as People*, Phoenix House, London, pp. 88 and 107.
[2] W. R. Fraser, "Tensions in Soviet Education", *Studies in Education*, University of Hull Institute of Education, July 1961.

and diversity exist legitimately within a firm structure of ideology and law as expressed in the preamble and terms of the Act of December 1958. The legislation sets bounds and gives direction to the teachers' search for an approved solution to difficulties amounting to confusion each time the educational machine is geared to a new type of product. Controlled purposeful activity motivated by a still powerful missionary fervour, and directed by an all-embracing government which uses traditions as they answer to the sometimes conflicting demands of ieology and productivity, this is the feature which stands out as a distinctively communist framework for a pattern which is still recognizably Russian.

CHAPTER 5

The Role, Status and Training of Teachers in the U.S.S.R.

The "Soviet Commitment to Education"[1] (to use the phrase enshrined in the title of an official U.S. report) stems from the need, still urgent after forty years of communism, to raise the productivity of the country by means approved in Marxist–Leninist doctrines. Since education is seen as the key to the development of the economy of the Soviet Union, much of the country's money has been poured into establishing a complex system of pre-school, school and higher education, with a number of other educational services employing between them over a million and a half qualified teachers. Nowadays, probably between 10 and 15 per cent of the national budget is channelled into education of all types.[2]

Previously, although Tsarist Russia had a well-established educational system, it was not broadly based. For a large part of the country, therefore, and for a high proportion of the population, the communist era has provided a first generation of formal education. It has been claimed, for instance, that in the Tajik Socialist Soviet Republic there now are three thousand schools with seven higher and twenty-two vocational secondary schools, not to mention an Academy of Sciences, catering for a population which, at the outbreak of the First World War, was almost completely illiterate.

Such an example is only an extreme case of what is fairly general in many parts of the Soviet Union; and it is not as though educational provision were the only burden on Soviet finance. Educational buildings, equipment and staffing have been budgeted for in competition with other enormous demands on the national income – an income which at the beginning of the Revolutionary era scarcely existed.

---

[1] *Soviet Commitment to Education*, Bulletin 1959, Number 16, U.S. Department of Health, Education and Welfare, Office of Education.

[2] An independent 1962 estimate gives the percentage for education of the Gross National Product as $4\frac{1}{2}$ per cent. This gives a clearer indication than the budget (Ed.)

The history of the first forty years or so of communism in the Soviet Union has been one of the struggle to develop both its natural and its human resources. In the early days, administrators-in-a-hurry hoped to achieve higher productivity while neglecting or short-cutting education. This phase ended in the early thirties. More recently, education has become so established that there was a danger of its becoming an end in itself. Since December 1958, this tendency has been officially checked under the Law on Establishing Closer Links between School and Life and on the Further Development of Public Education.

Throughout this history, however, teachers have been recognized – albeit grudgingly at some periods – as key workers for the welfare of the nation. In this general context their status and morale stand high and their overall motivation is potent. In 1918 Lenin said: "A teacher of the people should occupy a high position such as he never occupied, does not and cannot occupy in a *bourgeois* society. This truth needs no proof." At the 1960 All-Union Congress of Teachers, over forty years later, Khrushchev said: "Each (Communist) party and Soviet worker, despite his position, has to remember that he owes much to school and to teachers."

What helps both teachers and pupils to keep the picture uncluttered and the motivation clear is the comparative absence in the Soviet Union of negative influences militating against education, the fact that "the U.S.S.R. has ... escaped the large-scale commercialization of the moron" as Alec Nove puts it in *The Soviet Economy*.[1] Money has been withheld from consumer goods, from debilitating commercial advertising, and from the titillating influences of cheesecake pornographic paper-backs, to be poured into education. Instead of women's magazines, racing news and crime fiction, people straphanging in the Moscow Metro read serious hard-backed books and *Pravda*, while young apprentices and even working girls may be seen studying textbooks connected with their part-time or correspondence courses. Much of what is read may be dull; it may be lacking in art for all I know (not being a Russian scholar). The point at issue is that the reading matter is not pulling in a direction opposite to that of the teachers or of the education system. If young people in U.S.S.R. reject the school system, there is little to support their feelings of rebellion. They cannot readily ape the behaviour or attitudes shown in glamorized pictures

[1] A. Nove, *The Soviet Economy*, George Allen and Unwin, 1961.

of having a "good time", when such models are wholly outside their experience.

Supporting the pragmatic necessities of the economy are the doctrines of communism which are studied in every school and college. Every student, teacher and administrator in U.S.S.R. has passed examinations on Marxist–Leninism. Every school-child is surrounded by quotations from their "gospels". Learning is enshrined in the doctrines as a good thing in itself. Under the glass tops of library tables or surrounding the dais on the school platform are exhortations to study and to labour. Lenin is the father-figure in education: his bust or statue is prominent in every school. Among other fruitful ideas, Lenin formulated that of creative collective work: in his view – and in that of many psychologists since his time – the answers found by a group being likely to be better than those found by any individual alone. No ignoramus, Lenin was himself master of several languages and a considerable scholar, while his wife, Krupskaya, was an enlightened authority on education. Had it not been for their explicit doctrines, it is by no means certain that the Soviet Union would have established anything comparable with its present educational machinery.

In the early days of communism, in the twenties and early thirties, there were many experiments and much confusion in education. But what emerged from all this experience was the conviction that Lenin and Krupskaya had been right. The Soviet authorities came to realize that no short-term or makeshift policies in education would carry them through the process of building a new nation. They realized that if the national aims of increased production, adequate defence and improved standard of living were to be brought within their grasp, then good academic standards had to be widely attained in the schools. The task of educators was accordingly to provide learning, i.e. knowledge and the skills to use it. Therefore a pattern of education was laid down which was maintained for more than a quarter of a century. The reorientation initiated by the Khrushchev Theses of 1958 has led to the first major change in education since the early thirties.

It is clear from the above that in the Soviet Union teachers are a respected group with the status due to key workers in the struggle for the economic uplift of the country as a whole.

But in a sense they share such importance with "all other workers and peasants", each of whom is supposed to feel himself as an important cog in the whole production machine. It is, of course, not certain that everyone does feel this significance, but there is still about Soviet effort a kind of back-to-the wall, pull-for-the-shore desperation which one feels in Western countries only during official wars. For the Soviet people it has been war time to all intents and purposes ever since they remember. As they see it, their country has been surrounded by enemies and their only hope first of survival, then of an improved standard of living, lies in disciplined collective effort: in putting first things first.

The present status of teachers in the Soviet Union relates largely to this pattern of a quarter of a century. Within it they fulfil a respected and traditional type of role. They do what almost all the world of laymen expects of teachers: they keep order, teach from textbooks, set homework, evaluate and report on the pupils' progress, and discuss their problems with the school principal. All this they do in a fairly fixed routine of class-lessons, free periods and teachers' meetings. They appear to maintain discipline without undue strain. This success may be due in part to the system of marking the pupils' work. Both classwork and written work are assessed out of five marks by the teacher, marks of two or one being considered as failures. The notice of the principal is attracted at once to any pupil who receives low marks at all frequently, and he "helps" the pupil to make greater efforts, the initial assumption always being that lack of scholastic success is the result of laziness. If the pupil's retardation continues, his failure may be reported to the parents. It can come up for consideration by the school committee, by a parents' committee; eventually by a committee of neighbours in the child's home area, or even by a committee of the factory or place of work of one or other of his parents. All along the line classroom discipline and attention to school work are thus reinforced. The pupil is soon made aware of the serious view of his work taken not only by his class-teacher but by all the other adults in his world.

In his turn, the teacher who is beginning to be careless in his work or to feel that certain pupils are "hopeless" at their work, soon finds that he is expected to achieve learning among a very high proportion of his pupils. His failure to do so will reflect not only on the pupil but on himself. Whilst the responsibility lies with the teacher to help to identify pupils suffering from brain damage or physical defects, the eventual ascertainment of such handicaps by specialist diagnosticians is on a conservative scale. A Soviet teacher is not encouraged to call out for remedial treatment elsewhere for his maladjusted pupils with learning problems. He is expected to cope with the situation and to achieve some success in terms of measurable academic attainment by practically everyone in his class.

As compared with that in the earlier period (of the twenties) the role of the teacher is nowadays clearly defined, and the daily life of the school is definitely patterned. If he teaches younger children below the age of about eleven years, he takes his (reasonable-sized) class for all their work. If he is teaching at secondary level he gives instruction in the one or two subjects for which he has academic qualifications. In either case he works to a defined time-table, a clear curriculum, with particular textbooks, aiming to cover a certain body of knowledge by mainly the age-old read and discuss, question and answer, revise and repeat, write and correct, mark and record, talk and chalk methods of schools the world over.

The roles of everyone connected with education are equally clearly defined, from the entering pupil aged 7 to the school principal, from the chief administrator to the part-time cleaner.

As soon as children begin attending school they are taught the "Rules for Pupils"[1] which obtain in every Soviet school. There are twenty-one of these and they lay down definite instructions for behaviour in school. It is, for example, the duty of every school child "to sit upright during the lesson, not leaning on his elbows and not slouching; to listen attentively to the teacher's explanation and the other children's answers, and not to talk or let his attention stray to other things". The stated purpose of the child's coming to school is "to acquire knowledge persistently in order to become an educated and cultured citizen and to be of the greatest possible service to his country". Some of the rules flow over from school life to the child's other spheres; he is admonished about punctuality, cleanliness, tidiness, respect to elders, care of property, kindness to younger children. At least one of the rules may be a little premature for the 7-year-olds: not to smoke and not to gamble; but no doubt the pupils accept it with the same tolerance that young children in our culture learn that they are not to commit adultery.

The younger children attend for a shorter day at first, but apart from that, the general routine of school with its adherence to the rules and associated code of honour continues for all on the established lines.

[1] Quoted from *The Changing Soviet School*, Ed. G. Z. F. Bereday, W. W. Brickman and G. H. Read, Constable, 1960.

The forty-five minute "hour" lessons are separated by ten or fifteen minutes of talk and movement. Homework is introduced at once and the homework time-table is compulsory for all. The pupils and teachers alike are trained to keep records of the work and of the marks given for it. A standard printed "diary" the size of an exercise book is used by every pupil. This treasured possession is ruled so that with six lines to a day and three days to a page the week's record can be seen at a glance. The mark one to five for each hour's work has to be initialled by the teacher. There are spaces for notes on absence, lateness, illness, as well as for the teacher's comments and the parent's signature.

Changes in the curriculum are not the responsibility of any individual. Any real educational "experiment" or "research" is initiated from above, i.e. by authorities external to the school personnel. A school may be selected for a special purpose; but, in carrying through these purposes, the school staff follow the lead and have the support of the authority, which has also to bear the brunt of any opposition, criticism or failure. An example here might be the selection by the authorities of School Number One in Moscow as an English school. Whereas in most schools English or another foreign language is begun when the pupils have completed four years of school, in School Number One English is begun in the second year, with special textbooks. The aim is to achieve such mastery of the language (by pupils and teachers) as will allow several subjects of the curriculum such as geography, to be taught in English by the time the pupils are about fourteen.

No doubt a school's being singled out for such an experiment can cause anxiety and additional work to the principal and teachers in such a case as that quoted above. The point at issue is that whilst they are of course expected to be utterly loyal to the policy decision of their authority, they are not also burdened with responsibility for initiating major changes in the curriculum. Except in matters of comparative detail, Soviet teachers and school principals are not burdened with policy making about what goes on even in their own school. The staff and head teacher have an important function in making official policy work and in helping pupils and parents to accept educational experiments; but they can hardly put themselves into a vulnerable position by going all out on some new educational line of their own, as can happen in England in private and, to some extent, even in local authority schools.

The anxiety apart, it is obvious that school staffs are often proud to be involved in some research. It adds interest to the daily work, brings notable visitors to the school, and opens the way for public discussion of their success. All this helps to build up the teachers' self-esteem and to focus local attention positively on the work of education. Since the project is officially sponsored, changes come down the line – perhaps apparently capriciously – but at least they are not dependent on such immediate changes as, for example, the appointment of a new principal or an increase in the number of pupils. Moreover, extra staff or relief in other ways are almost certain to be given to help the teachers to get to grips with their new problems (such as the learning of textbooks in a foreign language). Curriculum development and the findings of action research are the concern first and foremost of the Soviet administration, not a well-nigh intolerable burden borne by exceptional principals and outstanding teachers as, in the main, they are in the United Kingdom.

Of course teachers both in Britain and in the Soviet Union have other means than direct experiment of carrying into action their ideas for improved education. They can write articles for educational journals; prepare papers for educational discourses; or submit suggestions to the appropriate officer, committee or council.

In any country an educational administration which fails to take note of the more intelligent criticism and suggestions of its practising teachers is riding for a fall, for the resulting loss in the ardour and good will of both principals and teachers will reduce incalculably the effectiveness of the work of the schools.

In this regard the lines of communication in the Soviet Union appear to be more open than many visitors or critics suspect. Although at any one time the system of Soviet education looks extremely rigid, yet change is a normal expectancy. The schools have established many routines, habits and traditions, especially as described above in matters of pupil conduct and teacher-pupil relationships; but in certain important respects the schools are always changing. Within the rigid framework, the curriculum is always being modified to meet new needs, while the transitional nature of the school society is everywhere recognized.

The constant revision of textbooks well illustrates the fact of change being normal and universally accepted in schools. Some of the textbooks in use in U.S.S.R. may at a casual glance look old-fashioned.

Many of them are cheaply produced on poor paper with rather small illustrations and little colour; but the books in use are not old, and the standard of production is rising. Revising curricula and producing textbooks is a serious undertaking to which the concentrated efforts o numbers of educational experts are constantly devoted. Since the committees responsible for textbooks are anxious to meet the real needs of teachers, before each new book is published for general use it is tried out in hundreds of schools and may be revised to meet the criticisms and to incorporate the best suggestions of the teachers in those schools.

As well as meeting these expressed needs the textbooks are an important vehicle for spreading new curricula. A teacher of English with whom I discussed textbooks in Kiev knew in September 1958 that new books were pending, and she was looking forward with some eagerness to receiving them. When they became available as expected, she very courteously sent me samples, pointing out where the new books were better. I mention the detail only to illustrate the point that ordinary classroom teachers are aware when new textbooks and curriculum are imminent. Some of them even feel involved in helping to make the changes.

The more far-reaching changes which were anticipated in 1958 were also (to some extent) under discussion among teachers before they passed into law on 24th December. Although the words being bandied about at this time were mainly to do with technical developments, the real issue which the Soviet teacher has had to face is much bigger. Recent changes in the law have brought him right up against the fact – tacitly denied in schools in many countries – that the school is not fulfilling its function if it becomes a static society and an end in itself. A school is a changing milieu in which dependent children grow towards a life of adult service.

Whatever changes are made in the role or functions of the teacher, two points remain important in the Soviet Union: the teacher is kept clearly apprised of what he is expected to do and he can be sure that his work will not fall outside the range of what is thought of by teachers as "professional" work.

Teachers, of course, share the very special responsibility which all adult Soviet citizens are supposed to accept for the moral guidance of the younger generation; but the teacher's part in this has to be achieved through the content of the curriculum and through the normal discipline of the classroom.

It is this exclusively professional function of teachers which helps to give them status. Within the school they are identified with the holy purposes of education pure and simple. Other qualified persons fulfil a variety of ancillary and of menial tasks. This system helps to place the teacher at the top of the hierarchy, whilst of course giving him the chance to do his job adequately without distractions. In a well-equipped, well-staffed town school in addition to what in England would be named the headmaster, deputy head and assistant teachers, there are a chief training teacher, librarian, nurse, visual-aids or other technician, part- (up to half-) time doctor, administrative officer and deputy, as well as clerical and domestic helpers. There may be full-time youth workers too.

The exact staffing ratio varies. Good schools, including experimental schools, appear to be heavily used as training grounds; and the internship, apprenticeship, or practice system of learning a profession results in large numbers of staff in many institutions, including schools.

What is important, however, is that all these people, and I am here only concerned with teachers, have their definite role and duties. They know what to do. Other people also know what the teachers are expected to do and the whole system combines to perpetuate itself and carry on with a momentum engendered by custom.

All this means that in the Soviet Union the public image of teachers as well-qualified, competent professional persons is not too often damaged by stories of weakness or ineptitude.

In our own country nothing is more prejudicial to the status of teachers in the eyes of parents than sons and daughters revealing at home that certain teachers cannot keep order; that "old so-and-so" never really teaches anything; or that no teacher turned up to give a certain lesson and the children had a high old time; unless it is when stories of indiscipline in school reach the Press or are made into films of the type of "Blackboard Jungle". Such stories also undermine the confidence of the student teacher and the self-picture even of experienced teachers.

It is of great benefit to the status of teachers in U.S.S.R. that under the Soviet system teachers are thought of as being generally fairly successful. The impression at least is gained that few of them are obviously incapable of maintaining discipline or are blatantly unable to get through their quota of work.

No one of course would deny that in still having in their classes many children from semi-literate or poorly educated homes, Soviet teachers are up against a major problem without parallel in present-day Britain. What, however, we are unable to judge, is whether Soviet teachers as a whole are more or less intelligent than their opposite numbers in the West. We are equally without sufficient basis of facts to estimate the turn-over of staff, the wastage from the profession, and the incidence of health, including mental health, problems.

There is nothing, however, in what I have seen or read to indicate that Soviet teachers are not fairly comparable with teachers anywhere. They do not include many of the top-flight intelligences – or not for long – but they do appear to include a high proportion of people of considerable good will and fair intelligence for whom teaching is a life's work and a way of life. A number of teachers to whom I was introduced had spent many years in the same school. They were as engrossed in the welfare of their pupils and in the day-to-day trivia of their job as any teachers anywhere.

Because her letter illustrates so perfectly the attitudes and preoccupations of a Soviet teacher, I cannot resist quoting verbatim a letter received in November 1961 by an English private boarding school teacher from her pen friend in the Ukraine. Only the salutations are omitted.

> I got your letter a week ago but had no time to answer it. You are quite right, promotions mean a great deal of extra work. I am busy all day long and when I come home in the evening I am overtired. But still it is a very interesting work. To begin with our boarding school – it is a new one. It is here, in Kiev, not far from my home and in a very beautiful place. There is a great park there and our school is quite near it. We shall have only boarders – we are going to welcome our pupils in a couple of weeks. For these two months we have been working hard trying to make a real good home for our children. There are more than sixty teachers and tutors at the school. We take care of everything – painting desks and planting trees, buying flowers, visual aids, toys, books, pictures, carpets, crockery, mirrors, coats, dresses, blankets, etc. etc. Of course there are people who are busy with these things; but we are to help them, to prompt them, to control them. Every little detail must be looked at as we want our boarding school to be an excellent one. Then we must arrange their documents for payment. The thing is that parents

pay for their children and it depends upon the wages parents get. If there are some children in the family they pay little. If the wages are high and there is one child only the parents are to pay more. Of course the children have the same conditions of life and food and dressing.

There are thirty pupils at every class. They have one teacher if it is the 1st–4th form, and two tutors. The 5th–the 8th form have different teachers as it depends on the subjects the pupils are taught, and two tutors too.

Then we have a staff of cooks and a doctor and some nurses, etc. There are three buildings connected – a building of bedrooms and game-rooms, a school and a dining-room with a kitchen. When the weather is good my friend will take some pictures of our new school and I'll send you some.

When I wish to rest I re-read my English novels and it is a fine rest.

If you read the books I have sent you, write your opinion about them. I should like to know what you like among them.

This dedicated teacher has evidently gained some well-earned step on the ladder of promotion. What of the slightly less devoted, less hard-working general run of teachers? How can their best contribution to education be ensured?

In my view, for these average Soviet teachers there is great value in the clear definition of role and function which I have described as being now typical of the system of public education. Neither in the Soviet Union, nor in any other progressive country, is it reasonable to expect every classroom to be manned by a person exhibiting all the desirable characteristics of the perfect teacher. One task of the administration is to clarify educational policy and communicate it to the teachers, so that they are as effective as possible: and, one might add, for as long as possible.

This question of "effectiveness" is full of difficulty. The measure of a teacher's value is in the all-round progress of his pupils: but this, in turn, is not capable of reliable assessment.

This feature of the work of a teacher, the fact that his "productivity value" cannot be calculated, leaves education at the mercy of the theorists – and worse. Perhaps, however, some lessons for educational management can be gleaned from industrial practice, since nobody can gainsay that in industry the effectiveness of the management is reflected to some degree in the output of each firm. In this connexion the following quotation from the "Objectives of the Glacier Project"[1] seems relevant.

> ... Managerial effectiveness is partly a function of the personality and character of the manager. Training can do little to change these personal qualities.
>
> A manager's behaviour is, however, strongly influenced by the correctness of definition of the role he occupies, the relationship of this role to other roles in the total system, the terms of reference governing his role and the degree to which the manager understands these matters. Modification and clarification of such conditions can, therefore, produce significant changes in managerial behaviour and effectiveness. Moreover, these conditions can be scientifically studied and taught...

I am not sure that the Russians are "scientifically studying and teaching" "these conditions" in the sense in which these phrases are used by Glacier; but I have gained the impression that there is in effect a continuing definition, clarification and communication of his role to the Soviet teacher which gives him confidence, harnesses his energies, and promotes his self-respect.

It has been pointed out that not every serving teacher is a scholar-saint. Nor, if it come to that, is every Soviet school pupil. But just as the administration has structured a system which gives fair support even to quite average teachers, so in the classroom the basic assumption has to be that all the pupils can do the work. With adequate teaching and encouragement almost every boy and girl can be enabled to master the curriculum at least to the point of attaining minimum pass marks.

Except for the few children who receive separate (special) education on account of brain damage or by reason of some other severe handicap, every pupil begins a foreign language or two. All embark upon mathematics and science. The programme is there for all without distinction of sex, race, or ability level.

As in State systems in most other countries, teachers in the Soviet Union have little or no choice in the matter of which pupils they will teach. A pupil who makes little or no progress may eventually be expelled, but except in fairly extreme cases the teachers have to keep on

[1] Quoted on the cover of the Prospectus of the Glacier Project of the Glacier Institute of Management, 1961.

trying with those with whom their work seems unrewarding: they can neither avoid them within the system nor get rid of them out of it.

Whilst this leaves the question of status equal among teachers in general, the inability to choose or select the pupils means that the area of professional choice is more obviously limited than it is in countries where some teachers achieve higher status through working only with selected pupils. In the U.S.S.R. there are selective schools, but these are only for pupils with marked aesthetic gifts. In such schools, special work in music, dancing and/or art is added to the curriculum of ordinary schools. Teachers in boarding schools are in a rather special position: but not from the point under discussion. A boarding school is intended to serve the needs, for instance, of a collective farm or of the orphans in a city. Entry or not to the school is decided by the authorities, the teachers concerned having no say in the matter.

Not only have Soviet teachers no power to select pupils; they have no choice of curriculum. The textbooks they use are prescribed by the State; the system of correction and assessing of class work and homework is defined and the general formal way of conducting class lessons is laid down, as are the sanctions for school discipline. These features have been established by the Ministries for Elementary and Higher Education and are universal. Soviet teachers accept these conditions unquestioningly along with winter snow and summer heat.

Despite these conditions, Soviet teachers answer in the affirmative when asked by foreigners if they exercise discretion in their work; if they share responsibility for their programme; and if they can use their initiative on behalf of their pupils. Let me indicate that there is at least some substance in these claims.

Quite certainly the principal has some discretion over the time-table and the general conduct of the school. In regard to these matters he is expected, perhaps required, to call regular meetings of the teaching staff. Through these meetings teachers feel they have some say in administrative decisions affecting their programme. Teachers are also called into consultation in connexion with the progress of their classes, of their subject, or of individual pupils. Within the school their opinions and advice are officially sought in these matters which immediately involve them.

School examinations very intimately concern Soviet teachers as well as their pupils, since the practice is for the teachers to play a part in the State examining process. The main topics to be examined are decided upon by the central authority. These are sent to the schools some weeks in advance of the examination dates and, within those topics, the examples or particular questions to be answered by the pupils are made up by the teachers.

Alert teachers can, however, find ways to stretch their professional wings. Textbooks are always being written or revised, and every book is tried out widely before being officially adopted. Where such books are tried out the teachers are invited to make criticisms and suggestions. Making such pertinent observations on new textbooks is one of the means whereby an able teacher can become noticed outside his own school.

Other opportunities are given for able teachers to show their quality at "pedagogical readings" at which teachers' papers are read aloud to an audience. Where these ideas seem to justify it, the State will publish and distribute the paper. Any teacher may, of course, write a text or other book, but its use in school depends upon the approval of the State and upon State publication.

This scope for engaging in educational research and curriculum development broadens the horizon of the above-average teacher and may serve to draw him into a higher echelon. The opportunity for upward mobility means that a teacher is not confined to a work-to-rule situation. He may take part in the process of making the books and changing the curriculum if he prove himself competent and acceptable in the task. These opportunities are not dependent upon the particular personnel of the school or upon the chance circumstance of a good or bad Principal but are understood to be open to all through teachers' circles, clubs and in-service centres connected with Pedagogical Institutes, or with the Educational and Scientific Workers' Union.

All teachers belong to the same union as all others engaged in the work of education. This union accordingly embraces personnel ranging from school cleaners to university professors, from laboratory technicians to research engineers. Within it, all are "workers" by definition, but it is obvious that some are high prestige workers. Near the top of the ladder university professors in the Soviet Union have very high salaries.

The question is whether or not Soviet school teachers tip the scale towards professional standing. In any country teachers form so large a group that they seem to "dilute" the ranks of professional staff by sheer weight of numbers, and the more select professions are often keen to deny them such status. In the Soviet Union, however, the status of teachers in general appears to be higher than that, for instance, of most medical doctors; and my view is that the teachers, if not yet all fully accepted as professionals, are well on the way to that position.

Teaching in the Soviet Union offers the security and the career possibilities associated with professional status. No doubt conditions vary from school to school with differences in local administrative personnel; but the general structure of the educational system is universally the same, and within it the life and career of a teacher can be progressive, respected and satisfying.

What is most noticeable about the position of a Soviet teacher when we get down to brass tacks is the straightforwardness of the deal. The salary scale relates to the post whether occupied by a man or by a woman, although it is differentiated as between primary and secondary teachers. A primary teacher is paid an inclusive salary; but a secondary teacher is paid extra if his hours appreciably exceed the normal eighteen hours of class contact whether because of additional shifts or because he stands in for a sick colleague.

It is to the advantage of the Soviet teacher that decisions as to the numbers of teachers to be trained and the salary and conditions of their employment are made centrally. The status of teachers is thus secure and is not, as in school systems in some parts of the western world, at the mercy of local political jacks-in-office. To be the butt of irrational prejudices is in any case one of the burdens of the teaching profession and one which probably cannot be entirely overcome. What ought to be obviated, however, and what seems to be avoided as far as possible in the Soviet Union, is exposing teachers to the spleen of frustrated local committee men – of whom no doubt the country has its due share.

To describe the psychology of the "burden" to which reference has been made would carry this discussion outside its proper range. But one or two other aspects besides the administrative one are worth considering. It may be that the classroom situation in itself puts a severe emotional strain on teachers and that is unavoidable. If Jersild's researches[1] in New York have any general application, it seems that teachers typically suffer anxiety, loneliness, hostility and near despair. What is the more necessary therefore is that on the one hand teachers should be aided to come to terms with their situation; and on the other,

[1] A. T. Jersild, *When Teachers Face Themselves*, Horace Mann-Lincoln Institute of School Experimentation, Teachers' College, Columbia, N.Y., 1955.

that everything possible should be done through the administrative structure to protect teachers from wanton attacks and sadistic denigration.

These attacks, with their lowering effects inwardly on morale and outwardly on status seem to be most commonly directed against teachers of the younger age groups. The stereotype is either the schoolmarm, or the man teacher who is sneered at as a man among boys but a boy among men.

To some extent this eroding of the morale and status of teachers in any culture relates to the status of women. Where women's status is low, that of the teachers as a whole is inclined to suffer; or else the profession becomes so divided that its status-as-a-whole can scarcely be discussed. Since in the Soviet Union the status of women is high, the fact of the teaching profession's being predominantly female is not a depressing influence on its general standing. From this point of view teachers as a whole in the Soviet Union benefit from its being what G. Rattray Taylor[1] describes as a "Matrist" society: i.e. one which, among other characteristics, gives high status to women and accords high esteem to research.

In many countries even where in recent years discriminatory practices and restrictive legislation affecting the employment of women have been reduced or rescinded, history still takes its toll. Just as the "colour" problem is most severe among races which have grown up together but without equality, so the difficulties about applying the open-door principle to the employment of men and women can least readily be resolved where the cultural habit is to accord status to women only for their womanliness, but to concede full human stature to men.

In this matter, as in so many others, the Gordian knot was cut for Soviet citizens soon after the Revolution of 1917. Education and the careers to which it alone now leads are open alike to men and women. Marital status is officially irrelevant to professional appointments, whilst much has been done to relieve employed women of undue strain in connexion with the birth and upbringing of their children.

In the Soviet Union the patriotic thing (recalling again the "wartime" feeling of the country) is for women to be in paid employment. This is not, of course, exactly a requirement: but when some of the most pressing problems of care for their families are shared with the State, many educated women find they can compass the demands both

[1] Taylor, Rattray G., *Sex in History*, Thames & Hudson, about 1955.

of home life and of professional duty. Their service is less interrupted by domestic crises than it is in countries where teachers have no claim on or access to nurseries and kindergartens for their own babies and young children.

The totality of the revolution in the official attitude to women comes home most vividly to the foreign visitor in a Moslem area. At first glance much of Russia may look like a Western country, but a visit to Central Asia provides a new perspective. In Uzbekistan, for instance, the prospect for girls in pre-revolutionary days was not only a complete lack of education but a stifling existence behind a veil, deprived of nearly every kind of human intercourse and doomed to a life of physical and mental sickness. Nowadays in these desert towns and villages, little girls and boys leave their homes together, dressed in school uniform, and carrying their satchels. In school they are taught by newly trained young men and women, full of hope, good will and confidence in the future. What a tragedy that these generations, although enlightened by much scientific study, are also burdened by out-of-date, though newer, mystical doctrines and confused by irrational myths and prejudices!

The point has been reached in the Soviet Union where education is snowballing. There is no problem of recruitment for higher education or for training for teaching. The school experience of these young aspirants to higher education has been such that they see teaching as a respected profession. Their desire to get into it is not inhibited by fear of indiscipline in the classroom. A flood of young people is graduating from ten- and now eleven-year schools with no other aim than to pursue their education and attain the status of professional persons whether as teachers or scientists.

What must be very encouraging to Soviet teachers and to their recruitment is the great development of the educational system. In earlier days, say thirty years ago, the national drive was for bare literacy, for the rudimentary "three R" skills. Whilst this primary work remains basic and has been increasingly supported and underpinned by nurseries and kindergartens, the spectacular strides forward of the last decade or two have been in the secondary stage of education (the word "secondary" covering, in general, education up to the age of eighteen years).

Within this period the aim was at first simply to extend the period of schooling, but once the four years of primary education (from age seven to eleven) was more or less universal, the policy was to achieve seven years of school for all. Before this provision was nation-wide, the need for full secondary education for all was recognized. Then, for some years the aim was ten years of schooling, from age seven to seventeen (with an extra year for special schools and for schools in areas where the spoken language was not Russian).

This upward extension of the age-range has meant a great concentration on the curriculum and on the organizational problems of the older age-groups. More and more teachers are dealing not with little children but with maturing adolescents. To the man in the street (if not always to the woman) and often to the educational administrator, such work with the older pupils seems more professional. Rightly or wrongly, more esteem attaches to teaching mathematics, physics or a foreign language to sixteen-year-olds than to guiding junior hands along the flowing lines of Russian cursive writing.

Since the end of the Great Patriotic War (World War II) developments in education have changed the whole emphasis of education from the primary to the secondary stage. Teaching these older age groups is quite a different matter and official pressure is now on the teachers to recognize even more fully than they have done, just how different it ought to be.

A school can so easily become a little world of its own. Under the guidance of class-bound teachers, pupils can learn to accept examination-bound horizons. They may eschew almost all practical work – home chores and every other kind of manual effort – because of the bookwork always waiting to be done. Judged, as they feel themselves to be, by their pupils' results in examinations based mainly on textbook learning and classroom experience, most teachers unwittingly encourage this attitude which may result in young students in their teens growing up almost insulated from the world of work into which at some point they are to be jettisoned.

It is these problems that the most recent developments in Soviet education, dating from the Law of December 1958, are intended to meet. The effect of this law on the status of teachers can only be to raise it. Full secondary education now occupies eleven years, of which the last three years are not compulsory. During those last three years all pupils, even those aiming at higher education beyond the age of eighteen, must include some work practice or employment in factory, farm, hospital or wherever it can be arranged. Under the new régime, the teachers of pupils of age fourteen or so who are coming towards the end of eight years of school, advise them and discuss with their parents the possibilities of the future.

There are now open to these young people, in schools defined by the 1958 Law, four types of ways of completing secondary education: the parents have the right of choice. The general secondary school offers a completed secondary course in three years, covering approximately the same school studies as were formerly taken in the ninth and tenth years of the ten-year school, though with some radical changes in content and method. During this three-year course, fifty-four days a year are spent in industry, in farm work or in other work-training. After completing such a course the 18-year-old may try to get acceptance in a university, pedagogical institute or other centre of higher education. (It is necessary for nearly all applicants to spend a further two years in full-time employment before being admitted to higher education.) In future, it will be by this route that teachers in the Soviet Union will in the main reach their training or higher education, though higher education is open to all who complete their secondary education and "matriculate", however or whenever they do so. If however the young man (or woman) on completing his "general secondary school" course does not want further education or is not accepted for it, he already has a starting point in the world of work. With some experience behind him he is in a position to seek full-time employment.

A second way of completing secondary education is through the technical and other specialized secondary schools. Entry to these depends upon satisfying entrance examinations and is not restricted to students just leaving the eight-year school. Some young people who have already done a few years' work and have qualified by part-time study can get a coveted place in the secondary technical school (*tekhnicheskoye uchilishche*, or *tekhnikum*). Others, again, who have completed their secondary education elsewhere, may join the secondary technical school. For these older students there is a short course, but for the regular students a course of up to four years is now the general rule. A high level of theoretical training is offered and sound practical knowledge is gained, usually at the works, though farms and workshops are also being set up actually in some technical schools.

The third kind of school, the vocational-technical school (*remeslennoye uchilishche*) is for those who go to work after finishing the eight-year school. This does not provide a complete secondary education but offers a one-, two-, or three-year part-time course related mainly to the chosen vocation, and the pupils are paid apprentice wages. These schools replace the old railway and mining schools where many orphans and children from large families were formerly kept at the expense of the State.

Finally there are the evening (or shift) secondary schools of general education which offer an opportunity to anybody to complete his secondary education whilst still holding down his employment. For shift workers, these schools also offer day courses. Those who make good progress in their studies are helped by a day or more off work during the week, on half pay, whether the works managers like it or not.

This whole nationwide drive to link the schools with work and to keep young employed people in touch with the schools is a magnificent experiment in which teachers play a leading part and in an expanding variety of roles. The possibility is open to them of helping a very high proportion of Soviet young people to grow up under their custodial care during the impressionable years when trends in personality take shape. There is the opportunity not only to help their charges to establish themselves in the world of work, but also to support them through their crises as they feel their way into the realm of adult emotions and loyalties.

It is quite clear that the new policy offers teachers not merely professional status but something approaching full human stature. In the words of M. I. Kondakov,[1] "Special attention is being devoted to the qualifications of the teaching staffs as well as to the measures aimed at enhancing the role and authority of the teacher" (p. 22).

This is the ideal: but a very practical solution to the stubborn problem of what to do with the least academic teenagers is also inherent in the 1958 Law. Under the new law the eighth grade becomes the year of decision. At the age of 15 some pupils are to all intents and purposes allowed to leave school (although their position is safeguarded in that they continue studying part-time and they may later return to full-time education if they can establish their claims). The effect of this clause is nevertheless to relieve the schools of certain pupils at the point at which, in any country, it becomes increasingly difficult to hold them successfully in school.

[1] Kondakov, M. I., *Education in the U.S.S.R.*, Foreign Languages Publishing House, Moscow, 1961.

Any fear on the part of the teacher, or failure to cope with the problem posed by unduly extending the term of compulsory education, seriously undermines his confidence and causes loss of face. Since as pupils grow older, the individual differences in their attainments become more marked, the last two years of the former ten-year Soviet school must have imposed a severe strain on teachers and pupils both geared alike to a lock-step curriculum.

Now, after finishing the eighth grade, those who want to escape need have little more to do with ordinary school. This releasing of all the remaining pupils from their desks for part-time practical work-experience and training must complicate the organization of school work in the ninth, tenth and eleventh grades. Yet such a departure from fixed routine should be welcomed by intelligent teachers whose status can only rise as they are seen to be dealing successfully not only with pupils who are under the full weight of tutelage in the classroom, but also with young citizens who give at least part of their time to productive labour in the national interest, earning as well as learning their place in the Soviet world.

Moreover, as time passes, the new recruit to the teaching profession will himself have had some contact with the world of work outside of the school-college-school circle of experience. As part of the price of a place in a college or university, he will have had to work seriously at some practical task, showing a proper respect for the basic superiority of productive labour.

There is then no problem of recruitment to the teaching profession in the Soviet Union. In recent years approximately two out of three applicants for training college places have been turned down, and the struggle for university entrance is not less severe. Yet in interposing work-experience for all during the secondary stage of education, and in further reinforcing the practice of a two-year working experience, before higher education for most students, the Law of 1958 reduces one danger inherent in advanced academic education: that of producing a cultivated élite qualified and determined to pursue a professional occupation or to lead the executive life, but practically incapacitated for work in productive enterprises and socially alienated from those who are so employed.

When a young student enters a training college or university, he is paid an allowance. This is increased for the more mature students so long as successful study is being recorded, the initial level being also to some extent related to the parents' economic position. Whatever the latter, however, a clever student whose attitude and studies are highly approved, is paid enough during full-time study to enable him to live an ordinary life, comparable with that of "other workers and peasants". He can marry and live in his own room or flat (if he can find one), or he may be housed in whatever lodgings he can get, or in the residential quarters attached to his university.

To a visiting American professor such a student's economic standing may not seem high; but the important thing is that there is no great discrepancy between a young person's standard of living whether he is student, apprentice, workman or farmer. Study is a serious business, and while successful is awarded a living wage.

This condition means that young people in the Soviet Union can work for far-off goals in their careers without having to sacrifice too greatly either their parents' standard of living or their own independence.

For teachers (among others) this financial support is important, and the situation in U.S.S.R. contrasts favourably with conditions in many countries where teaching is the subsidized profession *par excellence* (as far as the costs of training are concerned). In these countries teachers are characteristically from homes in the economic stratum below that to which, when professionally qualified, they claim to belong. The upward struggle is often accompanied by guilt feelings if parental sacrifice has been incurred, and by immaturity of personality development where economic dependence has merged into personal inability to stand alone.

It is worth while for any administration to try to avoid causing such mental health problems in teachers. Whether these are more general among teachers than in the rest of the population, it is impossible to say: but it is incontrovertible that they are of great consequence when they affect teachers, because of the incalculable influence exercised by the profession on the rising generation.

It is also worth while in preparing teachers to carry their education to the point at which they have a real interest in their subject and a capacity to enrich the more elementary units of the work which they may later teach in school.

That this is the aim at present in educating intending teachers in the Soviet Union is indicated by the fact that the bulk of teachers now graduate through the four-year courses for primary teaching (after the age of fifteen) or through five years in a pedagogical institute or a university (after the age of eighteen or twenty). The latter alternative is coming much more to the fore. As the qualifying conditions for entry to all these courses are now highly competitive, and the courses of study formidable both in hours and academic rigour, no one can reasonably challenge the claim of a recently qualified teacher to the status and respect due to a professional level of education.

Further, the Soviet policy is to continue on the lines already established and to raise the level of educational attainment even of the primary teachers (as of others dealing with young children) by providing a five-year post-secondary school education on the university or institute plane for all teachers. It is, in effect, aiming at what we should describe as a fully "graduate" profession, although the words used are not always the same as ours, and the avowed aim is not the status of the teaching profession but rather the fulfilment of Lenin's vision. Lenin wanted a "thoroughly developed and thoroughly trained people, people who are capable of doing everything" and he felt that this could not be achieved unless the teachers were themselves well qualified and deeply imbued with the spirit of communism.

These twin aims of Lenin are well illustrated by the way in which geography is taught at the secondary school and as an advanced study; although, no doubt, the point could be equally well established by a consideration of the teaching of mathematics, languages or the sciences, since these are all felt to be vital subjects.

In geography all the familiar basic "grammar" is covered in the detailed five-year course which all pupils undertake between the ages of eleven and fifteen or sixteen years: map work with physical, human, economic and regional studies. As in other countries, the homeland is stressed. Outdoor fieldwork and excursions are included from the first year and geographical clubs are recommended. "Problems arising in the study of geography are frequently connected with other school subjects and so the problems of soil, vegetation, zoology and agriculture are connected with biology, physics, chemistry and other subjects. It is, therefore, necessary according to the syllabus to apply knowledge gained in other studies to the study of geography and to rely on it frequently."[1]

[1] C. F. Bednar, "Geography in the Soviet Secondary School", *Studies in Comparative Education: Teaching in the Social Sciences and the Humanities in the U.S.S.R.*, U.S. Department of Health, Education and Welfare, Office of Education, Division of International Education, 1959.

The Economic Geography of Foreign Countries[1] which forms the text-book for Grade eight (age 14) looks like a fairly ordinary textbook of the kind used in many countries for preparing for examinations. After an introductory chapter on the political map of the world has made a distinction between (1) the U.S.S.R. and People's Democracies and (2) the Capitalist Countries, each country is dealt with according to a similar pattern of description. Under the heading of Europe, the Polish People's Republic is given eight pages, the Czechoslovakian Republic, six pages and so on. Later in the book the U.S.A. is dealt with in twenty-four pages and Canada in five. For each country there is a factual statement of area and population followed by paragraphs on geographical position, physical features, minerals and resources, population density, standard of living and economy (industry, agriculture, transportation, foreign trade, cities and towns). Many of the countries are illustrated by one or more maps (relief, rainfall, distribution of population, industrial development); by one or two pictures and sometimes by a chart or a graph.

At intervals of approximately three pages a few questions are included. These usually call for regurgitation of facts, rather than for deductions, and by occasionally making reference to maps not included in the text indicate that atlases need to be used. Some textbooks have their own map book. Excellent reference atlases are available (and cheap) but I did not see any large-scale maps (equivalent to our Ordnance Survey maps) in use in schools.

Especially if he attended a university, however, the teacher will himself have followed an arduous course of study of geography, including detailed field study, map reading and map making. As A. M. Ryabchikov says in his account of "Geography in Soviet Universities"[2] (p. 26): "A considerable part of physical geographers and economic geographers teach pupils in secondary schools. Geography teachers with a university background as distinct from pedagogical institute graduates have a great deal of experience in research work and often carry on investigations of local regions."

There seems no doubt that recently qualified graduate teachers of geography are able to deal very adequately with the actual contents of

[1] I. I. Mamayev, *Economic Geography of Foreign Countries*, State Text Book Publishing House of the Ministry of Education of the RSFSR, Leningrad Branch, 1957.
[2] A. M. Ryabchikov, *Geography in Soviet Universities*, Published for VIth World Festival of Youth and Students – an international gathering of students of geography, Moscow, 1957.

the secondary school curriculum. They should have enough knowledge and experience to enrich the work outlined in the text except perhaps in regard to "scientifically derived information about other people and their cultures."[1] These shortcomings of the text it is probably not possible for the teacher to remedy. On the other hand, especially if they have themselves taken part in advanced fieldwork studies, teachers can feel involved in the overall purposes of geographical study in U.S.S.R. It is not only, rather crudely, to "promote in the student's mind the development of a materialistic world outlook and educate the student in a spirit of Soviet patriotism and friendship of nations."[2] More specifically, the advanced study is nationally co-ordinated to provide the data upon which the next stage of the coutry's development can be based: the stage of economic and administrative decentralization. A university field worker in geography or in an allied discipline has glimpses of this future, as he helps to build up knowledge concerning the natural resources and economic potential of some region of the Soviet Union, and as he helps also to convey to farmers, quarrymen, miners and transport workers in perhaps a remote area some notion of the ways in which their efforts are contributing not only to the national effort but to a realization of regional self-dependence.

By means such as these, what may look like routine textbook work in the classroom can be illumined with national purpose. There is little danger of the teacher's thinking of himself, or being sneered at by others, as just an academic recluse, when the aim and purpose of the subject he teaches are so explicitly related to national development. Status is aided by this identification of schoolwork with the needs of a changing and developing national economy; an identification which is found not only nominally in government-issued instructions to teachers, but also genuinely in the experience and training of those teachers.

The high level of preparation for initial entry to the teaching profession, illustrated at length in this discussion of the place of geography as a subject, provides a firm basis for high status. It also reduces the feelings of utter hopelessness from which many trained teachers

[1] *Soviet Education Programs*, U.S. Department of Health, Education and Welfare, Office of Education, Bulletin 1960, Number 17, page 205.

[2] U.S.S.R. Ministry of Education on the motives for the study of geography in Soviet Schools, quoted by C. P. Bednar, op. cit.

elsewhere appear to suffer. A well-qualified subject specialist does not feel tied to teaching whether he likes it or not. He knows that he can command congenial employment in other spheres. He is a teacher by choice and on that account, a better teacher.

He is, moreover, likely to avail himself of in-service opportunities of further improving his quality as a teacher. A city such as Leningrad offers impressive programmes for such mature study. Teachers there may be given one-year full-time academic courses (on release with salary), summer courses, seminars (twice a month) and conferences (during spring vacations). The in-service centre has a full-time staff of over a hundred teachers, of whom fourteen are full professors.

No doubt, as in other countries, the promotion system for teachers is less than satisfactory to some of those left behind. But apart from achieving higher responsibilities and salary, some teachers, like other "productive workers", may be selected for special recognition by tokens of merit and honour. Such awards no doubt provide compensations: as I saw it, no disillusionment or sophistication clouded the glory of a teacher rewarded for a meritorious forty years of classroom service by the title and decoration of "Honoured Teacher".

Most teachers, however, whether in the Soviet Union or elsewhere, do not progress more than a step or two up the promotion ladder and are not singled out for personal honours. The high status of these regular teachers in the Soviet Union is indicated in the Report of the First Official U.S. Education Mission to U.S.S.R.[4] in these terms (pp. 85-6):

> In general, teachers appear to be relatively well paid; they have very good working conditions; and as a group they appear to be highly motivated and well educated professionals who are happy in their work and proud of it.

A few pages later in the same book *Soviet Commitment to Education*[1] Mr Derthick and his colleagues identify a cause of success in Soviet education to which attention should be drawn before this chapter is concluded. They say (p. 102):

> Due very largely to the work of the Academy of Pedagogical Sciences, education in the U.S.S.R. is not static but is constantly

[1] *Soviet Commitment to Education*, Bulletin 1959, Number 16, U.S. Department of Health, Education and Welfare, Office of Education.

changing and improving. The strong belief of the Soviet people in education is matched by an equally strong effort of educators to find the best ways of accomplishing the educational objectives. Because of the central and influential position of the Academy of Pedagogical Sciences, improvements in education can be introduced in the U.S.S.R. much more rapidly than in a country where education is decentralized. It is something of a paradox that the Soviet Union, which in many respects is monolithic and inflexible, is in its educational program flexible to a degree and, even more surprising, responsive to grass roots experience with experimental programs. . . .

Probably no one in the Soviet Union receives or deserves higher esteem than an Academician. Few earn higher salaries. And this unique Academy is in fact the peak of the teaching profession to whose humbler base the bulk of this chapter has been devoted.

CHAPTER 6

Selection and Differentiation in Soviet Schools

I was struck again and again on visiting Russian classrooms by the fact that they seemed as much "European" as "communist". The attitude to work, the present concept of what is academically respectable, the use of well-hallowed academic terminology – all these appeared to me, an outside observer, reminiscent, to put it mildly, of French and German classroom practice. Before getting to Russia I had hoped, as a result of my visit, to write an impressionistic account of the feel of the classroom, including such things as the teacher-child relationship, the attitude to marks, and anything else which would have conveyed, if the word be allowed in this context, the general "spirit". My reason for this pre-occupation was that what many people and countries *say* tallies only slightly with what they *do*, even when they have fully developed ideologies. However, although I made very careful observations and notes about what one might call the phenomenology of the classroom, I was so often involved with Russian teachers and officials in arguments and discussions about the selection and "streaming" of students that I have been asked to contribute this present chapter.

I formed the strong impression, which of course might be quite mistaken, that teachers and officials were so powerfully defending the *theory* of no selection and no "streaming" that in fact there was about to be a change in practice in this matter. In many discussions they went to extreme lengths in maintaining that there should be no selection for schools, and that there should be no streaming within schools. They seemed to be saying that all children should (and could) have exactly the same education. On this last matter particularly there were many heated discussions. During one of these I was moved to ask a very wise and much experienced lady whether she thought that the child who had consistently scored two marks, on the famous five point scale,[1] over a period of one year had in fact done the same sort of work

[1] Restored by Party directive in September 1935, when progressive education was on the way out. From as early as 1920 Dewey had been well known and followed; but by July 1936, he (and other "progressives") were definitely out of favour.

as the child who had consistently scored five, simply because both had been exposed to the same syllabus. Certainly if one is going to maintain that any streaming is "undemocratic" and therefore undesirable, then the only solution would be for the same teacher to teach all the children who come into any given school, whether they numbered 50 or 300. Be that as it may, during our tour in 1960 I developed an interest in the question of selection and grading of students in the Soviet Union.

The question is a complicated one, and writing about it is no easy task. Soviet officials made a special point of saying that all young people receive the same kind of basic education, that there is no streaming, that selection in the United Kingdom sense is anathema, that what differentiation there is in educational offerings in the U.S.S.R. is based on the differing attainments of the children as they go forward on the educational road, and that the educational road is quite wide enough to take all the traffic.[1] They criticized the United Kingdom system, and, *mirabile dictu*, the United States system, for being over-selective. But the palmy days are long since over when Lenin could sign, as he did in 1918, a decree, concerning admissions to the universities in the R.S.F.S.R., which contains the following:

1. Every person, regardless of citizenship and sex, reaching the age of 16, can be admitted as a member of the student body of any of the higher institutions of learning without submitting a diploma or testimonial papers attesting graduation from a secondary or other school.

2. It is forbidden to demand from persons seeking entrance any certificates whatsoever, except their identification papers.

[1] "The Soviet system has obviously unleashed the floodgates of ambition and desire for advancement through education. This raises serious questions as to whether or not the educational channels are sufficiently large and the control points open wide enough to contain the flow."
The Soviet Citizen, Alex Inkeles and Raymond A. Bauer, Harvard U.P. 1961, p. 156.

"In 1932 the Central Committee of the Party passed a decree relating to the schools which decisively reversed the trends in education, setting the school back on the path of conventional study.... The accent was on formal studies, involving primarily book learning. Grades and examinations were emphasized as they had not been since Tsarist times, with individual competition for high grades encouraged." *Soviet Society*, ed. Alex Inkeles and Kent Geiger, Houghton Mifflin, Boston, 1961, p. 435.
This decree marked the reverse of a phase which had started in the '20s, during which experimental ideas from the U.S., Germany and elsewhere had been much employed.

All systems of education are in some sense selective: some directly on educational grounds; some indirectly on socio-economic (or other) grounds. The European tradition of Russian education was bound to come through the revolutionary and communist theory and practice. The already remarked-upon European feeling of the classroom is certainly symptomatic of something deeper. The European tradition of élites, of the lower status of manual labour, of the high importance of learning, was bound to reassert itself in the kinds of education which were considered appropriate, and necessarily so, in the selection of students to pursue these different kinds of education.

Yet two samples of indirect selection, chosen outside Europe, but not entirely outside the European tradition, might well throw light on our present considerations. The first is the Harvard/Newton programme for the Masters of Arts in Teaching; the second, the recently instituted common entrance examination in Jamaica, West Indies. These should remind us, incidentally, that the whole question of selection and its problems are not peculiar to the U.S.S.R. They are very much "our" problem. As I have had reason to mention elsewhere[1] one of the most interesting things about the Harvard/Newton programme is the fact that it has encouraged people into high school teaching from a socio-economic background which had not previously provided many high-school teachers. This was not aimed at, as far as I can make out, in the original planning of the programme. The process of selection which seemed to the originators to be a purely academic process was in fact, in a very important way, a socio-economic process. To begin with, the colleges which co-operated in the Harvard/Newton plan tended to have a high percentage of students from a definite kind of background. But more important than this, since each college was particularly careful, in selecting its two candidates (for work at Harvard), to use not only academic but general criteria, the selection in fact turned out to favour those who came from homes which had concepts of service, of high standards, and of academic achievement. So at any rate, it seemed to me when I looked closely at the workings of this imaginative attempt to provide high grade teacher training and teacher education at the university level.

Similarly, the common entrance examination in Jamaica was not intended to select children from a certain geographic or social area. It was intended to select those people of the best general ability, and of

[1] *Universities Quarterly*, Vol. 13, No. 1, November 1958.

the best preparation for secondary schooling of a markedly grammar type. It has turned out, however, that in the rural areas only a small percentage of children score high enough marks in the common entrance examination to demand places in the grant-aided government secondary schools.[1] Moreover, it is noticeable that the people winning many of the free places and scholarships are people from certain socio-economic background. This is only to be expected because, however objective the examination might be, it cannot help favouring those people who come from a tradition of literacy and book-learning. In a society such as Jamaica people who come from such a background tend to belong to certain socio-economic groups, although a notable exception to this is to be found among primary school teachers and their children. Many of these teachers, especially during the period thirty or forty years ago, developed, without the benefit of financial status, an interest in book learning, and a belief in certain values and

---

[1] A 10 per cent sample of all children taking the common entrance (or "11+") examination yields the following percentages:

Secondary urban	$\dfrac{29 \text{ gained places}}{89 \text{ sat the exam.}}$	32·6%
Secondary rural	$\dfrac{17}{72} =$	23·6%
Private urban	$\dfrac{21}{117} =$	17·9%
Private rural	$\dfrac{6}{41} =$	14·6%
Primary urban	$\dfrac{35}{229} =$	15·3%
Primary rural	$\dfrac{53}{1156} =$	4·6%
TOTAL	$\dfrac{161}{1704} =$	9·5%

TOTAL RURAL (all types of schools)

$$\dfrac{76}{1269} = 6\cdot0\%$$

TOTAL URBAN (all types of schools)

$$\dfrac{85}{435} = 19\cdot5\%$$

So 6 per cent of those sent up by rural schools get places; whereas 19·6 per cent of those from urban schools do so. These figures are from Dr Douglas Manley, recently of the Department of Education, U.W.I. (cf. also *Selection for Secondary Education in Jamaica*, by P. E. Vernon, Government Printer, Jamaica, 1961).

behaviour patterns which are undoubtedly helpful in academic work and in the preparation for examinations of an academic type.

Whether these two examples are accurate in their details or not, the point that I should like to make is that every society does in fact select – and not necessarily on criteria that are easily uncovered. Nor is it easy to extract from the whole social complex those factors which are purely academic, or based entirely on the intellectual potential of the individual being tested.

For one thing, once a society, for whatever reasons, sets up different types of schools, or sets out to meet different manpower and production requirements, with the help of its schools, it has at least to connive at a system of selection.

A society might appear to be selecting only on academic grounds. But it is clear that academic achievement, and even to a certain extent potentiality, rests upon habits and values which are sometimes developed by factors, such as family conditions, which are not openly and clearly connected with academic matters. Certainly non-academic factors are likely to be at work at a level well below the surface in the Soviet Union. But an enormous amount of research would be needed to trace clearly and accurately their operation. There also must be some sort of selection according to what one might call geography.[1] The ten-year schools were first started in non-rural areas. The non-rural areas had a start on the other areas, for in the latter illiteracy and ignorance were rife. At present there are still remote rural areas with four-year schools only. In all countries which are not completely industrialized one meets this problem of the development of the potentiality of the rural children.

It is as well to remember that despite the amazing steps forward which the U.S.S.R. has made in so many fields[2] it is still in some ways an underdeveloped country. If it shares much with Europe in educational ideas and practice, it shares also some of the problems of Asia, Africa and South America. It is in part "European", in part industrial, and in part "under-developed"; this last characteristic explains much.

There is another general point worth noting. Both the internal and external strength of the Soviet Union rest very much on its system of

[1] cf. Nicholas DeWitt, *Soviet Professional Manpower*, National Science Foundation, Washington D.C., 1955, p. 53.

[2] cf., for instance, Georges Jorré, *The Soviet Union*, Longmans, London (2nd edition), pp. 207–10 and passim.

long-term planning. Citizens are apparently perfectly willing to accept certain hardships at certain times not only for ideological reasons but even more because they know that the plan aims at easing their present difficulties. It might be that "Western" countries, and all particularly under-developed countries, have not taken into account the fact that human beings are perfectly willing to sacrifice, if they know what they are sacrificing for. Sir Winston Churchill, great war leader that he was, appealed to the people more and more to face "toil, blood, sweat and tears". Similarly, I have often felt that what many new countries need is the equivalent of a Sir Stafford Cripps, someone who does not believe that people work only for personal gain and for consumer goods. If the whole Soviet economy and social growth rest on long-term planning, can the society afford not to plan and select the careers which their students should follow? Once again, this selection might not be direct, or it might be. But it would appear that contrary to what even the most capable officials tried to imply, there must be differentiation in education in quite basic ways, there must be selection, and at least some of the selection will be based not on native and individual ability but on usefulness to the country and the party, and this is almost bound to involve sociological and family background.

One field in which selection is definitely practised and justified is in the field of the fine arts. In schools for gifted children special training is given in the ballet, music of all kinds, painting, modelling and other arts. This is an interesting example of what I meant by saying that Russian education gives the impression of being in some ways very European, and is not completely cut off from pre-revolutionary history.[1] No doubt the tradition of nurturing talent in the fine arts was too strongly embedded in the Russian nation for even "the great October Socialist Revolution" to disturb it.[2] It is of course true that now it is not only talent from the aristocracy that is developed. On the whole there is "an extensive system covering the whole nation for the purpose of discovering, motivating and developing giftedness and

---

[1] Note the reported words of a Lutheran pastor in 1673 to the effect that "though Moscow had not yet composed elementary schools for the teaching of letters, she had succeeded in organizing an academy of drama". V. O. Kluchevsky, *A History of Russia*, J. M. Dent & Sons, 1913, p. 283.

[2] "Many of us are to blame for spoiling our children, asking them when they are still in their rompers: 'What do you want to be when you grow up?' and falling into raptures at their answers – an academician, a ballerina, or something else of that sort. And now these same children are called upon to be steel smelters, rolling mill operators, forge hands; dirty, hot and hard jobs." Quoted from *Oktybar*, No. 10, 1944, pp. 120-1.

talent. The Soviet educators explain such inconsistency by the rationalization within the scope of their political theory that special talents must be identified and encouraged but not recognized as innate endowments."[1]

Selection is either for full-time schools or part-time special art schools. Apparently selection for the part-time special music schools is not based on examination. But for the full-time schools there are highly competitive examinations: it is reported that for the Central Musical School, which is an eleven-year-school, in 1958 "out of 250 children admitted for entrance examination only forty were accepted". In a school like the Central Musical apparently the usual circles such as the Pioneers do not function. This means that any of the "socialization" or political education which goes on through the various circles will be missing in the life of these specially selected students, even though a formative part of their curriculum, as in any other secondary school, will consist of indoctrination in the ideology of Marxism–Leninism. One wonders whether selection for these special arts schools, and the kind of education which is received in them, is not even if unwittingly, leading to the creation of an élite. It did appear that one of the privileged classes in the Soviet Union consisted of the artists. It is worth noting that the schools for the gifted in music and art were unaffected by the School Reform Law of 1958. The absence of circles in some of these schools can well be explained by the fact that the children carry a very heavy work load, for they have to pursue usual academic studies as well as develop their special talents through arduous study and practice. But might we not have here another case in which what is apparently selection on artistic or academic grounds has clear socio-political significance?

It should be mentioned, before looking at selection outside the field of special art education, that there are good schools for defective children just as there are for the artistically talented. The work in defectology seemed to be outstanding and has been much stimulated by the contribution of such people as Professor A. R. Luria, whose basic Pavlovian orientation is well illustrated by his statement:

[1] Bereday et al, *The Changing Soviet School*, Constable, 1960, p. 364. The stress on environment, and the emphasis on Lysenko and Pavlov, explain the need to deny innate endowments, and explain the fact that they can be dismissed. Also cf. the article by E. M. Williams and Norman Larby called "Educational Standards", *Times Educational Supplement*, 22. 7. 60), which refers to the shadow of Lysenko across the whole educational system. To me the influence of Pavlov seemed as great.

"Only when, either at the pre-natal or at an early stage, a child has suffered serious brain disease which profoundly disturb his further development and makes him defective intellectually, may we speak of intellectual backwardness of a kind which makes the child's education in the common school impossible and calls for his transference to an auxiliary school."[1]

Selection to higher education, except in the case of "schools of closed access"[2] and of the higher party schools, is fairly straightforward. Full-time higher education is nominally open to any student – if he has finished the eleven-year school on the academic side, has passed certain highly competitive exams, has done (or is exempted from) a two-year stint of work experience, and is under thirty-five years of age. But as higher educational institutions usually conduct evening and correspondence divisions alongside full-time day divisions, the question arises whether a student "selected" for evening work, or pursuing such courses while earning a living, is really doing the same sort of university work as those attending full-time in the day.[3] Evening work is not limited to those under 35.

The entrance examinations to higher education are fiercely competitive; Moscow University had, in 1957-8, 8,000 qualified applicants for 2,800 vacancies.[4] In some cities up to nearly one third of those eligible for higher education have been unable to secure admission. The school-leaving diploma awards gold and silver medals for good performance; but no longer can gold and silver medal holders from the eleven-year schools enter universities or institutes without taking the

---

[1] *New World Review*, June 1958. Also quoted in *The Changing Soviet School*, p. 339. Of great interest, incidentally, both for its intrinsic worth and for the ideological set of its introduction is the book by A. R. Luria, *Speech and the Development of Mental Processes in the Child*.

[2] cf. p. 15, DeWitt, op. cit.: In theory entrance to these schools is reserved primarily for the descendants of living or killed-in-action members of the Soviet Armed Forces. In practice, however, access is reserved for sons of the Soviet Officer Corps.

[3] At the Polytechnical Institute, Leningrad, we were told that evening students did four hours per night, four nights per week. They get ten days' leave twice a year, and for doing their thesis. About 88 per cent we were told, pass every year.

[4] "A successful student through a system of stipends and scholarships gets paid for going to school" (at the university level). "And it is largely by lessening the economic burden of education upon the individual and his family that the Soviet state is able to apply such stringent selection and to channel by means of incentive the national talent into fields of specialization it deems most desired." Taken from N. DeWitt, "Soviet Scientific Education and the School Reform", *School and Society*, Vol. 88 (1960), pp. 297-300. Cf. *Soviet Society*, p. 442.

entrance exams, although they are given preference once they have passed. A candidate must pass in all his subjects.

In *Uchitel'skaya Gazeta* Mr Orlov (cf. *Times Educational Supplement*, 29 October, 1960, p. 563) advocates the reform of the competitive examinations for entrance to higher education. He points out that brilliant science students fail to get places because of weakness in literature and history. Similarly, he says, weakness in foreign languages tends to bar some scientists at the postgraduate level.

It is also worth noting that Mr Orlov "inveighs also against the tyranny of the seven-year economic plan which demands for each department a certain number of postgraduate workers each year, irrespective of excess or deficiency in the supply of suitable candidates".

The pedagogical schools also, which are being replaced by more selective faculties in pedagogical institutes, recruited ten-year-school leavers by competitive entrance examinations. Such pedagogical schools as continue to exist offer two-year courses for kindergarten and primary school teachers. This kind of humbler post-secondary institution is mentioned to show a selective process at work here too. The promotion of teacher-training, even for infant schools and the early grades, to the university and institute level is bound to increase the degree of selectivity.

Two points should be made here, and they are possibly best stated by King in the first edition of *Other Schools and Ours*.[1] First, "the term 'ten-year school' (i.e. before 1958-9) does not necessarily mean formal classes in conventional subjects during the whole of that time. Even during the most typically Stalin period the last three years might be spent (and certainly were for the less 'academically' suitable children) on projects closely associated with work, and particularly linked with the current Five-Year Plan" (p. 155). Thus an element of internal selection preceded the end of school life even before the introduction of the Khrushchev reforms of 1958-9; and this is made all the more obvious when we recall that children with unsatisfactory academic performances were (and are still) made to repeat grades. Consequently, in the autumn of 1958 Khrushchev complained several times of the very large number of children who did not complete the ten-year-school programme. Second, even if they did, "The selection at seventeen years of age is ... harsh and relentless. No fees are charged in higher education; but most students get scholarships or grants, which are

[1] *Other Schools and Ours*, Edmund J. King, Rinehart, 1958, and Methuen, 1960.

conditional upon progress" (ibid., p. 163). We shall soon return to some of these considerations, but should note at this point that since the ten-year school has been extended to eleven years, university and institute selection has been effectively restricted to diploma-holders from the academic upper school or the technicum. Between them, these do not amount to more than 40–50 per cent of the age group, and of these most of the technicum group do not proceed further.

The mechanism for selection at the age of fifteen, after completion of the now compulsory eight-grade general education school, has been described in several places.[1] Therefore it is sufficient to recapitulate only its main features here. These include the gradual introduction of "polytechnic" elements of work experience during the years thirteen to fifteen, to bring schools closer to life and also to offer a profile of abilities and interests different from those of the classroom, and thus valuable as a diagnostic aid; and, above all, the division of children at the age of fifteen into three quite separate kinds of school.

At least one of these would hardly be called a school in other countries' terminology. It consists of full-time engagement in regular factory or farm work, with afternoon or evening instruction of between fifteen and eighteen hours a week – or its equivalent differently arranged. The instruction includes both vocational theory and general education. At its best, this programme can be very successful; but there is no doubt either in the minds of Soviet theorists or on the part of any observer of these classes that the children are considered to be intellectually less advanced – for we can hardly expect the authorities to use a word like "endowed". Such vocational schools or apprenticeships do not give a "complete" secondary education. That is to say, they do not lead to the school-leaving diploma which entitles its possessors to compete for higher education. But the door is never absolutely closed; and able boys and girls are encouraged even at this late stage to seek entrance to a technicum, either at the end of their vocational school course or at some stages before. Undoubtedly, some very able pupils have proved their prowess and achieved great distinction later – either in their vocational field or some other.[2] About half of all Soviet children pass into these vocational schools or apprenticeships at the age of fifteen, for one, two or usually three years.

[1] See Bereday et al., ed., *The Changing Soviet School*, chapters 8–10; and Edmund J. King, *World Perspectives in Education*, 1962, especially chapter 7.
[2] Major Yuri Gagarin, the first space man, is a case in point.

Higher in the academic scale is the technicum, to which about 25 per cent or less of the 15-year-olds go. The normal course is one of four years, and gives both a medium-grade technical or managerial qualification and a school-leaving diploma that entitles its owner to apply for admission to higher education – usually on the technological side. However, the majority of pupils do not go on to further study, at any rate for the time being; and the technicum course is intended to be terminal. Its technical side is specialized and relatively advanced. The ingredient of general education is closely integrated with the vocational interest, but is of a high quality. Therefore these institutions can fairly be compared with the more selective academic grades nine to eleven in the more conventional school soon to be described. An interesting feature in some parts of the communist world (e.g. in Czechoslovakia) is that the technicum or its equivalent attracts proportionately more boys than girls, and the upper "general education secondary school" appeals more to girls. It is said unofficially that the reason is found in the better paid jobs available to people with good technicum qualifications, especially if they proceed later to institutes of technology at the university level.

The third alternative after the age of fifteen is the three-year "general education secondary school", leading straight on to the school-leaving diploma. This, therefore, is a school to continue the tradition of academic excellence; yet its teachers still sometimes complain of some dilution of standards because of insufficient differentiation before the age of fifteen, and even more because of the "polytechnic" requirement that the pupils must spend one or part of two days each week actually engaged in production. Whereas "polytechnic" work under the age of fifteen is usually done in a school workshop, over the age of fifteen it is usually in a factory, farm, or comparable enterprise. The senior pupils thus engaged are increasingly expected to acquire a marketable vocational certificate in addition to the academic school-leaving diploma which is their main objective. Some 20–25 per cent of the age group are in schools of this kind. It is almost undoubtedly from this group that the most favoured 20 per cent of all the university entrants, exempt from the compulsory two-year work-stint, are recruited. So the outsider can be forgiven for construing the threefold differentiation of children after the age of fifteen as being a plain mechanism for selection, especially as this impression is reinforced in unguarded moments by the terminology of their teachers and of university professors.

Moreover, the communist school itself is far from being the whole or indeed the predominant factor in total education. The extra-scholastic youth organizations are staffed with paid "educators", one or more of whom may be found in every school of any size. The "circles" of the youth organizations not only foster socialization, provide recreation, and facilitate the "activity" and practical work so conspicuously absent from many aridly didactic classrooms; they also provide challenging opportunities for the able child and actually coach him either in additional subjects (such as foreign languages) or in the higher flights of the conventional school subjects. They take the academic competitions ("Olympiads" – of which more later) as much under their wing as the athletic competitions called Spartakiads. All these points have been made elsewhere; but it seems necessary to recollect them here, when interpreting the significant phenomena that suggests differentiation to non-Soviet observers.

It will therefore be noted how very important are four factors in the selective process as set out above:

1. selection for secondary and technicum education at the age of fifteen;

2. success in the selective academic stream of eleven-year schooling, with uniformly good attainment throughout school life, and gold or silver medals in the school leaving examination;

3. full utilization of all the extra-scholastic or para-scholastic encouragement that may be acquired in the youth organizations;

4. the whole question of "work experience" before and after fifteen years of age, and especially in relation to the two years of compulsory work which so many university and institute candidates must undergo before proceeding to higher education.

Let us turn our attention briefly to direct selection on the lower levels. If the diagrams on pp. 136–8 are carefully studied, it will be noticed that, despite claims made for the spread of basically the same education for all (which, ideologically and culturally speaking may be truer than we suppose), increasing differentiation of both school experience and of vocational or professional training is a marked and growing feature of Soviet education. The Party embrace and the

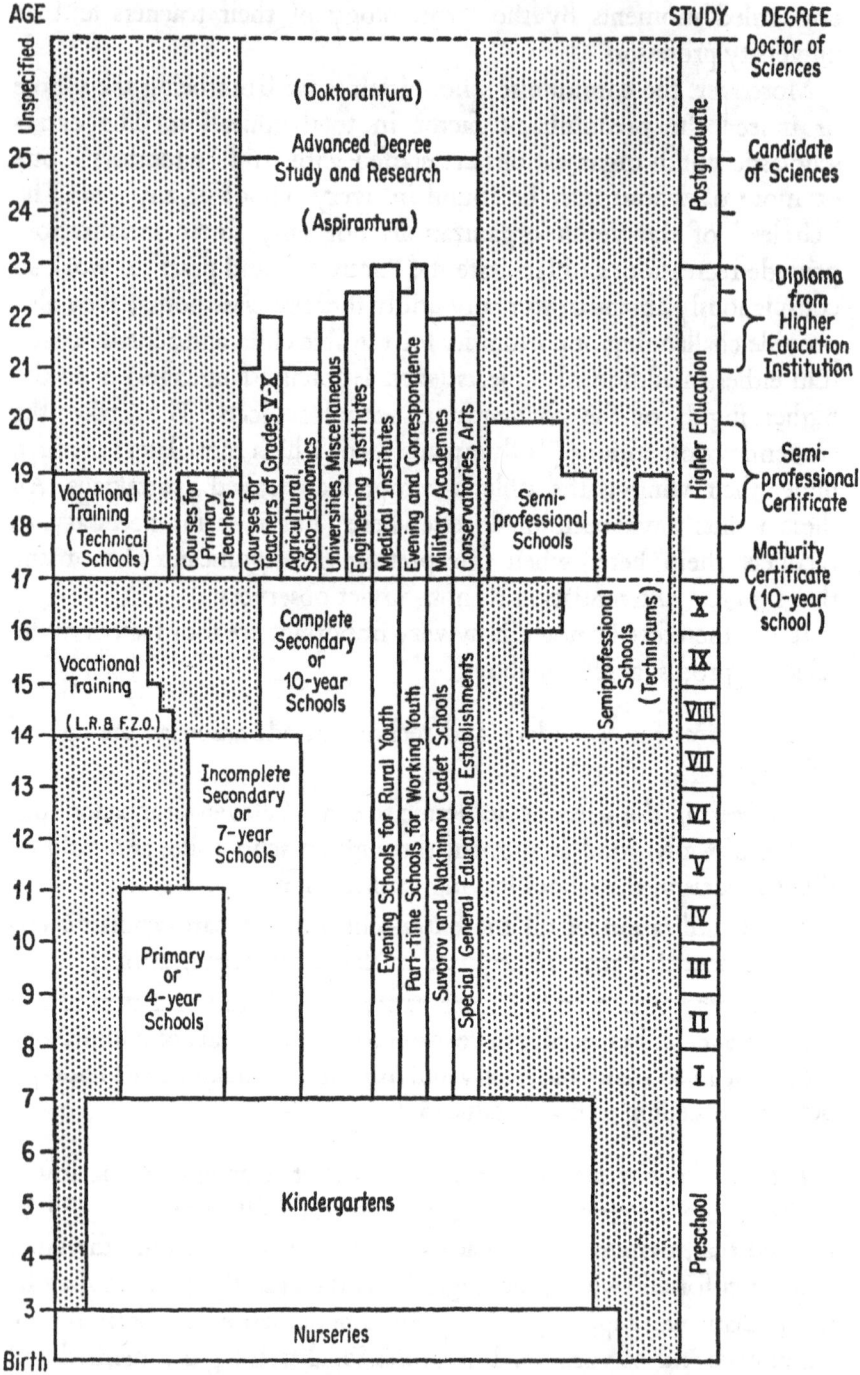

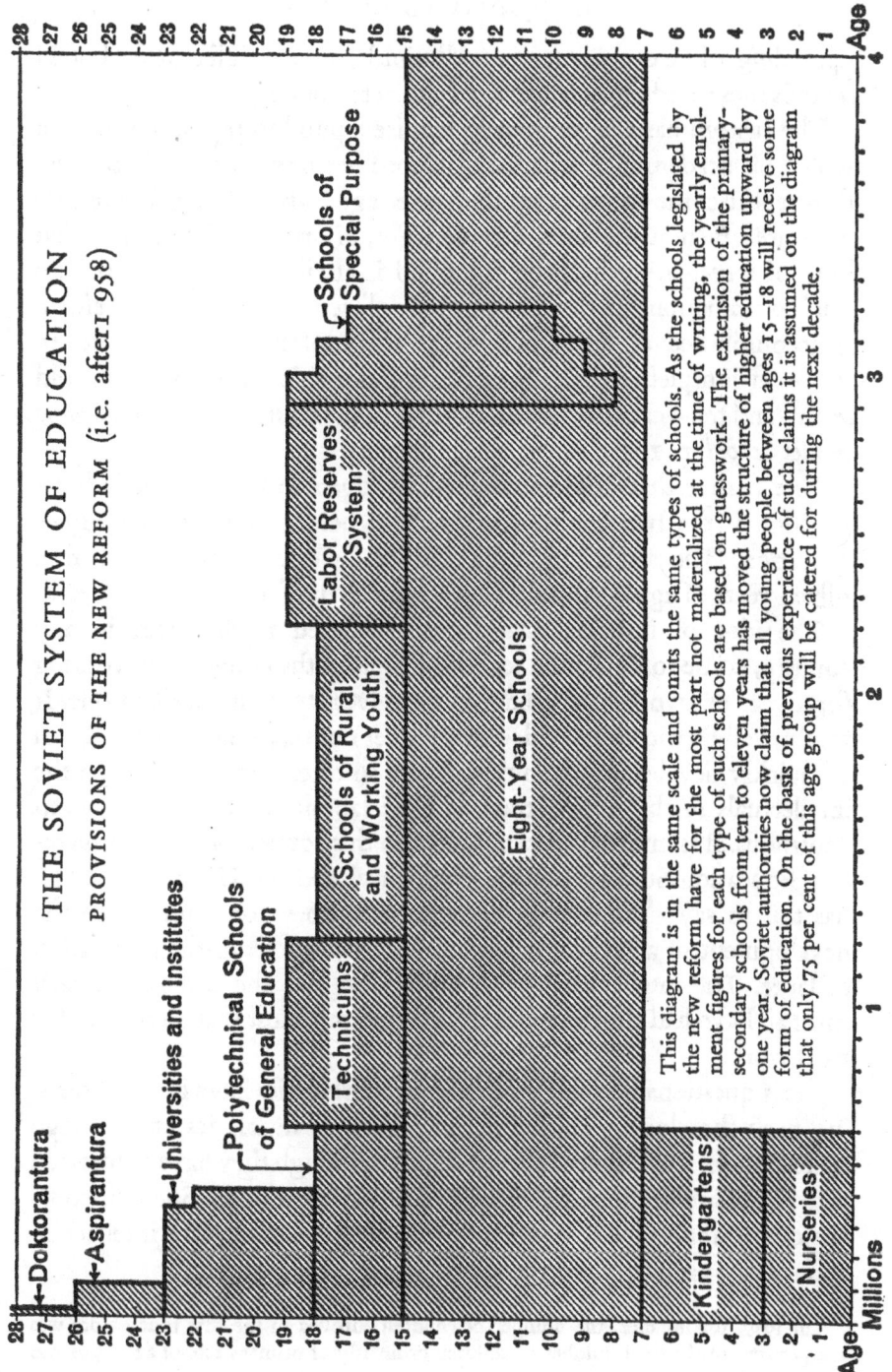

Note: The diagram on p. 136 is taken from Edmund J. King, *Other Schools and Ours*, Methuen, 1960; and that on p. 137 from G. Z. F. Bereday *et al.*, ed., *The Changing Soviet School*, Houghton Mifflin Co. of Boston, Mass., 1960.

upgrading of many occupations diminish certain differences; but in schools these are firmly recognized and acted upon.

The custom has always been to require a pupil to repeat any year in which his academic or attendance record has been poor.[1] Those who thus repeat come to make up the "over age" group. "Final examinations are given at the end of grade eight, in order to determine what kind of secondary education the pupil is eligible for. There are also final examinations at the end of grade eleven. Until the new reform is accomplished eight grades in the incomplete school and eleven grades in complete secondary school will not uniformly replace the old seven- and ten-year structure in all parts of the country" (*The Changing Soviet School*, p. 103).

One matter that appears particularly open to the uses of indirect selection is the business of work service before going on to higher education. The same might be said of "work experience" before fifteen years of age. I should like to consider the former in some detail.

The idea of insisting that future so-called intellectuals, in any country, come to know the real conditions of the country by working for a year or two before going on to university is an excellent one. It might well be tried – provided that it does not retard development – in all quickly developing countries, where so often the gap between the intellectuals in the upper strata and the labourers in the lower is so enormous. It is interesting to note that in this connexion the Comparative Education Society (U.S.A.), which visited the U.S.S.R. in 1958, has this to say: "The Soviet government does not want to see the development of a broadly educated élite remote from the population at large. The intellectual, the technologist, and the ordinary citizen must all have had similar work experience and must share a respect for hard work.

"It is questionable whether the Soviet authorities have in mind turning back the clock – abolishing all difference in salaries and prestige according to achievement and position – although they have eliminated some of the substantial differences in the past year or so. Such differentiations doubtless led to a widening of the gap between the intellectual (not to say political) and the average man."[2]

---

[1] In 1939, for instance, the number of children enrolled in the first four grades was 124 per cent of the total number of children ordinarily of primary school age – this was because of "repeats".

[2] Bereday *et al.* (ed.), *The Changing Soviet School*, Constable, p. 98.

SELECTION IN SOVIET SCHOOLS

If the young people are persuaded to do their stint of work as a service to their country, then clearly so much the better. And one has the feeling that many Russian youths will think of the community first. However, since in the U.S.S.R. not 100 per cent but approximately 80 per cent of the students are required to do "work service" before going on to higher education, we must ask to what extent are the 20 per cent who are being allowed to go straight on, selected entirely on academic grounds. Someone from outside the society cannot help feeling that this system could be used so as to make certain that those who favour the ruling classes in the Soviet Union, and those favoured by the ruling classes, are the ones who will get special consideration for direct entry to the university. Such selected persons would be two years ahead of their colleagues in the race for power and position, whether social, political or economic. Certainly the recommendations of the secondary schools are bound to favour those people who have been "good boys" in the Komsomol.[1] Those who have proved themselves to possess "a negative attitude", or still to hanker after "anti-social *bourgeois* tendencies" can hardly be expected to be included in the 20 per cent who go straight to university. Perhaps this is as it ought to be, but it looks very much like offering possibilities of selection on non-academic grounds.

As we will see later, the academic reasons given for allowing 20 per cent to go directly to university are quite respectable ones. It is said that Khrushchev was the person who pushed very hard for the compulsory year or two of work service, between the end of an eleven-year-school and the beginning of higher education, as he felt that the intelligentsia were losing touch with the ordinary people. In this connexion it was most interesting to hear one of the outstanding Russian educationists explain the existence of the teddy boys, the *stilyagi*, by saying that the trouble was that "these people are nobody; but they think they are smart". This came surprisingly from a brilliant man who had been putting forward egalitarianism as well as communism and atheism for about two hours. But it no doubt underlines the problem. Another

[1] "The method of awarding scholarships has been revised to take more account of the material needs of the student, and somewhat less of his grades; special courses are being organized to help *V.U.Z.* applicants who have not completed secondary education (that is, those from "Work Schools" or apprenticeships – *Ed.*), or who have been out of school for a while; and all applicants must present recommendations from places of work and also from party, Komsomol, or trade-union organizations, whose representatives in addition sit on admissions boards." *Soviet Society*, p. 578.

official, in explaining the false pride, the negative attitude to manual labour that had grown up among the academically educated, said; "After eight years of education, on finding no university places nor technical nor engineering jobs, some stayed at home, read books and filed their nails."

Of interest is the fact that in a case reported in *The Times* (London) of April 5, 1961, the fathers of the girls detained by a Voluntary People's Police detachment for "being dressed in a way too fashionable for their age" were, one a university professor, the other, an engineer.

Some people in the Soviet Union have "never had it so good", and as in any other society some of their children see no reason why they should go out and work and make a contribution to the society when their parents can well afford to keep them at home in what one might irreverently call *bourgeois* ease. But there is the problem of the widening gap between these and the proletariat who should have inherited the land. Khrushchev recognized it.[1]

One wishes that in other countries – particularly under-developed countries – more people would recognize the danger of this widening gap. Khrushchev's cure, as far as one can discover, was to insist that young people be forced to work before they went on to what is bound to be a privileged position for a minority, namely that of university student. He also stressed the urgently re-emphasized idea of polytechnicization. The academicians are said to have opposed very strongly the idea of working before going on to university. We were told that the only issue which has been openly debated in *Pravda* and such journals for many many years was this one. Any covert reasons which might have existed for the academicians' strong feelings are not easy to discover. But they did give a sound academic argument. Their contention was that in certain subjects it was most unwise to lose the fine edge of the enthusiasm and skill of the young people leaving the secondary schools. They pointed out that in such subjects as mathematics and modern languages it would be most improper to have a break of two years. Mathematicians are said to mature young, and linguists would

---

[1] Note the following statement of Florinsky's (quoted by DeWitt, op. cit. p. 49): "The gulf between the educated classes and the masses was the basic and fatal weakness of Russia's social structure." Vol. 11, p. 1256, *Russia: a History and Interpretation*.

The reference is specifically to the period just before, and at the start of World War 1.

In our concern with "communism" in general we must not forget that in the U.S.S.R. we are dealing with *Russian* communism.

lose touch with their languages. On the other hand, they argued, some real and tough experience of the world might be useful to students of history, literature and so on. In the end then, the decision was taken to allow 20 per cent of that minority of young people (some 20–25 per cent of the total age group) selected for higher education to go directly on to university and to insist that the other 80 per cent of that still favoured minority do work service.[1] Certainly in a society which is undoubtedly monolithic, one must wonder whether processes of selection according to usefulness to the Party and previous "good behaviour" will not be in constant use.

It should also be mentioned that university graduates are directed, as are the products of specialized secondary schools, to their first jobs on leaving their schools or universities. Knowledge of this direction must act as some sort of "selection" process both from the point of view of the student and of his advisors – and is perhaps intended to do so by the main planners in the society. It would seem unlikely that ministries and other agencies would allow people to train for jobs which could be non-existent or scarce. Intending pupils will no doubt keep their eyes on development plans so that they train themselves in fields in which they are more likely to be sent, say, to Leningrad than Siberia, supposing that they would prefer the former to the latter.[2]

There are so many people willing to exploit anti-communist propaganda at all costs that there is always the danger of being considered a professional anti-communist whenever one criticizes the U.S.S.R. or brings under analysis its various claims. In indicating my strong feeling that more selection than is admitted does take place I have referred to the monolithic nature of the country and its organization. Lest it be thought that I am merely using anti-communist propaganda I must later on say something detailed about the way in which almost every action is designed to tend towards the greater glory of communism, "the bright future for humanity".[3] Even when the Russians were being friendly and understanding this overriding communist aim was

---

[1] It would be useful to discover exactly what percentage of the 20 per cent are in fact going to pursue studies in maths, physics and languages. They are in any case described by their professors as "the most brilliant".

[2] The importance of this direction to the first job and its effect on students were clearly admitted in conversation in Moscow. See also DeWitt, op. cit. p. 86.

[3] "Hail to communism the bright future for humanity" was the motto prominently displayed over the Lenin bust in Boarding School No. 7, Leningrad. Its bright red letters accosted us as we stepped out of the watery, melting snows into the warm vestibule.

apparent – the more so as with many it is a basic and hidden assumption. But first, let us recapitulate.

At all levels, then, there are two main factors operating in the selection of candidates moving on to further stages of education:

1. The demand for outstanding performances throughout all phases of schooling, in competitive exams, and in such things as the "Mathematics Olympiads".[1] (Remember also the omnipresence of marks on the five point scale.[2])

2. Certain ambiguous matters,[3] geographical, socio-economic, political, such as the Labour Draft, "work experience" before fifteen, the polytechnicization of the last years of the ten- to eleven-year-schools, and the "work service" demanded for 80 per cent before they proceed to higher education.

The truth is that even over the question of special schools for "gifted" children there was a sharp division of opinion. While schools for the fine arts, as described above remain – so strongly are they embedded in the Russian tradition – special schools for those "gifted" in science, mathematics and physics were strongly opposed by the ideologists, and were not mentioned in the 1958 reform even though Khrushchev himself had at one time argued for them. As in other countries there were those like M. Laurentiev who stated quite simply "All classification of children is bad, and in our society we should make

---

[1] These are public contests on a city-wide, regional, and national scale. An account of one such was given by Professor Smirnov:
"In 1957–58 the Moscow University organized a Mathematics Olympics. The Olympics was attended by pupils of the ninth and tenth grades. The questions and problems were those concerned with mathematics in the secondary-school program. If the student does well, he is identified as a gifted pupil.
Children from each unit compete by solving difficult mathematical formulas. The winner in the region competes for the city or *oblast* contest; the *oblast* winner competes at the republic level; the republic winners compete in the All-Union meeting."
The Changing Soviet School, p. 373. Since that book was written new types of scholastic Olympiad have been established, and the old ones intensified.

[2] Almost every bit of class work I saw at secondary level was given a mark, often after discussion with the class. A young boy would be called out in front of the class to read or to answer questions on a text: "Is it the past indefinite or the past continuous?" "What is the infinitive" etc. etc. The teacher would then say "Go to your place; I give you a 4". She would record it in her book; and the boy would also enter it in his.

[3] cf. p. 157 – *The Soviet Citizen*: "But it is undoubtedly the case that the probability of obtaining a higher education which society 'awards' at birth to a boy born into a peasant or working-class home is still much smaller than the probability for success possessed by a boy born into the home of a professional or administrator."

no distinction between intellectual and manual labour". Others followed the line that only through the selection for special schools – even if these were the exception rather than the rule – would the state properly encourage and develop the talents of its people. The great tension that arises over this question in the U.S.S.R. seems to be based on the intricate relationship which has to exist between a strong "proletarian" ideology, a strong desire to impress this ideology on outsiders, a strong desire to surpass the U.S., an ever increasing experience with mass education, a strong academic and artistic tradition with its concomitant socio-economic implications, and the predetermined objection to such things as intelligence testing[1] and other non-Pavlovian psychological instruments.

The situation with regard to selection has been constantly changing, and, as I suggest later, is probably moving towards greater variety of offerings and greater selectivity. Perhaps some very brief comments on the pre-1958 situation are in order. We read in *The Soviet Citizen* on page 146: "Far and away the outstanding obstacle to a superior education for those from upper class social backgrounds was not money, but rather the régime's evaluation of such backgrounds.... Most frequently, however, they either disguised their origins or 'won' status as workers by taking on manual jobs for a specified period of time." The upper classes referred to here are those who were going to school in 1920 to 1935. In other words their origins were pre-revolutionary upper class. The *Times Educational Supplement* for the 25th of May 1960 refers to "the introduction of the so-called 'class principle' of admission from 1923 onwards". This is of admission in reference to higher education. This same article refers to "the proliferation at this time"

---

[1] By the decree "On the Pedological Perversions in the System of the *Narkompros*" (July 4, 1936) "intelligence and other psychological tests were discontinued". *The Changing Soviet School*, p. 72.

"As against a survival rate of 50 per 1000 among those who started in 1929, of those who started in 1945, 250 per 1000 completed the ten-year school in 1955. This is a tremendous increase, and speaks unequivocally of expanding opportunity to attain secondary education" (p. 156, *The Soviet Citizen*). However since 1955 higher education has not been expanding as rapidly as secondary.

Of two-fold interest is the following: "In the summer of 1956 one high educational official listed as her prime difficulty the fact that too many children wanted to go to college. Another expressed interest in the reintroduction of intelligence testing" (p. 157, *The Soviet Citizen*).

[While this book was in the press, news was received from a leading Soviet educator that some intelligence tests (not attainment tests) were brought into use again on 1st September, 1962.—Ed.]

(approximately 1930) "of Communist party schools of various kinds, 113 of which were classified as higher educational establishments in 1932". There are many other indications that from time to time between the first impetus of the October Revolution right up to the time of World War II various at least indirect selection mechanisms were at work. This placed the planners in a difficult position because they considered the school as an important "ideological arm of the Party", as a source of influence on the hostile or indifferent elements in their population (cf. p. 431, *Soviet Society*). At the same time they wished, when schooling was scarce, to get the working classes into schools, and therefore to exclude the very people whom they hoped to affect and whose support for the new régime they were trying to win.

Moreover, it must be remembered that seven-year education for all youth was not made compulsory until 1949 for the whole Union. Even then, of course, the compulsory law did not automatically ensure that all youth would receive such education. Up until 1949 it had been very much a privilege of the city youth (cf. p. 432, *Soviet Society*). At the level of the four-year "elementary" schools it was not until the mid-thirties that enough buildings had been put up, and enough teachers had been trained to make attendance at this level possible throughout the Union. So, as there was not enough schooling for all, there was a problem of selection and admissions. This problem was not always, nor in the end, solved by Party decree. To a large extent it was the logic of the situation that helped enormously with the selection. Mostly because of tradition, one supposes, the children of the lower classes did not go to school in the early days, while many of the children from professional homes did obtain both primary and secondary education because of the importance which their families placed on such education. It is only proper to point out that during the 1920's the Soviet schools were "strongholds of democracy relatively speaking ... racial and sexual equality was taught by verbal means and by the policy of complete equality with regard to the admission of members of racial minorities and girls in the schools" (cf. p. 431, *Soviet Society*).

The system of fees was introduced in 1940 at the secondary and higher levels, so that the ability to pay entered at that time into the process of selection. Fees have of course now been abolished, except for residence (not tuition) in boarding schools.

During the whole of the pre-1958 period and right up to the present time one of the very interesting aspects of selection has been the fact that the U.S.S.R. has tended to select its women as well as its men. As C. P. Snow puts it: "They have regarded women as providing half the brain-power of the human race . . . there are 233,000 women engineers . . . 1,250,000 women teachers. In Moscow University alone 1,000 of the lecturing staff are women" (*Times Educational Supplement*, 26. 2. 60). Of course there are many sides to this story because women, in 1948 for instance, were to be found also in such occupations as compressor operators (27 per cent), stevedores (17 per cent), steam boiler stokers (6 per cent). Further, women are paid directly for their day labour on the collective farms; the reward for their labour does not go into the general family fund. "Sir John Maynard regarded this change as having produced one of the fundamental social sources of support for the régime, by putting the village women 'on the side of the Soviets'" (cf. p. 562, *Soviet Society*).

From a woman's point of view the following remark of an informant is interesting: "Women knew that even if they did get married they would still have to work. Education meant better working conditions on equal terms with the men." It is very important for us in thinking of the question of selection for education to remember Snow's emphasis in this matter.

It is necessary now to recall what has been mentioned earlier about the overriding and all pervading[1] nature of the general aims and particular objectives as set out by the main planners, and to give an example or two of it.

It is difficult for people living in a sort of *laissez-faire* Western democracy to realize just how all pervading certain aims and attitudes are in a society like that of the U.S.S.R. But Khrushchev puts it well enough: "literary criticism must be merciless and relentless when the issue at stake is the defence of our ideological and political principles and attempts to infiltrate alien and *bourgeois* attitudes and views." In commenting on the speech in question, delivered July 17, 1960, but not reported in *Kommunist* until May 1961, Monitor (*Times*, London, 23. 5. 61) says:

---

[1] Note, for instance, ". . . sport is not of the amateur or professional kind enjoyed in England as a means of recreation or amusement, but is classified politically and is designed to produce worthy representatives in international competitions". Jorré, op. cit., p. 209.

"At the present stage according to the Soviet leader, the ideological work of the Party is concerned with the 'complete eradication of remnants of the old exploiting world from the consciousness of the people'. The Soviet Union needed 'such books, films, shows, music, painting and sculpture as will educate the people in the spirit of communist ideals, will awaken in them a feeling of exaltation with all that is wonderful and beautiful in our socialist reality and will instil in them a readiness to give their strength, knowledge, and capabilities to the service of the people'."

Education is the instrument of ideology.[1] It and everything else in society must play its part. In order to make this point quite clear, I should like to describe at some length an experience of mine which took place on Holy Saturday night in Moscow in 1960. I was specially invited to visit a school at which a concert in honour of *international understanding* was to take place. I gladly agreed to go, on the understanding that I should be returned to Friendship House by about 9 p.m. where I was to meet an important official of the Russian Ministry of Education. The teacher who was looking after me, and who turned out to be in charge of the whole function, arrived at about 6.30 p.m. instead of the promised 6 p.m.

When we arrived at the school there was real chaos. He tried valiantly to reorganize the children. But it look a long time. There was one youth with a camera who was very much like a certain type of extrovert American. One's every action, facial expression or yawn was most important to this youth and to the Radio Moscow and Television people. They always tried to get me while I was applauding.

One of the most important items in the concert was a chorus sung by many of the children in English, German and Russian. Clearly good work had been done in teaching the children English and German.

[1] "The attitude of the Soviet rulers toward education is exceedingly complicated. Marxism, being a rationalist school of thought, places a high value on education and learning *per se*. Education is 'good'. It would be a mistake, however, to believe that the Soviet leaders cherish the educated man in the classical sense of the intellectually curious, free-roving, skeptical enquirer" (p. 131, *The Soviet Citizen*). Professor I. A. Kairov, the President of the Academy of Pedagogical Sciences of the R.S.F.S.R., whom we had the great pleasure of meeting and engaging in discussion, describes communist education as a preparation for active participation in the building of communist society, and for the defence of the Soviet Government which is building that society (in *Pedagogika*, Moscow, 1948). Kairov said that communist education must be an extension of socialist education – atheist and scientific.

Some who sang the chorus were remarkably young. Their performance was clearly not simply a matter of brute memory of a few stanzas in two different languages. The interesting chorus line which came quite often, and was vigorously sung, was "But we are strong, we are strong". No doubt it referred to the youth of the world as a whole, but the children could be excused for feeling that it referred to their country, to its Sputniks, and to the fantastically large missile carriers which were in a few days to be parading in the Red Square on May Day. "But we are strong, we are strong." This chorus with its implications came during and after all the generous sentiments about peace and international understanding.

In the same way the playlets which were performed in English made a contribution to what my hosts understood to be a concert contributing to international understanding and peace. The general aims and orientation of Soviet government policy were never forgotten. Children between twelve and fifteen, or a bit older, had learnt enough English at school to act quite reasonably in English. They had not all caught the tune of the language, but they did well. And all the while one kept wondering whether children of the same age, from similar schools, in U.K., U.S.A., or the West Indies could have done anything like this in Spanish, or French, or German (not to mention Russian!). No doubt here and there in some places!

More interesting than the linguistic achievements of the children were the subjects, or themes, of the playlets. Both were placed in the U.S.A. One was no doubt "original", the other based on Tom Sawyer. One or the other had taken a prize at the big drama competition which had apparently just taken place between schools in Moscow – I had seen groups of children outside a large building waiting to mount their entry. They do take their cultural activity quite seriously!

There was no doubt about the implications of the theme of the Moscow playlets. Remember it was the night especially put aside for international friendship! The original sketch was placed in a staff room of a high school in the northern U.S. The lady teachers are discussing a certain child. Will she really be allowed to take up a scholarship that she has won? One lady seems doubtful, the other (the head?) vows to fight for her. Why there are such stress and strain only becomes clear when we discover that the girl in question is a Negro, and so she'll probably be discriminated against. As the playlet goes forward, and it seems likely that she *will* get the scholarship, hopes are expressed that soon racial discrimination in the U.S.A. will end. But the sting is in the tail for the curtain comes down soon after it has been pointed out that it is a good thing that the girl had come to the north as in the south she would not have had any chance at all! Loud, loud applause from the children who could thank whatever gods there be that *they* have no racial prejudices! If only there had been a way in which the loud and innocent applause could reach the ears of the *Jewish* doctors who "conspired" to put Stalin away, and who suffered suitably for their wickedness!

The second sketch did take us to the south – to Tom's classroom. The teacher was dressed in tails, and caused much amusement by his sadistic clouting of all and sundry with a large ruler. The boy who played the teacher did it excellently – and one wondered where he had learnt such behaviour! Shades of Dewey! How he rampaged around! The children fought; no work was done. Tom saved a girl by saying that *he* tore the page which, in fact, she had (in a scuffle). Tom is going to catch it; she realizes that he has saved her. "Tom, how could you!" A look of love. Curtain. Roars of cheering, applause, laughter. What schools they have in the U.S.A.! "Tails", and beatings and all!

But *we're* strong, *we're* strong!

After much talk I was sent on my way with a long farewell speech made by one of the more lively teachers. He ended with faith and conviction: "Finally, I consider it one of the greatest omens for the peace of the world that your Easter tonight coincides with the birthday of our Nikita Khrushchev".

As I rushed to Friendship House (where I was too late for my appointment) the question did just come to my mind: Would people who planned international peace days with such an awareness (almost unconscious at times) of their own ends and policies, trust to chance to ensure that by the end of university years the requisite number of electrical engineers, atomic scientists and Bantu experts[1] happen to appear on the scene ready for assignment to important posts.

There are many lesser points about selection that ought to be mentioned. What, for instance, is the place of the boarding school in any possible selection process? The suspicion of one going from the Western world to the U.S.S.R. tends to be that the growth of boarding schools

---

[1] Note *Times Educational Supplement*, 26. 8. 60, p. 237: "The Soviet claim to be training a large number of cadres in modern Asian and African languages 'in order to communicate with the common people who do not know English or French' is amply borne out."

is yet another step in the indoctrination process. But this might be a mistaken view. We were assured during our visit to Boarding School Seven in Leningrad, and elsewhere, that parents really desired to have the boarding schools, partly because in many homes both parents are at work. (It was hard, in fact, to find a housewife who was not also out at work.) We were told also "We think that the boarding school can cope with education better than can the parents". In this connexion we must remember the constant distinction made in Russian theory and practice between education and general "upbringing". Although indoctrination would of course go on in the boarding school, perhaps it is only our prejudgements on the issues of Russian education that make us look at boarding schools mainly in the light of such indoctrination. The boarding schools might in fact be an instrument of a certain kind of selection. For one thing, we were assured, as others have reported, that priority for entrance is given to lower income families.[1] Moreover, it is reported that on some occasions at least the boarding schools tend to take difficult children, and children who are not doing well in their academic subjects in the day schools.[2] This tendency is one that is well known in other countries. But the interesting thing is that if this kind of selection does go on with regard to boarding schools – and I believe that it does – it has not affected the general assertions, made especially in criticism of non-Soviet countries, that all must have the same sort of education!

It should also be remembered that promotion is by no means automatic in the secondary schools and that pupils who average less than a three on the five point scale are kept down. This must mean that the children with the higher marks will get to the top of the school more quickly, will therefore be ready for work service or selection to the university earlier, and might well if they fall among the 20 per cent who avoid work service, also avoid the military draft. This is possible because of the complicated arrangements whereby if one gets to a certain age without having been drafted one may be exempted en-

---

[1] But fees for lodging, food, and clothing have to be paid on a sliding scale according to need and parental resources; cf. p. 210, The *Changing Soviet School*.

[2] P. 208, *The Changing Soviet School*: "When questioned on this issue, Gmurman stated: 'It must be admitted that the academic level of boarding schools, generally speaking, is lower than that of the ordinary schools. This is attributable to the fact that boarding schools often get pupils who have been rejected by the ordinary schools, pupils who have proved to be hard to handle. Much work must be done with such children, before they can be expected to catch up with their contemporaries in the ordinary schools.'"

tirely.[1] So that despite protestations that the brighter children do not get special treatment, it is quite clear that the bright boy might go straight through a secondary school, straight through university and be given his first posting anything from three to five years before his slower companion of the same age, who is following the same sort of education through the secondary school and through the university.[2]

It might be that as secondary education is given over a larger number of years, and as the number of secondary school-leavers greatly increases, that selection will be forced, or is being forced, upon an ideology which is not supposed to approve of it. For instance, entrance requirements for the technicums have changed.[3] Leavers from the seven-year schools used to be accepted; later, however, places had to be fought for, and those who were accepted just before the 1958 reforms had mostly passed through the ten-year school. Since 1958 the technicum has been a highly competitive parallel to the final three academic grades. The interesting thing to notice will be the sort of ideological justification that will be given for the selective processes which have already slipped in, or have been introduced, and for any more marked steps that might have to be taken in this connexion.

To sum up, then, the Soviet theoreticians certainly started by being anxious that equal education should be given to all. This might explain the amazing statement already quoted from Lenin that virtually no entrance requirements were to be demanded of people entering the university. It might also express a very healthy awareness of the danger

---

[1] Cf. pp. 27–28 DeWitt, op. cit.: "Today, therefore, the Soviet Union has a clear-cut policy of preferential treatment toward higher education students concerning the military draft. *Successful* secondary school graduates can enter higher education unperturbed by the draft law at age 17.... In other words, if one manages to enter and stay in a Soviet higher education establishment, he is not likely to be inducted into military service.

"... On the whole the impact of the military draft policy creates an additional element in the selection of students both in secondary schools and in higher educational establishments. A student whose grade progress in secondary school is at least normal for his age has a good chance, because of the one-year escape clause, to enter higher education. This is not feasible in the case of repeaters or for pupils entering school at an age over seven. In higher education, the draft policies exercise an additional force for maintaining a satisfactory academic record since failures lead to expulsion and subsequent loss of preferential status as far as military service obligation is concerned."

[2] Cf. DeWitt, op. cit., pp. 13–14: "The second category (i.e. who were drafted into Labor Training Schools) included over-aged pupils (*pererostki*) attending the intermediate grades (5–7). Over-aged pupils in most instances were those who were required to repeat a year in one of the lower grades because of poor scholastic or attendance records. In the third draft category were regular students in the intermediate grades of rural areas only."

[3] Cf. pp. 72 and 73 DeWitt, op. cit.

to a society of that kind of social structure in which an élite is very clearly marked off from, and very nearly unconnected with, the rest of society. Or it might be simply a matter of communist ideology wanting to persuade the proletariat everywhere that they are indeed coming into their own.[1] However, from what was seen on a brief visit to the Soviet Union and from many written sources it seems quite clear that education for all is no longer meaning the *same* education for all. All kinds of differentiations have come into being. I have tried to point to many of these and to their significance. It is hard to produce conclusive evidence. But I am willing to chance the assertion that in the not too distant future differing abilities in other things than the Fine Arts will be openly admitted and taken cognizance of by the education system.[2] I remember particularly the expression on the faces of many teachers when high officials from the Ministry tried to explain to us that the difference in the performance of various children was in no way connected with their various innate abilities. On that occasion one official said "No one in the U.S.S.R. says that people are of the same ability; but we want them in one class because they can help each other. We are against the élite". He went on to say that they were interested in the individual but then immediately mentioned the needs of society. As he spoke on this matter of varying abilities and the élite I jotted in my note-book "some of the Soviet teachers here present do not quite agree with what the top brass is saying about differences in ability". I noted further "differences of ability – this is what they will not face *in the open*". It is my considered opinion, for what it is worth, that they have been facing these differences, and have been dealing with them – in a fairly indirect way. They will no doubt institute further, and perhaps more open, ways of meeting them.

In all known societies selection for education and other apparent

[1] P. 46, DeWitt, op. cit.: "In the Soviet education system the selection process is of great importance. It is a device through which Soviet propaganda can make extravagant claims that every Soviet citizen has a right to education and to the limitless development of his intellectual capacity. In reality, however, it operates to give extensive education to a few of the fittest and limited education to the many, who get what Stalin has called 'education sufficient enough to become active participants in social development'. What constitutes a 'sufficient' amount of education is determined primarily by various factors which occur in the process of selection."

[2] P. 267, *The Changing Soviet School*: "Many members of the Academy of Pedagogical Sciences, appeared to favor schools for those gifted in mathematics, physics, chemistry, and biology. Provisions for these schools were eventually dropped from the Education Law of December 24, 1958."

privileges are never simple matters following ability only. The remarkable thing about the theoreticians in the U.S.S.R. is that they claim not to be selecting on any other grounds than those of attainment. It is difficult to square this assertion with the existence of such schools as the Higher Party schools and the schools of Closed Access,[1] with special Fine Arts schools, with the exemption of certain people from work service and from the military draft, with the severe competition for university and other places, and with the fact that the Communist Party in the U.S.S.R. is not open to every well or ill-meaning dolt who comes along. It is itself a carefully selected élite.

[1] Cf. p. 15 DeWitt (already quoted p. 11).
Also notice p. 437, *Soviet Society*: "There is no doubt, however, that children of prominent Party officials obtain educational privileges, as teachers and school administrators are eager to retain the good-will of influential parents. Furthermore, one of the determinants of 'merit' in the judging of pupils is a complete knowledge and acceptance of Party doctrine, so-called Marx–Leninism." (This was written in 1954.)

CHAPTER 7

The Polytechnical Principle[1]

The origins of "polytechnical" thinking

The polytechnical principle has become one of the major components of communist educational theory and practice in recent years. It is intended to contribute decisively to the unification of school and life, and to constitute an essential foundation for linking school instruction with productive work. Yet the word "polytechnic" itself is not new. For Western European students it will be associated with the idea of an educational institution offering high-level training in several technologies, such as the French "école polytechnique" and the Regent Street "Poly" in London. This coincidence of terminology is in some ways unfortunate, as the social and educational philosophies underlying these usages are quite other than those underlying the modern communist use of the word. For the true origins of the modern concept of polytechnic education we have to turn, not to institutions bearing that name, but to the educational ideals of social reformers; for the idea is not merely the basis for modifications in the curriculum, or for the imparting of technological bias to traditional subjects, but is a fundamental principle embedded in the educational system emerging from a radical transformation of society and a radical reassessment of the nature of man and of his place in his society and in the cosmos. For this reason, although communist educationists pay some tribute to the so-called Utopian socialists of earlier times, such as Thomas More, Thomas Campanella, Charles Fourier and Robert Owen, and although they date the beginnings of modern didactics to Ratke and Comenius, they attribute to Karl Marx the credit for the first valid systematic formulation of educational theory. These and other earlier thinkers may have seen into the ills of their own societies, and may have produced creditable schemes for the extension and improvement of

[1] Owing to the writer's inadequate knowledge of Russian, most of the sources for this essay are East German, including German editions of works originally published in Russian, Czech, etc.

L 153

education, but only one who was simultaneously educator, economist, and revolutionary could, we are told, see into the character of polytechnic education as an integral part of a socialist society of which it shares the historical inevitableness.[1]

Marx and Engels (and later Lenin, Krupskaya and Stalin) derive their ideas on education from their comprehensive study of society as a whole, and although Engels acknowledged that Fourier and Owen had already demanded "the greatest possible variation in occupation for every individual, and correspondingly, a training of youth for the most comprehensive technical activity", his analysis of capitalist society led him to the conclusion that polytechnic education, as distinct from polytechnical training, could only be realized within a higher social and economic order.[2] This is implicit in the Communist Manifesto's demand that the workers should make their educational policy the dominant one in the new order,[3] and more explicit in *Das Kapital*, where we find a detailed study of the growth of manufacturing industry showing the development of the various specializations going to make up a productive process and of the various levels of skill within each specialized field. Most industrial workers are seen as machine-minders, or as really no more than ancillary, the real control and understanding of a mechanical process being vested in a "numerically inconsiderable" staff – a higher form of working class which is outside the definition of factory worker proper. The development of specialization led to each individual worker's being regarded not just as an adjunct to the machine, but as himself a part of a part of a machine, exposed to exploitation as the machine itself was exploited, in the interests of the capital-owners who instituted the system of mechanized production. Hence arose the paradox that the machine, which opened up prospects of enormous improvement in the living standards of the people, became an instrument for the degradation of the majority. The cause of this degradation was not the machine itself, but its application within a capitalist economy. The overthrow of the capitalist society was therefore seen as a prerequisite for the liberation of the workers from their educational as well as their political and economic restrictions. Only in a socialized industry would it be

---

[1] *Geschichte der Erziehung*, Volk und Wissen Verlag, Berlin, 1957.

[2] Engels, *Herrn Dührings' Umwalzung der Wissenschaft*, Dietz Verlag, Berlin, 1948, p. 365.

[3] Marx-Engels, *Manifest der Kommunistischen Partei*, Dietz Verlag, Berlin, 1948, p. 28.

possible for each individual worker to enjoy life on an ever higher level of material prosperity, enriched by the full development, training and employment of his innate capacities. For the worker to understand and control the whole of the means of production, his intellectual, physical, moral and aesthetic education would have to be completed and shaped by "polytechnic" education.[1]

This outline of the argument is necessary in order to show that although there may be points of contact between certain of the phenomena of polytechnic education and some of the proposals of non-communist educational reformers, the idea of polytechnic education must be looked at against a background of Marxist economic and political thought. Numerous communist writers have made the point explicit, that "it is a *bourgeois* hypocrisy that the school can stand outside politics. . . . The school stands in indissoluble connexion with the workers".[2]

The argument starts with this consideration of economic and technical needs in a new form of social organization, but leads ultimately to the realization that "all the upbringing, education and instruction of the youth of today must be an upbringing to the communist morality".[3] But communist educationists had still to be weaned away from the seductive doctrines of school reform along "vocational" lines as propagated by non-Marxist reformers. Dewey's ideas on the school as an embryonic society, and his appreciation of the need "that each shall have had the education which enables him to see within his daily work all there is in it of large and human significance", are paralleled by Kerschensteiner's plans for a school programme based on practical activity, using the vocational as a principal incentive. ("Work with the hands is the foundation of all true knowledge.") These ideas appear to have been developed pretty fully by the Russian, P. P. Blonski, in the early years of Soviet education, although most modern communists are silent about him. There was, and still is, much of great value in the thoughts of the propagators of the "work-school" idea, and much which must have appealed greatly to left-wing visionaries. Kerschensteiner starts with the conception of an ideal "organization of society, which accords to every individual whatever is to the moral

---

[1] Marx, *Das Kapital*, Dietz Verlag, Berlin, 1947, Vol. I.

[2] Lenin, *Works XXII*, p. 474 (Russian edn.), quoted in Dorst, *Erziehung, Bildung and Unterricht*, Volk und Wissen Verlag, Berlin, 1954, p. 170.

[3] Lenin, speech in October 1920, quoted by Dorst, op. cit., p. 179.

benefit of all his nature", and bases his "work-school" on the desirability of uniting theory with practice and school with life. For Marxists, however, these are dangerous doctrines, implying adherence to the then accepted forms of citizenship and the stratification of society according to occupation. A counterblast was necessary, which should elaborate upon the basic premises of Marx and Engels and indicate the weaknesses in the "reformers'" case.[1]

It is Nadezhda Krupskaya who is nowadays given most of the credit for establishing a firm foundation for communist educational theory, and especially for developing the polytechnic idea on unambiguously Marxist lines. She was not opposed to the idea of practical work as the core of the life of a school, but considered that "in present circumstances a work-school can of course only exceptionally be free" (i.e. from *bourgeois*-capitalist pressures) (*Svobodnoye vospitaniye*, 1910, No. 10). She proposed a complete re-examination of the school curriculum and syllabuses, with a view to ensuring that all children have the possibility of reaching the highest level of scientific and technological knowledge integrated into their training in manual skills. In the preparation of syllabuses, research workers and technologists should come to the aid of teachers in discarding out-of-date material and working out the polytechnic approach. She saw the possibility of a new subject of study, "organization of work", acting as the connecting link between the school curriculum and the political-economic society in which the school functions. Productive work by the children should not be carried on under school auspices in isolation from the outside world, but in factories and farms side by side with the workers normally active there, whose participation would serve as an aid in the extension of the polytechnic principle to the adult community and in the involvement of working adults in the whole educational process.

Krupskaya stressed that the productive work of the children should not be too highly specialized: experience in the factory should be so organized as to lead to an understanding of the function of each department within the total effort of the factory and of the role of the factory in the total economy of the area and of the country. Productive work should be both industrial and agricultural; it should be explicitly related to the content of classroom work; it should lead to an under-

---

[1] Kerschensteiner, *Begriff der Arbeitsschule*, 14th edition, Oldenbourg, Munchen, 1961. For the relations between Dewey, Kerschensteiner and Blonski, see Anweiler, "Der internationale Zusammenhang der Reformpädagogik", in *Bildung und Erziehung*, Laumanns, Lippstadt, July 1961.

standing of chemical as well as mechanical production; and it should be a training in initiative and intellectual adaptability as well as in manual skill and scientific knowledge. At no time did Krupskaya regard children as a source of cheap labour (in fact she inveighed against any possibility of exploitation, in several speeches to both teachers and youth movement leaders) but saw the necessity for adjusting programmes of school work and productive work to the physical and mental aptitudes of the child. Her ideas on the organization of polytechnic instruction in school and in industry are supplemented by a deep interest in the role of youth organizations and their "socially useful work". She must be regarded as a major source of Marxist educational theory; and after making acquaintance with her ideas one realizes how derivative most subsequent thinking is.[1]

This is not the occasion for a detailed analysis of the ebb and flow of interest in the polytechnic principle, as this subject has already been fairly fully explored.[2] The principle does not appear to have received detailed study before about 1952 or 1953, and it is possible to place several interpretations upon the relative neglect before then and the enormous resurgence of interest since. It is probably outside the scope of this essay to conjecture whether the explanation is purely political, or whether it is legitimate to consider that the close of a post-war period of reconstruction led naturally to a desire for new educational planning. In either case, the new polytechnic thinking takes account of the need for the consolidation of educational systems on approved Marxist lines, especially in those countries only recently received into the socialist camp; of the manpower needs in countries becoming more industrialized, especially in view of the "second industrial revolution" brought in by automation; and of the need in modern society for a new impetus to extra-curricular guidance of youth and to further education of adults.

The polytechnic infant

In a communist educational system, which concerns itself explicitly with upbringing as well as education, there is no room for amateur

[1] Krupskaya, *Ausgewählte pädagogische Schriften*, Volk und Wissen Verlag, Berlin, 1955. Another major Russian writer is A. S. Makarenko, some of whose main works are available in English; but his approach is much less political, less systematic and more empirical.

[2] Bereday and Pennar, edd., *The Politics of Soviet Education*, Atlantic Books, 1960.

approaches. "We need a communist upbringing for children, and this demands that they are looked after for a considerable time in kindergartens."[1] Mothers are encouraged to make their contribution to the nation's productive efforts, so the very lavish provision of nursery schools serves the twofold purpose of aiding production and of bringing children under the aegis of the educational system at the earliest possible age. (East Germany has 355,000 nursery school places, Hungary 177,000, England and Wales 26,000.)[2] At this stage one can hardly claim to be discussing polytechnic training, but one can think of ways in which the young child's attention can be directed towards an understanding of the kind of society he lives in and of his place within it. He can be presented with the idea of technology in action, of the kind of jobs grown-ups do, and of what is meant by useful work. Children can hardly avoid hearing of technical matters, and their desire to be tractor-drivers, air-pilots, and so on is a well-known one, leading to the desire in play to simulate mastery of the appropriate skills. Where the polytechnic principle is adhered to, a conscious and systematic effort is made to lead interest towards productive work. This is seen in both formal and informal activities. Through play, influences are exerted by means of picture-books and the books which parents and kindergarten staff read aloud to children. One finds fables such as *The Grasshopper and the Ant*, *The Cock and the Two Mice*, in which there is explicit praise for hard work; descriptions of life on the farm; the awakening of respect for miners, bakers, tractor-drivers and so on. Of course it is not exclusively in the socialist countries that one finds toyshops permeated by a technical atmosphere, but in so far as so many playthings are designed and produced in the first instance for use in nursery schools, the Western visitor does notice a certain lack of the less didactic kind of toy (and an almost complete absence of purely military vehicles, aeroplanes, rockets and guns). These remarks apply equally to the kind of toys school children have up to the age of nine or ten. Construction sets are encouraged, and those designed for slightly older children are made to conform to higher standards of accuracy. For example, a set intended for the construction of a model tractor conformed to the general design characteristics of a specific type, and the accompanying leaflet explained in simple terms how those design

[1] Krupskaya, op. cit., p. 160.
[2] *Vergleichende Pädagogik*, 1961, I, Volk und Wissen Verlag, Berlin. *Statistisches Jahrbuch der D.D.R., 1961*, Zentralverlag, Berlin. *Education in 1960*, H.M.S.O., London, 1961.

features came about. This development is of course associated with the growing popularity of construction sets intended to facilitate the performance of specific groups of experiments in higher classes (especially in mechanics, electricity, &c.). Even a standard game like "Happy Families" can be made to contribute to the furtherance of the polytechnic principle if its sets are designed to show productive workers in appropriate groups.

Special periods for systematic polytechnic instruction (under any name) are not envisaged at the nursery school or primary stages, but this does not mean that practical activities and instruction on polytechnic lines are not undertaken. Formal and informal contacts with co-operative and nationally-owned industries are encouraged, and "socially useful work is for the primary stage an essential form of the connexion between school and life, which should permeate the entire teaching process". These outside contacts are in a sense extra-curricular, whilst the socially useful work is usually carried out under the auspices of the youth movement. There are, however, opportunities for polytechnic approaches within the time-table, through participation in the work on the school garden (even from Class One) and through practical activities associated with formal lessons, in addition to the one or two periods a week officially earmarked for craft-work.[1] Children are introduced to the properties of various easily worked materials such as paper, cardboard, clay, plasticine, wood, wire, thin sheet-metal, &c. They learn how to handle basic tools, such as scissors, knife, awl, hammer, file, &c., as well as learning some of the basic processes of gardening. All this obviously bears a close resemblance to standard practices in good primary schools in non-communist countries, but there is rather more to it than the simple desire to develop children's aptitudes by many-sided activities. They are not only learning the qualities of materials and the capabilities of tools, but are (it is hoped) beginning to learn how to apply in practice their theoretical knowledge of counting, measuring, drawing; to acquire regard for the value of materials and for the need to use them economically; to understand the value of work and to gain respect for those grown-ups who sustain the community by their productive labours.

The youth movement probably does its most important work with the children from ten to fifteen, and leads them to membership of the

[1] *Lehrplan der zehnklassigen allgemeinbildenden polytechnischen Oberschule*, Ministerium für Volksbildung, Berlin, 1959.

Komsomol or equivalent organization; but it also throws its aegis over practical activities arranged by its primary section (Young Pioneers in East Germany, Sparks in Czechoslovakia, &c.). Interest circles are formed for "young handymen", rabbit-rearing, modelling; or *ad hoc* groups perform useful tasks within their capacities, such as sweeping up leaves, killing colorado beetles, or tidying up the school area; and individual children are urged to help mother in the home. All this, too, bears a superficial resemblance to the activities of the Wolf Cubs and Brownies, but in the socialist countries the majority of children are involved and the "socially-useful" activities are in constant progress. "All the forms mentioned are directed towards bringing up the children to a communist attitude to work."[1]

The polytechnic content of general education

The development of the idea of polytechnic education has been linked from start to finish with a consideration of political and economic needs in a socialist society. At the same time it must be conceded that the introduction of a technological element into general education for adolescents is something which has received serious consideration in many schools in non-socialist countries where economic prosperity is based on industrialization, and where even agriculture is being approached as a form of industry in which efficiency can be achieved only if production units are large and machinery employed to replace unskilled manpower. The use of electric power, automatic and semi-automatic machinery, and chemical products leads to an increase in productivity – but also to increasing demands on the scientific and technical knowledge of the workers involved. The technological advance of the Soviet Union is not an isolated phenomenon: in Czechoslovakia productivity increased by 8 per cent in 1959 and capital investment by 12 per cent; whilst "in fifteen years Rumania has discarded a way of life which has hardly changed since . . . the Middle Ages, to emerge as an embryonic industrial state".[1] There is clearly a temptation to try to ensure that school-leavers have a foundation of technical knowledge by simply tacking a technical subject on to a

---

[2] Trajer and others, *Základy výroby na střední škole*, Prague 1960; German edition entitled *Der Produktionsunterricht an den Mittelschu en der Č.S.S.R.*, Volk and Wissen Verlag, Berlin, 1961. School textbooks and the Young Pioneers' programme also give clear indications of what good children are expected to do.

[1] *Times Review of Industry*, London, March 1960 and May 1960.

traditional time-table. There is the other temptation (to which many English head teachers yield), to disregard the tendency of the times as a trend towards "mere" vocationalism and to adhere to the traditional curriculum as a perfect vehicle for a kind of general education the worth of which is said to have been adequately demonstrated. Advocates of the polytechnic principle would argue that its implementation must involve simultaneously the acquisition of a basis of technical skill and also a broadening of the field of general education to maintain a true relationship with a new form of society. In order to make clear what this statement means, it is necessary first to indicate what it does *not* mean.

It might be thought possible to consider the polytechnic principle as a principle of teaching method and of syllabus- and curriculum-construction, involving the identification and explanation of all possible connexions between what the teacher aims to teach and its technological aspects. This "technicalization" of the school programme, which might apply to cultural and aesthetic subjects as well as to mathematics and sciences, has its defects.

One is that it could well impair the natural system and discipline inherent within each subject. Another, more serious, is that it would probably not be effective for the polytechnic purpose, in that there are thousands of different production processes, and it is possible to acquire a superficial knowledge of a large number without necessarily arriving at an understanding of the whole system of production or of the basic principles. Yet another is that this superficial view of what "polytechnic" means could endanger the underlying principle of general education on which the curriculum is founded. (There is a training school for watch- and instrument-makers in Paris, where every subject is approached from a "horological" angle: this is indeed a razor's edge on which few teachers would care to walk.)

A second misunderstanding could arise if we were to regard polytechnic education as synonymous with workshop training. It is true that workshop training appears on the time-table. Other subjects however, all play a part in the whole process of polytechnic education – sciences, geography and drawing in particular. Workshop training is important, even essential, in leading to familiarity with tools and materials; but it makes one contribution amongst many. In this connexion it is necessary to lay stress on the relationship between workshop training and the study of industrial production. In England, and presumably in other non-communist countries, there is a certain emphasis in handwork lessons on the aim to produce a "thing of beauty" or to gain personal satisfaction through self-expression. In the communist setting, workshop training is the beginning of training in industrially useful skills and of understanding of industrial processes: aesthetic considerations are secondary. Associated with this possible misinterpretation is a third, though minor one: that training in any form of practical skill, including cookery and needlework for girls or "handyman's courses" for boys, is necessarily a furtherance of polytechnic education. Although these skills may be necessary and desirable, they do not in themselves constitute a "polytechnic" approach.

Having, it is hoped, indicated and obviated misunderstanding, it is possible to look at what is in fact aimed at and at the effect on the school programmes of this aim. The aim at this stage of compulsory general education after completion of the "primary" stage (varying from one country to another but usually at about ten or eleven) and before the beginning of more specifically vocational education, is a threefold one. First comes what may be called the "polytechnic horizon", that is to say, a broad view of the whole system of production. In this are included a knowledge of the main branches of production, of the relations between these main branches, and of the geographical distribution of productive units, sources of raw materials, and the role of the pupil's native area and native country in the system.

It is clearly impossible to cover all the hundreds of different industries that exist, but an attempt is made to study a few, as examples to indicate the four main categories into which industries may be divided: mechanical, chemical and agricultural production, and energy. By mechanical production is meant all branches of production which change the form of the raw material whilst leaving it unchanged in its chemical composition. Within this category fall the textile industry, optics and instrument making, furniture manufacture and (probably most important) machine-manufacture. Chemical production implies change in the composition of the raw material, such as is seen in metallurgy, dyestuffs, oil refining, petrochemicals, pharmaceuticals, plastics. Agricultural production includes plant and animal production whether looked at from the point of view of food production or of production of raw materials for industry (timber, leather, &c.). The term "energy" means the exploitation of natural energy sources to provide energy in technically usable forms. An acquaintance with these four main categories and the development of sufficient insight to be able to fit facts about any specific industrial process into this basic scheme is what is meant by the requirement now imposed on syllabuses, to provide a polytechnic horizon. There are characteristic relationships between the main branches of production. For instance, mechanical production furnishes all other branches with machinery and equipment; chemical production supplies mechanical production with much of its raw materials, especially metals; agriculture receives fertilizers and pesticides from chemical industry, and on its part yields wood, leather, &c., whilst energy production is vital to the others.

It is clear that pursuit of the general aim of achieving this polytechnic horizon must have a profound effect on syllabuses. For example, in chemistry, practical applications of inorganic chemistry can be seen through the study of coke and gas manufacture, the blast furnace, sulphur and its compounds, chemical fertilisers for agriculture, whilst the East German 14-year-old is already starting his organic studies with fifteen periods devoted to paraffins, olefines and acetylenes, in the setting of oil-refining.[1] This contrasts with the sterile emphasis on allegedly "basic" laboratory "experiments", with a limited number of inorganic substances, which has become traditional in England, and from which only a minority of pupils advance at last by embarking on a Sixth Form organic course noted for its tedium.[2]

Similar relationships are established between biology and the scientific bases of agriculture, and between physics and mechanical and electrical engineering. Changes in emphasis in the syllabuses for science subjects bring in their wake less obvious but also significant changes in the approach to some other subjects. The approach to mathematics represents a departure from the emphasis on pure mathematics which is normal in Western countries, and which is based on the assumed inherent value of mathematics in contributing to all-round intellectual development of the individual. The polytechnic mathematics syllabus does not deny that mathematics "is to develop intellectual abilities, especially logical thinking", but goes on to stress that "pupils must acquire necessary mathematical bases and pre-requisites for their further activity in a vocation and in society". There is a conscious effort

---

[1] *Lehrplan der zehnklassigen allgemeinbildenden polytechnischen Oberschule*, Ministerium für Volksbildung, Berlin, 1959.

[2] *Technical Education*, London, December 1961, p. 15; *Technology*, London, January 1962, p. 15.

to relate mathematical procedures to a body of knowledge of how those procedures are applied in industry and commerce. Descriptive geometry is explicitly related to engineering drawing; percentages and statistics to book-keeping problems in socialized industry; and tables and a slide-rule can be *used* long before they can be *understood*.[1]

History can contribute towards the acquisition of a polytechnic horizon by the emphasis on economic history and the development of productive enterprise, and geography helps "especially by working at questions concerning the exploitation and transformation of the environment, interconnexions of individual branches of the economy within a socialist country and within the whole socialist world-system".[2] In literature and art, there is no denying that the primary aim of developing command over language and appreciation of aesthetic values is retained, but again the intimate connexion between school and life is striven for. An American educationist is said to have pleaded for "just one picture of a man in overalls, dirty, and with sweat on his brow".[3] There no shortage of such themes in communist schools, which are animated aesthetically by the spirit of "socialist realism". "The most beautiful thing in life is the work of man, and what more noble task than to portray faithfully the new man, the toiler, the richness of his spiritual interests, his fight against all that is obsolescent . . . the romance of communist labour."[4] The application of the polytechnic principle to all the curriculum is alleged to lead to the release of greater interest and energy through the realization of the practical value of scientific knowledge, the purpose of skills and the relevance of social and aesthetic studies to the wider world. Success cannot be achieved, however, without imposing on teachers the demand to select their material carefully, to revise it constantly, and to present it systematically. It is this educational necessity which, as much as political expediency, dictates the selection, supervision, and further in-service training of teachers, and which, as much as considerations of prestige, leads to the constant revision of syllabuses and textbooks and the development of audio-visual aids and teaching equipment.

[1] *Lehrplan der zehnklassigen allgemeinbildenden polytechnischen Oberschule*, Ministerium für Volksbildung, Berlin, 1959.

[2] *Lehrplan der zehnklassigen allgemeinbildenden polytechnischen Oberschule*, Ministerium für Volksbildung, Berlin, 1959.

[3] Mayer, *The Schools*, Bodley Head, 1961, p. 187.

[4] Khrushchev, Report to the 22nd Congress of the Communist Party of the Soviet Union, 17th October 1961.

Discussion of fundamental aims of education always proves to be a rather embarrassing topic, the precise nature and degree of embarrassment varying usually according to the distance from the classroom of the people concerned. *Quot homines, tot sententiae!* The verbalism inherent in the English academic tradition has led, not unnaturally, to an acknowledgement of English language and literature as representing the core of the curriculum, and to a misunderstanding of what is really meant by the word "communication" (the recent coming of the word "innumerate" is a belated recognition of this). The communist philosophy seeks to provide an unequivocal definition of the aims of education and simultaneously to give a clear indication of what is the core of the curriculum. According to Professor I. A. Kairov, President of the Academy of Pedagogical Sciences of the R.S.F.S.R., "The school must impart to its pupils the foundations of the scientific attitude, the communist views on nature, society, and man's thinking, the passionate conviction of the greatness of communist ideals, of the historical inevitability of the decline of capitalism, and the complete victory of communism. . . . The scientific attitude is the materialistic attitude. The school must seriously improve the scientific-atheistic education of its pupils, in the first place through the instruction in the natural sciences and in the historical-philosophical subjects, as well as in extra-curricular work."[1]

The achievement of this aim through formal lessons demands more than the application of the polytechnic principle to the standard subjects: the hitherto rather amorphous subject "civics" can be presented in a much more systematic way, and a new subject "introduction to socialist production" or "foundations of production" can ensure that no important gaps are left in pupils' knowledge of the bases of production in a socialist economy. Although much can be learnt from the practical work in production, about which something will be said later, it was soon discovered that a formal course of instruction would be necessary if children were to acquire the desired insight into the meaning of polytechnic education. In the R.S.F.S.R. a syllabus was devised for Classes 8 to 10 of the middle school, to supplement the gains made through the introduction of the polytechnic bias in standard subjects and through the practical work. In the syllabus for mechanical technology, children learn about the make-up of a machine, different types of machine-tools and the internal combustion

[1] Speech to 22nd Congress of the C.P.S.U., quoted in *Schule and Nation*, 1961, II.

engine. In the syllabus for electrical technology, they learn about electricity generators, transformers, metrology, motors, and about the application of electric power in mechanization and automation. In the syllabus for "foundations of production seen in individual enterprises" it is envisaged that they will learn about the raw materials, technological processes, and production organization in individual works, through visits and observation, lectures, and discussions. A separate set of syllabuses has been devised for rural schools, of course, providing for the study of mechanical and electrical technology through agricultural machinery, as well as the basic theory of agriculture. Through theoretical and practical study of one enterprise they will get to know the basic principles of energy supply, and technical and economic planning. "The teacher must guide the pupils' attention especially to the general that manifests itself in the particular."[1]

"Principles of production" forms part of the curriculum in the middle schools (that is, the schools catering for children from about fifteen to eighteen) in most communist countries; but it may be assumed that it will be introduced in classes of younger children as these countries catch up with their educational arrears. The educational problem facing the new Soviet Union in 1917 is now well known; but what is not so well known is that most of the countries now forming the socialist *bloc* were educationally well behind Western Europe. (For instance, Bulgaria has only recently introduced the compulsory eight-year school; most Hungarians left school at twelve under the Horthy régime; and Czechoslovakia has had to double her provision of academic secondary-school places.) East Germany started from a much more favourable position, and has therefore been able to develop syllabuses for "introduction to the principles of production" for all children from the age of thirteen as well as for those who attend the academic secondary school from the age of fifteen.

The East German syllabus is as follows (in outline only):

CLASS 7
We get to know the production of our socialist enterprise   9 hrs
From the history of our socialist enterprise   3 hrs
CLASS 8
The socialist attitude to work   4 hrs

[1] Shapovalenko, *Politekhnicheskoe obuchenie v sovietskoi shkole v sovremennom etape*, Moscow, 1958; German edition entitled *Polytechnische Bildung in der sowjetischen Schule*, Volk und Wissen Verlag, Berlin, 1959, p. 36.

Technical development in our enterprise	7 hrs
The planning of our production	8 hrs
The organization of our labour	8 hrs
Revision and summary	4 hrs
CLASS 9	
Our agricultural enterprise and its production	22 hrs
Excursion to another enterprise	4 hrs
Survey of the main branches of industry:	
I Energy	7 hrs
CLASS 10	
Survey of the main branches of industry (continued):	
II Metallurgical industries	5 hrs
III Mechanical engineering	11 hrs
IV Chemical industries	10 hrs
V Our local industries	7 hrs

For schools in rural areas, the syllabuses are essentially similar, but items are given different emphasis and different sequence.[1]

When we come to look at the syllabuses followed by pupils in the academic secondary schools, we find an extension and elaboration of this same basic plan, but with two important provisos. One is that care must be taken to avoid duplication in Classes 11 and 12 of work already done in Classes 7 or 8 (this caveat applies to the syllabuses for practical work as well as to those for "introduction to socialist production"). The other is that by Class 12 it is assumed that a more strictly vocational element will have entered into the school programme as a whole and this will have its effect on the syllabuses in most subjects. The kind of practical work done will depend on the facilities available in local industries, which will determine to a considerable extent the nature of the technical specialization inevitable at this stage and will also influence the content of the technological theory, the "polytechnic" syllabus for sciences, technical drawing, &c., and the "introduction to socialist production". Teachers of chemistry, for instance, are to "use all possibilities of linking chemistry with other subjects and especially with socialist production in industry and agriculture, and take into account regional peculiarities".[2] We shall have to return later to a

---

[1] *Lehrplan der zehnklassigen allgemeinbildenden polytechnischen Oberschule*, Ministerium für Volksbildung, Berlin, 1959.

[2] *Lehrplan der zwölfklassigen allgemeinbildenden polytechnischen Oberschule*, Ministerium für Volksbildung, Berlin, 1960.

more detailed consideration of the polytechnic principle at work in the "extended high-school" of East Germany and the "middle schools" of the other socialist countries.

For the present, however, let us turn our attention to the third main component of the polytechnic general education obligatory for all children, that is, the practical skills to be acquired. Handwork in wood and metal has for a long time been established as part of general education in the schools of England, but its acceptance in the curriculum in many other countries is a more recent phenomenon. In those countries which have accepted the polytechnic principle as a guiding one, the place of handwork has been established beyond question. Its justification consists, at the eleven plus stage, as well as at the primary stage (as already indicated), in its value as part of moral training. Further, some forms of manual work help to an understanding of the basic principles of production, whilst a general introduction to manual skills is a necessary preliminary to the specialized vocational training which is to come from the age of fifteen onwards. This last point is taken very seriously; all available policy documents make it quite clear that the polytechnic elements in the education imparted to children up to the age of about fourteen are indeed part of a scheme for general education, and are not to be regarded as inherently vocational. It is assumed that specialized training for any specific occupation will not be given at this stage, and that the skills acquired will be the basic ones:

> elementary wood- and metal-working processes, using hand tools;
> familiarity with basic measurement techniques and tools;
> technical drawing and interpretation of drawings;
> laboratory work in sciences;
> elementary practice with electrical circuits;
> elementary agricultural procedures.

Again, as far as one can judge from available information, the East German approach is rather more sophisticated than elsewhere, but it is probably reasonable to expect that when the nine-year school in Czechoslovakia is firmly established, and the eight-year school in Bulgaria, Hungary, &c., these countries will strive towards a closer integration of the as yet rather embryonic polytechnic features in the general education up to fourteen and the whole-heartedly polytechnic, vocationally-biased programmes beyond that age. The "manual skill" components in the time-tables of "general" schools in socialist countries do not appear to take up any more time than they do in non-selective schools in England, the exception to this generalization being East Germany, which has its "instructional day in production" once a week for Classes 7 onwards. It will be interesting to see whether East Germany will remain an exception.

The polytechnic "general education" secondary school

The establishment of a clear distinction between general education and vocational training has preoccupied many Western educators, and the search for a clear-cut solution to the problem has perhaps done as much to confuse as to clarify the position of many English non-selective schools. Communist educational thinking has had to face up to the difficulty too, and in particular, has had to seek a solution to the specific problem set by those young people who entered a school offering general education up to the age of seventeen or eighteen and leading to courses of higher education. At this stage the theoretical difficulty cannot be denied, and two heresies have arisen. On the one hand, it was maintained that the object of a "general education" school was the development of all sides of the human personality, and that the introduction of a vocational specialization would work against this. At the other extreme is the view that vocational education is identical with polytechnic education and that production training is simultaneously polytechnic. Both these heresies have arisen through ignorance of the nature of polytechnic education and of the nature of modern society. The modern state is based on industry and "industrialized" agriculture; most of its citizens are engaged in production[1] and it is highly undesirable that any should be left in ignorance of production processes. These production processes are becoming more complex and making ever greater demands on the technical knowledge of the workers involved, (at all levels), who must have not only a high level of specific skill but also an acquaintance with a wide range of related knowledge and skill. Possession of several basic skills is necessary not only so that the worker can be truly master of his own specialist skill or technology, but also so that he can be rapidly re-trained to meet the changing needs either of his own industry or indeed of the whole economy.

In this connexion it is perhaps not irrelevant to observe that in the

[1] 85 per cent in the U.S.S.R., according to Shapovalenko, op. cit., p. 142.

Renault motor works, described as the most highly automated in the world, an almost identical basic training is given to future craftsmen, technicians and some technologists – a basic training of a "polyvalent" technical worker. The same tendency underlies the British development of Diploma in Technology courses open simultaneously to holders of General Certificate of Education Advanced level and Ordinary National Certificates;[1] it is also seen in the new "diagnostic" year for craftsmen and technicians proposed in the 1961 White Paper.[2] The distinction between vocational and polytechnic general education is inherent in the idea already quoted of "seeing the general through study of the particular". The "middle" school (or equivalent) cannot give a comprehensive polytechnic education any more than it can produce a fully-trained mathematician, but it can aim at imparting an understanding of basic essentials. In order to achieve an understanding of foundations, the pupil must study one branch of industry in depth, and this can only be done effectively if he himself participates in the production process – for which he must be trained. As a Western writer has put it, "adolescents are still in the process of achieving the quality of insights into experiences they have not yet absorbed".[3] So even at the level of the 15–17-year-old, specialized technical training is justified as part of general education, provided that it is properly linked with studies in sciences and social and aesthetic subjects. In contrast with this, vocational training proper is a preparation for a specific job, in a specific kind of enterprise.

Of the three main aspects of polytechnic general education, i.e. the "polytechnic horizon", the study of the bases of production, and the acquisition of practical skills, it is the first which receives most attention at the level of compulsory general education, and those children who leave school at fourteen or fifteen may be presumed to gain the benefits of the other two elements through their vocational training, accompanied as this is by part-time further education (at least in principle). Those children who stay on at school to seventeen or eighteen must continue with their practical training and with the acquisition of knowledge of and insight into the "foundations of socialist production". As at the lower level, teachers are expected to select

[1] That is to say, Diploma in Technology courses are open both to those satisfactorily completing "general education" pre-university "grammar school" courses and to those obtaining a more directly technical qualification.

[2] "Better Opportunities in Technical Education", H.M.S.O., 1961.

[3] Mayer, op. cit., p. 205.

material which will indicate the industrial applications of scientific knowledge. In chemistry, for example, "a system of knowledge of important chemical technological processes and of basic principles of chemical production" is aimed at, based on a knowledge of essential types of process such as analysis, synthesis, oxidation, reduction, polymerization &c.[1]

The explicit study of "socialist production" is both theoretical and practical, and takes place within a production enterprise. It can be divided into two main categories, namely, general study of fundamental scientific, technological and economic principles and general organization, followed by detailed study of the technology and organization seen in a specific enterprise. In East Germany, a lot of the ground in the first category has already been covered in Classes 7 and 8, but in the other countries much of the general work has to be done in addition to the specific training, during the three- or four-year "middle school" course. This may be a reason why Czechoslovakia and Bulgaria (for instance) appear to devote much more time to the "production practice" than East Germany does, as the following time-table shows:

Hours per week devoted to "production"

	CLASS 10	CLASS 11	CLASS 12
Czechoslovakia	8	8	8
Bulgaria	5	10	12
East Germany	4	4	4

It is not envisaged that the specialist training will be given by teachers belonging to the school, but by workers in the factory or farm, selected for their technical skill and their attitude towards the task of teaching it. Nor should the practice take place in any enterprise that happens to be handy. In principle, an enterprise should be chosen that is sympathetic to the project, that offers facilities for training in major skills and that is large enough for dispersal of the children through many work-places. Children do not, in principle, remain as a class for their production practice, but are attached as individuals or in as small groups as possible to a number of workers, once they have been taught sufficient as a group to enable them to take an intelligent interest in what is being done by individual workers. It is clear that local

[1] *Lehrplan der zwölfklassigen allgemeinbildenden polytechnischen Oberschule*, Ministerium für Volksbildung, Berlin, 1960.

exigencies may inhibit the complete observance of all these principles all the time. It is clear, too, that some forms of special training may be too highly specialized, or too localized, to conform with the educational requirements of the scheme, and that, with the advance of the so-called "second industrial revolution", some trades or even whole industries may decline in importance.

East Germany has specified six major groups of industries as being of permanent importance in the economy and therefore as suitable for study in connexion with the scheme. Syllabuses have been worked out for the theoretical and practical training in these six – agriculture, metal-working industries, textiles, building, electrical industries, and chemicals. County councils are empowered to approve locally-devised syllabuses for localized industries. In Bulgaria, mining, economics, transport and printing, as well as the East German six, were provided for from the start (1959) in a scheme involving recognition of fifty-three principal trades.[1] The training scheme would obviously collapse if it depended entirely on the unguided efforts of children working under craftsmen, however skilled, who had no instruction in didactic problems. The main way of overcoming this difficulty is to provide a systematic syllabus, of which the following East German syllabus for fitting and related crafts is an example:

CLASS 9 Agriculture, approximating to the syllabus quoted earlier.
CLASS 10–12

		Hours
I	Simple smith's work	18
II	Joints and assemblies	33
III	Cutting and shaping of sheet-metal and profiles	33
IV	Filing, tapping, &c., tolerances	66
V	Fitting	78
VI	Machine-work	63
VII	Heat treatment	42
VIII	Materials testing	18
IX	Quality control	21
X	Drawing office	15
XI	Driving practice	15
		402

[1] Wasileff and others, *Die bulgarische Schule auf neuen Wegen*, Volk und Wissen, Berlin, 1961, p. 22.

This total of 402 hours includes two continuous weeks of vacation practice in Class 10 (84 hours) and two vacation weeks in Class 12 (72 hours). This is of course only an outline: the schemes of work from all the six major industries occupy altogether 190 pages, and a growing volume of booklets and articles has been published for teachers, to supplement the guidance given by the syllabus and by textbooks. The amount of attention paid to the preparation of the syllabuses and the detailed care devoted to psychological and methodological problems are sufficiently clear indications that the object of the exercise is primarily educational, not productive. Even if this were not so, it is fairly obvious that an appreciable time must pass before a group of schoolchildren cease to be a liability and begin to be regarded as a productive asset in the firm which has them under its aegis. A Bulgarian source estimates that it is twelve to eighteen months before they are competent to carry out productive work unaided.[1] This does not mean to say that they are engaged in "producing scrap" in the early stages. Even the simplest processes can be productive of something – it has been jokingly said that "there cannot be many barn doors still lacking hinges in East Germany". The fact that something useful, however humble, is being produced, provides a certain incentive. If further incentive were needed, it is to be found in the acquisition of a recognizable level of technical proficiency. The level reached varies, but it is unambiguously related to the achievement required of a skilled worker in industry who has had full-time training. Generally speaking the great majority of these children can expect to gain a fully-fledged craftsman's certificate within a year of leaving school, whilst a few of the best can gain it almost immediately.

Conclusions – and some problems

As Kairov points out, "there is no doubt that the transformation of men, of their consciousness, the moulding of the man of communist society, is a complex problem, the solution to which will demand time".[2] One should not make the mistake of supposing communist educators to be barking up the wrong tree in assuming that educational measures can transform social and political attitudes. Nor should one

---

[1] Wasileff and others, *Die bulgarische Schule auf neuen Wegen*, Volk und Wissen, Berlin, 1961, p. 22.
[2] Speech to 22nd Congress of the C.P.S.U., quoted in *Schule und Nation*, 1961, II.

underestimate the effectiveness of programmes such as those outlined in breaking down traditional prejudices and preconceptions. One preconception which is fairly well entrenched in Western educational circles is that of the "pool of ability". It would be going beyond the scope of this essay to discuss this in any detail, but it is perhaps not without significance that East Germany is gradually reducing its provision for part-time further education of "unskilled" young workers by seeking out and developing their humble aptitudes, so that they can be trained to a modest "semi-skilled" level. No educator should despise a doctrine which leads to an enhancement of self-respect for even a small number of young people. Another shibboleth in England is the idea of selection and training for leadership. When the kind of general education imparted to the "selected" ones, (in this case the middle school pupils) does not differ in any fundamental respect from that given to the majority; and when those not "selected" are aware, as they are, that they can reach matriculation level in spite of having opted for a "vocational" training at fourteen or fifteen, then "selection" loses its crucial importance. Another established notion which leads to a great waste of talent in England is that girls are *ipso facto* non-technical. Out of 125,000 craftsmen's certificates awarded in East Germany in 1960, 50,000 were to girls; and most visitors to communist countries comment on the prominent part played by women at all levels in industry and commerce. All this makes nonsense of any calculations regarding manpower, at any level, which are based on the "pool of ability" theory or on present selection methods in England.

It is too soon yet to express any opinion on whether the ulterior aims of the polytechnic programme are likely to be achieved. Whether intimate contact with manual workers and engagement in manual work will lead to a positive communist attitude towards the working-class or towards work in general remains to be seen. What is certainly worth considering, as an ideological issue, is the fact that work, as such, has a central and positive value in the sum of communist educational theory. We tend to offer as our alternative to this a hotch-potch of half-baked factorial psychology (as justification for a curriculum that "just growed") and a part-time non-denominational (often non-anything else either) Christianity. In the words of an anonymous Quaker, "a society which accepts as inevitable the divorce between work and leisure, and cultivates its leisure as the only time for real living, is a sick society". For most schools here, extra-curricular activities are on the fringe of education, inherently valuable as being preferable to doing nothing. From this point of view, the jazz club members who listen to records are of nearly equal merit to the most earnest members of the geological or ecological group giving up their Saturdays to serious inquiry. This quantitative evaluation of leisure-time activity is not shared by the communist educator. The Pioneer movement works to a programme, and the Young Technicians' and Young Agronomists' clubs embark on solid tasks of real (if academically modest) significance. We should perhaps examine our "coffee-bar and ping-pong" approach to youth organizations and consider whether we cannot learn something from the communist world about the right use of leisure – or even about what the word "leisure" ought to mean.

The positive benefits to be derived from the application of the polytechnic principle should not blind us to the difficulties involved. There can be no doubt that an enterprise of this kind cannot be carried out by the communist countries on the cheap; schools require new laboratories and workshops; equipment for all this practical work is expensive; teaching aids of all kinds must be designed and produced. Especially in the sciences, textbooks and syllabuses need to be constantly revised. Above all, a new kind of teacher is needed, and the whole concept of teacher-training has to be re-examined to take account of the new demands made on teachers of all subjects. Many of the older teachers, including many outstanding ones, will need to be persuaded of the educational desirability of the new approach. Universities and "middle school" teachers will need to be convinced that time spent in a factory or farm is not time that could be better spent in formal academic work, and that academic standards will not drop. Parents will need to be persuaded, too, that their teenage daughters are not in moral danger when working in an as yet predominantly male industrial workshop.

The claim has been made that all this insight into industry, practical work and training, excursions to firms, participation in "socially useful work" and extra-curricular study – that all this facilitates an informed choice of career by the school leaver, "corresponding to the wishes of the pupil and the needs of socialist production". It is a pity that the undoubted effectiveness of polytechnic general education and especially of the production practice as a contribution to career choice is not enhanced by some use of standardized aptitude tests, interest blanks and systematic guidance procedure such as have been adopted with success in France and the U.S.A. ("tests" of any sort are anathema to the communist educator). A final problem, which can probably never be solved – even the production practice is organized by adults in the light of adult conceptions of what the child ought to want to know and ought to be able to grasp. To what extent is it possible ever to devise an educational approach which will depend on the child's initiative, on his voluntary acquisition of experience, knowledge and skill rather than upon his acceptance of those experiences and insights which adults want him to have? At least the polytechnic approach enables the child to progress from what Fichte called the "shadow-world" of words and abstractions, to the "kernel of perceptions, truth and reality".[1] The discovery and enlargement of fields of interest which contain the work of man, the satisfactions and the frustrations of that world of work, these may bring about the kind of life adjustment which is the major task of education for adolescents in an industrial society.

[1] Quoted by Kerschensteiner, op. cit., p. 109.

CHAPTER 8

Higher Education

The basic principles of Soviet Communism and their all-inclusive bearing on every aspect of education have been made clear in previous chapters. In treating in so limited a space of higher education, therefore, I propose only to touch upon the outline of the facts in the light of Governmental proclaimed aims, and then to offer some interpretative comments based on my own observations.

The U.S.S.R. education charter of 1938 was re-modelled to express changed circumstances and needs by the act of December 24th 1958; and this required that clear plans for its implementation should be drawn up within from three to five years. This was done by the statute of March 21st 1961. This document is explained in the July issue of the official periodical for higher education, the *Higher School Herald* (*Vestnik Vysshey Shkoly*) of the same year. Here the new statute is set out and its basic aims for higher education are shown as the fulfilment of the following seven tasks:

(a) The training of highly-qualified specialists brought up in the spirit of Marxist–Leninism to be well skilled in the developments of recent science and technology, both in the U.S.S.R. and abroad and in practical matters of production, who should be able to make use of modern technical knowledge to the utmost and be capable of themselves creating the technology of the future.

(b) The carrying through of research work which should help in the solving of problems of the building of full communism.

(c) The making of textbooks and other aids to study of the highest quality.

(d) Training higher education teachers and researchers.

(e) To furnish advanced training for specialists in different departments of the economy of the U.S.S.R. and its republics, in pedagogics, the arts, and in the health services.

(f) The dissemination of scientific and political knowledge among the people.
(g) Study of problems of the best employment of graduates and of their proper training.

It is clearly too early to assess the Soviet achievement along these lines, as the detailed plans for implementing the objectives just rehearsed are only this year being put into operation; but since they are mainly a repetition of the aims set forth in the act of 1958, it is possible to form an idea of the progress that is being made and of the results likely to be realized. Higher education may be said in general, both in the U.S.S.R. and in European communist countries, to cover three main types of establishment: (a) the Academy of Sciences and its distinctive special institutions; (b) the universities; and (c) separate technical and specialized institutes directly connected with the training of graduate students for particular functions. Each of the Soviet republics and autonomous states has examples of all three types, and this is also true of the other "people's democracies".

But before going further, I would remind the reader of some general points of special importance in approaching Soviet higher education. Russian does not distinguish, as does English, between scientific and humane or "arts" studies in its general terminology. The word *nauka*, commonly translated "science" (and its adjective *nauchniy*, usually rendered "scientific") is applied to all recognized fields of study: so that, for example, the *Akademiya Nauk*, always translated "Academy of Sciences", deals with such matters as literature, history and aesthetics, as well as the "sciences" in the English more limited sense. Literary criticism is thought to be treated by the same "scientific" principles and methods as biology or theoretical physics, and seeks to develop a scientific technology. The Soviet Academy has its Institutes of World Literature, of Russian Literature, and of *Yazykoznaniya*, "Linguistic Knowledge".

Secondly, everything in higher education is governed by what is called "the principle of democratic centralism". A universally applicable plan is directed from the central ministry, and under it by the relevant ministries of the constituent republics, &c. Fundamental plans and directives are devised at the governmental centre after consultations with every possible interested organization, and these are modified in detail only through the official determiners of regional needs.

In the universities and specialized technical institutes, for instance, of Georgia and Uzbekistan the native languages of these republics are freely used both in teaching and publication: but the basic principles and methods, as well as the academic curricula for these autonomous republics are applied exactly in Tbilisi (Tiflis) and Tashkent, their cultural centres, strictly on patterns devised in Moscow.

Thirdly, however, traditions inherited from pre-Revolutionary times still exercise a considerable influence. In the design, for example, of the academic ladder from first degree to doctorate much of the pre-Revolutionary external pattern remains. In Tbilisi and in Tashkent universities the natural admiration for the native heroic personalities of the past, and every aspect of the native culture which does not conflict with the idea of democratic centralism is keenly studied. The ancient poetry and folklore of Georgia and Uzbekistan are zealously "researched"; and scholarly work in such fields is vividly encouraged. An admirable scientific dictionary of contemporary Georgian, and immensely valuable studies of classical Georgian manuscripts have come from the academic institutes of Tbilisi; again, the best national Uzbek poetry of the middle ages has occupied some of the best Russian as well as native Uzbek scholars. All this, though of course the universal use of Russian along with the native languages is required everywhere.

Fourthly, the belief that human nature may be modified to fulfil the needs of the Marxist–Leninist state is everywhere implicit in all academic contributions towards the production of the fully developed Soviet "new man". This must always be a dominating factor in the development of the art or science of teaching in higher education as elsewhere.

Finally, since all publications treating of higher education are ultimately governmental, there must inevitably be the chance of some tendentiousness in conclusions based on Soviet published material. At the same time it must be admitted that Western studies of the subject present to some extent similar difficulties. Only with official aid can large and thorough works on Soviet higher education be carried through in the U.S.A. or in Britain, since the financial and other necessary resources are scarcely otherwise available for such lengthy and highly technical projects. Moreover, because of the consciousness of the needs of technological scientific competition with the U.S.S.R., nearly all the work done in this field in the West – and especially in the U.S.A., which has done the most – has dominantly emphasized "science and technology" and largely neglected what the Russians still call "humanistic" subjects. The best American survey, that by Alexander Korol of M.I.T., thorough and scholarly as it is, deals primarily only with what its title implies: *Soviet Education for Science and Technology*, though it includes valuable references to work in the humanities. It was published in 1957 by the Technological Press of the Massachusetts Institute of Technology jointly with commercial publishers.[1] It may seem at times to show the necessary limitations of official and political support, and in this way resembles the smaller survey by Nicholas De Witt of Harvard, entitled *Soviet Professional Manpower*, published by the National Science Foundation of Washington D.C. in 1955. This last, however, has been greatly expanded and brought up to date, and published by the same Foundation in 1961 as *Education and Professional Employment in the U.S.S.R.* Based on the work of the Harvard Research Center, it is now the fullest and most authoritative work of its kind.[2]

The excellent survey, *American Research on Russia*, published by a group of eminent specialists from Indiana University Press in 1959, though it covers literature, philosophy and religion, music and architecture, does not deal at all with higher education. As I have indicated, Russian surveys are much more definitely restricted by official needs. There is a well-written one entitled *New System of People's Education in the U.S.S.R.*[3] which includes higher education, issued by the Academy of Pedagogical Sciences from Moscow in 1960; and a popular *University Education in the U.S.S.R.*[4] published by Moscow University. Apart from the very numerous Soviet educational periodicals and the official monthly journal of the Ministry of Higher Education, there is easily accessible, in Russian, a very brief and summary survey of higher education, by A. T. Galkin, *Higher Education and the Training of Scientific Cadres*,[5] published by the official firm Soviet Science (*Sovetskaya Nauka*). In English there is a similar book by the same author,

---

[1] John Wiley & Sons Inc. of New York, and Chapman & Hall, Ltd. of London.
[2] Prepared for the National Science Foundation by the office of Scientific Personnel National Academy of Sciences – National Research Council. U.S.A. Government Printing Office, Washington D.C. 1961.
[3] *Novaya Sistema Narodnogo Obrazovaniya v SSSR*, Izdatel'stvo Akademii Pedagogicheskikh Nauk RSFSR, Moskva, 1960.
[4] *Universitetskoe Obrazovaniye v SSSR*, A. S. Butyagin, Yu. A. Saltanov, Izdatel'stvo Moskovskogo Universiteta, 1960.
[5] *Vysshee Obrazovaniye i Podgotovka Nauchnykh Kadrov v SSSR*, K. T. Galkin, Gosudarstvennoe Izdatel'stvo "Sovetskaya Nauka", Moskva, 1958.

designed for the Western general reader, issued by the Foreign Languages Publishing House of Moscow in 1959, *The Training of Scientists in the Soviet Union*.

We may now look briefly at the efforts being made to implement the aims of the new educational law of December 1958, as set forth in the 1961 list of tasks for higher education already quoted. But it should be remembered always that a basic motive for the new law was said to be "the establishing of closer links between school and life, and on further development of public education in the U.S.S.R.". This attempt to integrate more closely the intellectual with the practical productive life is reflected everywhere in higher education, from the institutes of the Academy of Sciences to the short specialist refresher courses in narrowly technical higher schools.

The general pattern of academic diplomas and degrees still bears the marks of its mainly German origin. The system of degrees and academic titles, abolished at the Revolution, was reintroduced in 1934. It is broadly the same in all institutions which grant officially certified qualifications. The normal undergraduate course extends over a period of five years, terminating in the examination for the diploma or first degree, which consists mainly of the writing of a supervised dissertation or thesis, agreed between the student and the supervisor and approved by the relevant higher planning authorities. A very heavy burden of lectures, as many as thirty-six in the first year of study, is perhaps the most superficially noticeable feature of the undergraduate course as far as the final fifth year in which the dissertation is written. A background of basic culture is always required throughout the course, in which social science is especially emphasized in the form of Marxist–Leninism universally applied. A foreign language is also obligatory. The major subject may be anything for which the student shows aptitude, provided this choice falls within the planned numbers of graduates needed for the various disciplines. The lectures are efficient and practical, given only by teachers who hold a licence to lecture.

Such teachers, beginning as "lecture assistants", must show by demonstration lectures that they can satisfy both students and the Faculty before being approved: and they must at least be working for the degree of *Kandidat*. After the five-year diploma course which leads to the first degree, those who are thought suitable for specialist training as academic practitioners proceed to a three-year course of post-graduate study in the *Aspirantura*, following mainly their special discipline with the aid of individual research supported by seminars, colloquia, &c., conducted by teachers who are at least of the rank of Kandidat. To pass the Kandidat examination, for which the *aspirant* prepares for three years, the student must produce a dissertation which is a definite contribution to knowledge, and considered worthy of publication. This three-year course of research as *aspirant* may for acceptable reasons take longer. Broadly speaking, this qualification of Kandidat is of about the same calibre as the Western Continental Ph. D. or that of the less exacting universities of Britain or the U.S.A. And again, of course, its cultural background must be guided in the spirit of Marxist-Leninism.

A majority of even fairly senior university teachers are *Kandidaty*; for the doctorate is in the U.S.S.R. considerably more exacting in standard than any Ph. D., approaching rather to the level of a D. Litt. or a D.Sc. in the more rigorous Western institutions. Usually it is only the more eminent and productive scholars and savants who hold a doctorate: and though this degree could in theory be obtained by a further two years' research after the *Kandidatura*, it usually takes a number of years. The three ranks of *Professor*, *Docent*, and Lecture Assistant are filled by the various institutions appointing staff, with the approval of the appropriate ministry. But there is a distinction between the holding of academic positions carrying these names, and the granting of the equivalent State titles. A State Board of Attestation "vets" the awards of all qualifications by the institutes of higher education; and the official titles of Professor, Docent and Lecture Assistant as distinct from the holding of these offices in particular universities are granted by the Ministry only. Thus a man may be a "Professor" in a given university though he holds only the degree of Kandidat, and though outside his university he has not the official title of Professor. Even the Dean of a Faculty is often a Kandidat rather than a "Doktor". Roughly, the ranks of Docent and Assistant correspond to those of Senior Lecturer or Reader or associate Professor, and Junior Lecturer, Assistant Lecturer or Instructor. Each main subject is directed in a department called a *Kafedra* or "Chair"; and the holder of this *Kafedra* is the Head of the Department, which is itself as a whole termed the *Kafedra*. In Leningrad, for instance, the English Department is known as the "Chair of English Philology", *Kafedra angliyskoy filologii*: and, taking "Philology" in its older European sense, it includes both the study of the language and the literature.

Graduates in their *Aspirantura* are taught in small classes or seminars or colloquia, while working individually with a supervisor who is commonly a professor. I attended two colloquia in The First State Pedagogical Institute of Moscow for *Kandidaty* in English. In one the group were working out problems of English lexicography and methods of producing the ideal Russian–English dictionary. In the other the aim was to apply rigorously scientific methods of criticism to English poetry, the particular task just then being to determine the relationship between the variations in rhythm and metre in different Shakespearean sonnets and changes in their emotional depth and intensity. In both colloquia, papers produced by the abler students were of the calibre that might often be met with in the better M.A. seminars in America or Britain, though of course the philosophic approach to Shakespeare's verse was conditioned by the always implicit assumptions of Soviet thinking. There is in quality and standard inevitably a very marked difference between the levels obtaining, on the one hand in major long-established universities like Moscow, Leningrad and Kiev, and on the other in recently formed academic bodies such as exist in the autonomous Soviet republics. Yet some of these latter, notably Tbilisi University, and the Kazakh University of Alma Ata, provide work of really scholarly quality and originality in fields where the material is closely accessible, such as the native languages and cultural history. But there is naturally a marked tendency for outstandingly promising students to be sent from the more remote centres to do their graduate work in one of the older universities, especially Moscow.

The first of the tasks set in the aims for higher education set in 1961 was the training of specialists. Here it should be borne in mind that, though science is inevitably much the most emphasized need, the Russian word *nauka*, translated "science", covers all branches of knowledge. Specialists of every kind, including higher academic teachers as well as technical scientific researchers are being prepared; and these are to be practical, in the closest possible touch with real life, forward-looking towards the new Soviet man, cognizant of all the scientific developments abroad, and consciously directing their lives towards the building of communism proper through the transition from the current "socialism".

It is not, however, the universities that are mainly concerned with the training of specialists, save for academic scholars and savants. Each type of specialist is trained, generally speaking, in particular institutions appropriate to the specialism or technique required. Thus, for instance, teacher specialists are developed in pedagogical institutes, agricultural experts in institutes of agronomy, and so on. Almost all the best scientific and scholarly research is done by developing specialists, not in the universities, but in the higher institutes belonging to the Academy of Sciences. For example, whereas chemical laboratories in even the major universities are relatively poor and not up to date in equipment, researches and the invention of new techniques in this field reach the highest and most productive levels, and have the finest and most lavish apparatus, in the special institutes of the Academy.

In the universities there is little important advanced work, again, in historical linguistics: but in the Academy institutes of general linguistics of Moscow and Leningrad there are most active staffs of researchers and deservedly eminent scholars guiding them. Whereas the books used by undergraduates in the universities for the study of Germanic languages historically are often old-fashioned and limited, the institutes of linguistics keep thoroughly up to date bibliographically, and a first-rate body of researchers are producing an outstanding comparative Germanic grammar, working as a joint team in Leningrad and Moscow at their respective Academy institutes. The two directors of this large project are Academicians, the one in Leningrad and the other in Moscow. It is from the Academy's multitude of scientific specialist institutes that the brilliant achievements have come. Moreover, the most promising specialist students commonly do their advanced work not in the universities proper, but in the relevant Academy's special higher institutes.

The social standing of the higher education teacher is rather higher than in Great Britain, and definitely above that prevailing in the U.S.A. Especially esteemed is the status of a university professor who has the official title as well as the local office: and the more so if he has a doctorate. This comparatively rare degree, *Doktor Nauk*, may cover work in any faculty, whether in the humanities or in science; for, as has been said, the Russian *nauka* covers both. If the professor is an Academician, *Akademik*, he belongs to a most limited and distinguished corps of élite. As such, he receives a good salary as an *Akademik* in addition to that of his university professorship; and he may be paid a further stipend as the Director of one of the Academy's Institutes. Broadly speaking, Soviet academic salaries, if one reckons the real economic value independently of foreign exchange, are much like those in

Great Britain in the various grades; but an Academician will be considerably better off than an ordinary British or American university professor; and one who directs an Institute proportionately more so. However, the relative inferiority of consumer goods in the U.S.S.R., the far more restricted housing conditions, and the frequent inaccessibility of foreign books (except in the admirably stocked Academy libraries) make his life in several ways less easy than that of his Western colleague. Moreover, in view of the re-iterated aim of integrating academic work as closely as possible with practical and industrial life, an Academician is expected to do often much of what may be described as *haute vulgarisation* for his special subject. He will often spend quite a lot of his time travelling about, visiting less advanced specialist centres and in lecturing in factories and centres of popular culture. The need to build up the new Soviet man who may eventually play his full part in a state in which communism has reached complete fulfilment must be always kept in mind by all higher education teachers: and always the background of Marxist–Leninism is adapted to a seemingly growing sense of Soviet patriotism and national pride. Consequent on the new law of education of 1958 already emphasized, there is of late augmented effort to encourage increased residence in university hostels, and to have as many as possible of the vastly increasing number of students who work by correspondence attend evening classes after their day's factory work is over, and thus make direct personal contacts with university teachers. This tendency is parallel to the immense growth of boarding schools and day boarding schools (where children remain each working day from 8 a.m. till 8 p.m.) which has been one of the most notable effects of the 1958 educational re-direction. Correspondent Members of the *Akademiya Nauk*, savants of special distinction who cannot carry out the full duties of *Akademik*, are esteemed often almost as much as the Academicians proper.

The social life of the university student is, as one would expect, thoroughly organized. There are all kinds of athletic, cultural and scientific group activities: and of late teachers have been urged to take a keener and closer interest in the whole extra-academic life of their students. As he advances in graduate status as an *Aspirant*, the student is expected to participate actively and productively in the appropriate learned societies. Publication of the specialist work of graduates too is readily obtained among the very large number of learned and scientific journals and periodicals which are everywhere officially sponsored and financed. In the best and most up-to-date students' residential blocks or halls, to be found in Moscow especially, and to some extent in the major capitals, students have facilities much like those on a good American campus. Two share a room in the best equipped buildings, and everything for complete living and personal development is provided. But in the more remote and rural centres hostels are usually overcrowded and inadequately equipped, as postwar reconstruction has not yet been able to deal with them, and the rush of applicants for places is almost unmanageable. In the most modern students' blocks and "dormitories", co-education extends to a point where the sexes are not segregated in anything beyond the sharing of rooms. Men and women, two men or two women to a room and small bathroom, may inhabit the same corridor, for instance, in the huge American-style skyscraper on the Lenin Hills outside the town where the scientific faculties of the Moscow State University are housed.

What strikes the visitor, however, who is familiar at all with pre-Revolutionary Russian life, is the relative flexibility which somehow seems to exist amid so much necessarily crowded conditions of work and organization. Especially in the first two years of undergraduate life the student is inevitably over-lectured and has too full a time-table; for as yet it is still found necessary to do at the university much that would preferably be done in the later years of school education; and the lack of individual teaching facilities, and the often limited choice of books, compel what would seem to most educators an unhealthy load of lecture-attendance and note-taking. For similar reasons the students appear to be submitted to a very great abundance of progress examinations and tests throughout their undergraduate years. Yet within these probably ephemeral limitations, the students manage to be far more alert and spontaneous than one would expect: and the amount of extra-academic activity beyond official requirements they succeed in fitting into this intense university life is astonishing.

Oral examination plays a great part at all stages of their work; and this no doubt has the advantage of developing in the more gifted students a quite impressive ability for self-expression. The Russian students strike the Russian-speaking visitor to Moscow or Leningrad who mixes with them in times of recreation as clearly having by no means lost their essential Russianness, not excluding its humour and romantic strain. The Georgians of Tbilisi University too seem to retain and freely express much of their traditional character. Comparing a visit to the U.S.S.R. made in 1960 with one just ten years earlier, I was impressed with a vastly increased flexibility of mind and the far more spontaneous expression of the immense natural curiosity among the Soviet students. The in many ways close regimentation remained: but somehow within it there seemed scope for considerable expression of the personality. Moreover, though the need for the speedy production and training of scientific experts of every technical kind makes any big relaxation of Soviet discipline and organization impossible, there has been of late a marked tendency to the humanizing of all aspects of university life. I say this after paying unsolicited visits to academic residential blocks, spending long days in living entirely with staffs and students, attending different types of seminars and colloquia with graduates, and myself taking graduate classes in a Pedagogical Institute without the presence of the teachers.

All students in the U.S.S.R. receive the minimum grants from the Government necessary for every kind of university or other higher educational residence and courses. Only those not adequate to the tests for admission may sometimes study at their parents' expense. Progress, as measured by examinations and teachers' reports, however, brings usually an increase on the minimal stipend; and a really promising and hard-working student may receive such grants as to enable him to live up to a comfortable standard. All are encouraged to undertake, whereever this has any relevance to their training, some form of practical productive labour during parts of their vacations; and such specialists as engineers are required to work in an appropriate factory for some part of their regular scientific training. Teachers and other workers are normally selected by their institutions for special study-leave so as to be able to attend short intensive refresher courses at suitable institutes, or to qualify themselves further in their technical speciality. Such students remain on full pay during these shortened special courses.

Within the inevitable socialist discipline of every aspect of academic life there is much informality in the relations between students and teachers, especially in graduate work. In the small seminar classes and colloquia in both universities and higher pedagogical institutes I have noticed a spirit of camaraderie between teachers and taught, with at the same time evidence of the respect and affection in which some of the more outstanding professors and *docenty* are held. On the other hand, in all higher educational centres the visitor from Britain will be struck with an atmosphere of what I might call serious uplift which seems pervasive. Uplifting slogans and admonitions are everywhere prominent on walls, though there are often so many of these that they tend to be taken as read or merely ignored by all concerned. In academic institutions the constant admonitions from the Party and the Ministry sometimes seem to be little more in effective direction than formulaic. Similarly, the attendance at lectures on social science, and the passing of the obligatory examinations in current Marxist–Leninist philosophy by the few students who will later be trained in theological seminaries for the priesthood, is probably little more than formulaic.

Little need here be said of the second of the tasks set in 1961, the carrying out of research work for the accomplishment of the full building of communism, that is, a fully communist society as a development of the present socialism. Marxist–Leninism, commonly taught in universities and specialist higher institutes as "social science", occupies something like a tenth of the working time of all students: as "social political" study in universities, and as "social economic" study in engineering and related institutes. In universities this teaching naturally includes communist ethics or philosophy, and historical dialectical materialism. Lectures and the resulting examinations are inevitably the least individual or the results of first-hand research, since a strict orthodoxy in accordance with the rulings of the Party at any given time is obligatory: and both teachers and students must in effect reproduce views taken as established truth. Teachers of social science for higher educational establishments are trained in specialist institutes for this work: but throughout the academic presentation of this subject and its reproduction by students there is an unavoidable danger of mere mechanical reception and re-presentation to the examiners. The preparation of the new Soviet man is more effectively to be sought in the basic spirit and ethos of his whole education.

The third task, the making of textbooks and other aids, is treated with the utmost care and thoroughness. The senior university teachers are much concerned with team-work for the production of textbooks which are tested experimentally and endlessly discussed by experts and officials before publication. Even Academicians are expected to take an active practical interest in textbook making. In Tbilisi, the most eminent authority on the Georgian language has himself provided the material for an academic grammar, and this was talked over and tried out by groups of graduate teachers with their students. A weakness in textbooks is at times the limitation of their material for political reasons, though, as has been indicated, the higher specialists in the Academy have access to all material without restriction. Another weakness is due to the vast official machinery through which alone anything can be published. Often too many copies are printed, so that a book is out of date before it has been fully distributed; or the right number of copies are distributed to the wrong centres. But for practical, and often almost encyclopaedic efficiency, within obvious limitations, many of the academic textbooks are of the most outstanding quality.

A good deal has already been indicated concerning the fourth task of the new planners, the training of teachers and researchers in higher education. Teachers are developed in the pedagogical institutes and the Academy of Pedagogical Sciences (*Akademiya pedagogicheskikh Nauk*): and researchers of all kinds are the concern of the Academy of Sciences and its specialized institutes, and of the universities working in conjunction with them. In teacher training, the best results are obtained in the graduate classes of the pedagogical institutes. Besides the well-known development of the finest technical researchers and applied scientific workers, in which very special efforts have been successfully made, really outstanding work is being done in the higher teaching and research into all aspects of the contemporary modern languages, especially English. Foreign language institutes and Translation Departments are attached to the leading pedagogical higher schools: and here, for instance, the study of contemporary English and methods of teaching it reaches quite marked excellence.

Though the modern literature selected for special study is often limited for semi-political reasons, the very best mechanical aids and methods at once scientific and vivid are employed. Really productive researches are being carried on particularly in all aspects of lexicography, notably in Moscow State University as well as in the Academy, and a stream of books and specialist papers pours from the presses on every conceivable point of grammar, lexicology, syntax and semantics. Though the emphasis is mainly on contemporary foreign (especially English) literature, literary history and the linguistic past are by no means excluded, though much seldomer opted for by students where a choice is allowed. If the Soviets are thought to show scientific practical pre-eminence by the production of the Sputnik or (with less certainty) the translating machine, it might be argued as plausibly that they have reached a leading position in the development of lexicography as a science, or in the methodology of the teaching of foreign languages.

Research in literary history, though to some extent conditioned in its temper by the always implicit philosophy, reaches a high level not only for Russian, but also for English, as may be seen in two recent volumes, the one from Moscow and the other from Leningrad. These are the *Outlines from the point of view of Stylistics of the English Language* of Professor Gal'perin,[1] and the collection of essays by Academician M. P. Alekseyev entitled *From the History of English Literature*.[2]

The training of specialists in Oriental languages, in which field pre-Revolutionary Russia had developed a very high tradition, is now being emphasized and improved: and immense amounts of all kinds of linguistic work are being produced, particularly in lexicography. The history of art is another field in which outstanding research is being carried on, and in which specialists are being produced, notably for the museum services, as these latter are a marked contributor to popular as well as academic education. Archaeology is not without its new specialists, in view of so much archaeological work now carried on in the U.S.S.R. Because, for instance, of the remains of ancient Greek colonies in Georgia, there are archaeologists with a real knowledge of Greek being occasionally trained in Tbilisi: and students take an active part in field-work connected with the excavations at Trialeta.

The fifth task, the provision of advanced training for every type of specialist needed in the various departments of the U.S.S.R. economy, provides for specialists in the arts, for higher teaching, and for all higher grades of the health services, as well as for the more emphasized economic, political and above all technical scientific departments. Naturally, some branches of learning in this connexion have been largely dropped since the Revolution, such as the Latin and Greek Classics and theology; but since 1952 experiments have gone on in re-introducing Latin into the higher grades of a few schools; and there are signs of the same experiment being considered for universities. In the very limited number of ecclesiastical seminaries there is, too, some advanced work for specialist theologians being attempted, though inevitably the resources available must be extremely slender. These seminaries are, of course,

---

[1] I. R. Gal'perin, *Ocherki po Stilistike angliyskogo Yazyka*, Moskva, Izdatel'stvo Literatury na inostrannykh Yazykakh, 1958.

[2] M. P. Alekseev, *Iz Istorii angliyskoy Literatury: Etyudy, Ocherki, Issledovaniya*, Moskva i Leningrad, Gosudarstvennoe Izdatel'stvo Khudozhestvennoy Literatury, 1960.

HIGHER EDUCATION

officially licensed, and come under the appropriate department of Government.

Advanced work for specialists needed in some of the traditional humanistic fields is, then, not neglected. The best Soviet museums, which work closely with archaeologists, art-historians, &c., in the universities, are equal in method and presentation to any in the world. There is immense specialist as well as popular interest in preserving the survivals of the ancient as well as the nearer past: the Hermitage Museum in Leningrad, for instance, which had been collected by the czars, was restored and cared for and enlarged with meticulous and affectionate care under the Soviet: and this is thought by many connoisseurs to be the best museum for art in the world.

The sixth task, the dissemination of political and scientific knowledge among the people, is, as has been already indicated, regarded as a duty, not only of the universities, but also of the highest category of scientists and savants themselves, the Academicians. The privilege of higher education in both the sciences and the humanities alike is held to imply the duty of and to include the necessary preparation for spreading the knowledge among the people which should lead to the building of full communism. Not only school textbooks, but merely propaganda works aimed at the common man, are produced by often eminent university teachers and workers in higher research institutes. In 1959 there appeared a brief but highly coloured patriotic account of higher education in the U.S.S.R. entitled *The Higher School of the Land of Socialism*.[1] It has been indicated earlier that specialists for the propagation of Marxist-Leninism are trained in institutes of social science devised for this particular purpose. As the communist way of thought penetrates and suffuses every aspect of life, there is a sense in which all knowledge is "political", and all that is exact may said to be scientific. Any young people, therefore, brought up under the new plan of integrating academic work with that of practical production or the factory, will be disseminating scientific and political knowledge simply by living and working among the people; and in so far as the building of the fully communist state is everything, nothing, however far removed it may seem from the state, can avoid being in some sense political.

But, as in Thomas More's *Utopia* in which so many communist ideas found partial expression, the dissemination of knowledge is

[1] V. P. Elyutin, *Vysshaya Shkola Strany Sotsializma*, Moskva, Izdatel'stvo Social'-no-ekonomicheskoy Literatury, 1959.

carefully limited, so that while freedom of personal belief and opinion is theoretically entirely admissible, any kind of knowledge which would seem to be harmful to the fulfilment of the current ideology is prohibited from public expression or communication to others. Thus, for example, while the Orthodox priest may conduct his divine liturgy for such of the faithful as may wish to attend his church, he must not seek to instruct the children outside his church; so that only those who have chosen to come to church can in effect receive any religious instruction at all. The visitor is often struck, in mixing with university students, and even their teachers, with a contrast between the accuracy and keenness of the knowledge displayed on aspects of learning thought to be of real value, and the large lacunae in these well-trained and lively minds in little esteemed fields. Thus, for instance, while recent Soviet history of every kind is generally well studied and expressed, it is common to find almost complete ignorance of medieval and early modern Russian history and economics among the educated. Again, there is commonly almost complete ignorance among otherwise well-developed graduates of everything connected with Christian history and traditions: so that even the ordinary names of religious festivals once important, or of essential parts of historically significant churches (or the museums which many of them have become) are entirely unknown.

Such limitations to the dissemination of knowledge may be largely due to the need to concentrate all on the building of communism in the U.S.S.R., and the clamant urge to provide vast crowds of efficient scientific technicians in the speediest possible way. Moreover, the real care which is taken in the conservation of the material results of past traditions may suggest that much of this deliberate confining of knowledge may be only temporary. One notices, too, quite a good deal of evidence of local patriotism among university students as well as teachers. Leningrad University, descended from Peter the First's technical academy, still cherishes exultantly the memory and even the living-quarters, and the apparatus as well as the final tea-cup of the world-famous chemist Mendeleyev. In the hugely long building put up by Czar Peter I, known as "The Twelve Colleges", one is proudly shown the room of Peter, the *Petrovskiy Zal*, where this builder of so much of modern Russia used to interview and preside. Moscow, too, in its academic circles is still vain of the great humanist and scientist Mikhail Lomonosov, after whom the older mid-eighteenth-century university was named, and where in the still graceful old building the humanities are taught.

The last of the major tasks of higher education listed at the beginning of this chapter is the study of problems of how best to employ the graduates produced by the universities and specialized institutes and how best to train them for their vocations. These problems are continually evident and their nature as constantly changing with the needs of the Communist Party and their reflexions in the centralized work of the Ministry of Higher Education, which through its multiform machinery in effect directs and controls everything.

The recruitment and tenure of academic and specialist teachers is one such outstanding problem. Another is the direction and proper distribution of all graduates into employments wherein they will be of the maximum value in the whole scheme of State economy. With regard first to the appointment of university and comparable teachers, since 1954 there has existed, at least in theory, a scheme of competitive appointment and re-appointment intended to keep all teachers constantly up to their best possible effort and capacity. Every academic appointment is thrown open to competition, the most suitable candidate is chosen by a small committee, and this competition is repeated every five years. Each teacher, then, must in theory show after five years of tenure that he or she is still the best or most appropriate holder of that particular post, and every holder of an appointment is required to submit quinquennially to a thorough testing in comparison with other new candidates. Thus there is no permanent tenure even for a professor or docent. Moreover, such competitions always include the production of a full dossier showing every aspect of political and other affiliations: so that a scholar or scientist whose outlook on life seemed unsuitable to the Ministry may fail to get the appointment even after successful competition; for every appointment made by any academic institution must be finally confirmed by the Ministry of Higher Education.

One thing which may very often interfere with the rigours of this method of recruiting academic teachers is the need, as directed by the Ministry under the guidance of Party decisions, to balance or adjust teaching against research, and both against the demands or applied science and technology. Teachers may be in serious short supply in certain fields in a university: but if the needs for researchers are thought to be clamant, graduates will be directed to the special research department most favoured. Another factor which militates sometimes against the proper distribution of teachers and researchers according to their abilities and aptitudes is the need to supply the provincial academic centres with good recruits without taking away outstanding people from the greater metropolitan institutions. There are never enough really able people yet in the various categories to go round: and the view of the Ministry on how best to distribute the best trained minds is almost inevitably constantly changing. Another difficulty which affects especially the provincial universities and higher institutes is the tendency to local inbreeding. Often local patriotism seems to require the retaining of graduates for higher work in the same academic institution in which they were graduated.

All graduates are directed at once to the employment considered most appropriate, as determined by the Ministry's view of the various needs. This should mean that the graduates are utilized in the most desirable manner: or in practice it may fall far short of this ideal because of the shortage of qualified people, the interference of the Ministry with choices made on good academic grounds, the desire to encourage certain institutions while leaving the others relatively neglected, or a local patriotism which the central authority cannot or does not find it expedient to control. Consequent on such difficulties, it is in the institutes of the Academy of Sciences and other higher specialized centres that the finest scholars and research-workers are to be found. Thus, for instance, some of the best teachers of higher English studies are at work in the Pedagogical institutes of Moscow and Leningrad rather than in the universities proper.

Every graduate, on completing his first degree course, must accept the type and place of employment to which he is directed. Furthermore, he must remain in that particular post for three years. But the conflict between the needs of the state as seen by the Ministry, and the wishes and aptitudes of the graduate, may often cause him to do less than his best work. Inevitably there must often be square pegs in round holes – especially when there is the added complication of the political needs overriding graduate potentialities. One whose vocation is clearly teaching may find himself directed to some type of technical scientific research project, because this is short of staff and is considered to be of immediate import; or a born researcher may find himself a teacher in an uncongenial provincial centre because staff problems in that university have got out of hand. Again, there may be conflict between the need for engineers to work in a factory and the needs of pressing scientific research.

In viewing these difficulties in the recruitment and distribution of higher teachers and in the choice of the most appropriate employment of graduates of all types, it is but fair to remember that, in practice, there is much flexibility in applying the interpretations of principles which arise from the constant planning of "democratic centralism". There seems to be much of what may loosely be termed pragmatism in the actual working internally of universities and higher institutions within the directives of the planners. No fixed method of applying the rule of quinquennial competition for academic posts has been formulated: and there seems to be much friendly adjustment to genuine needs in carrying it through. Similarly, most graduates do seem in the end to get to the type of work they are best fitted for, though often with a good deal of wasted application of effort in the process.

On the other hand, it is obvious that the Soviet principles of training and direction of higher educational labour would produce the best possible results were it not for the human factors in what Christians would call our "fallen nature", which the philosophy of Marxist-Leninism does not recognize. It is also important to realize that, in everything now being done in the field of Soviet higher education, what happens is regarded openly as experiment. If the newest methods fail to produce the results looked for, they may be "scrapped" at almost a moment's notice on orders from the Ministry. There is always a consciousness of movement and experiment in higher education. The eyes of both planners and graduate students are constantly looking forward to the next hoped-for stage of development. The Soviet "new man" is always in the minds of educators, who are thinking already of the vastly improved human beings of the next century.

It is, perhaps, significant that since the Revolution there has been an increasing tendency to substitute the Russian word *Obrazovaniye* for the older *Prosveshcheniye* as the official term for education. *Obrazovaniye* implies the *shaping* or *formation* of minds, while *Prosveshcheniye* is near to our "enlightenment". The possibility of giving a new shape or *Obraz* to the human personality has somewhat replaced the idea of letting the *light* go through him as in *Prosveshcheniye*. This change in terminology may be symbolic. Again, there has grown up in the last twenty years a strong tendency to distinguish "culture" (*Kul'tura*) from "education". "Culture" is the image of Soviet society at its ideal best which is officially sought to be projected, both to the peoples of the U.S.S.R. and to the external world. Higher education is disseminated through a number also of newly-established "Universities of Culture" (*Universitety Kul'tury*), in which what are taken to be the most valuable aspects of higher education are disseminated to ordinary working people who are not seeking diplomas or degrees but wish to participate in something like what is called in Britain "University Extension Courses". Many graduates who have excelled in foreign languages and contemporary literatures are employed as cultural agents, to serve as guides and interpreters to foreign visitors, to staff "cultural institutes" abroad, or to act as interpreters on all kinds of diplomatic occasions. Here a problem is often to prevent the necessary contact with non-Marxist foreigners from producing undesirable results. There is a Ministry of Culture which centralizes and controls such activities.

Undoubtedly the recent reforms, stemming from the plans of 1961 to realize the aims of the education acts of 1958, have markedly tipped the scale in favour of technical and specialized scientific training. Though qualitatively the new Soviet specialist or technical scientist may not be equal to the best that can be produced in Great Britain or the U.S.A., yet the mere fact of vastness of quantity and complete power of selection and direction of talent must lead to speedier and more impressive applied scientific results than any less centralized state can provide. Yet this technical achievement must also mean concentration on specialist development as against the broader humanistic growth of the whole personality, which was formerly a traditional aim. The creative faculties, both of intellect and feeling, the free search for truth regardless of the "usefulness" of what is discovered, and the development of the artistic or aesthetic aspects of the human being – these things must inevitably tend to be neglected or checked in the so rapid march of the Soviet mind. Yet, as has been said, if the time comes that the Soviet aims for its new citizens seem to be definitely near enough to realization, a freer and broader development of the human personality may perhaps be looked for. The greatest Russian poet of this century, Boris Pasternak, complained in the 1930's that "New Man has walked over me": but in springtime at the end of the war he was singing of his beloved Moscow that "There one is at home at the primal source of all with which the century shall flower".[1]

[1] Last lines of the lyric poem *Vesna*, in *Zemnoy Prostor*, Moskva, Sovetskiy Pisatel', 1945, p. 44.

Broadly speaking, the patterns and aims of higher education in all the European states dominated by Soviet ideology are alike – in effect, variations on the same themes modified by local conditions. The two communist countries which are in some degree definitely exceptional here are Poland and Yugoslavia. Poland, because of its retention among the majority of its people of the Catholic faith and its varying traditions, shows a good deal of individuality within the communist frame, such as the work of the Catholic University of Lublin, which goes on while having some not unfriendly informal relations with the State Marie Curie University in the same town. Or again, there has been a proposal of late to reduce the normal five-year first degree courses in Polish universities to four, on the ground of an expected improved effectiveness. Yugoslavia, with its centripetal federation of states somewhat resembling in superficial structure the U.S.S.R., in its higher education presents problems often similar to those of the Soviets. There are universities at varying stages of development, from that of Zagreb with its strong inheritance from an advanced humane Austrian tradition, to that of Sarajevo which serves the relatively backward state of Bosnia, with its considerably Moslem population, where the very new university is only just beginning to function fully. Moreover, recent developments in the central Yugoslav government, in directions quite independent of a purely Soviet ideology, have resulted in a good deal of academic flexibility and a far greater measure of internal freedom than is yet possible in the U.S.S.R.

Of course the Yugoslav centres of higher education, even more than those of Russia, suffer from the dislocations due to a too speedy development on the technical scientific side especially, and from an inevitable tendency to allot far more of the limited resources available to metropolitan centres (particularly Belgrade) at the expense of more remote provincial establishments. In Yugoslavia, with its strongly patriotic local elements and its often still unblended traditions from Byzantine Orthodox, Latin Catholic, and Moslem Turkish civilizations, there is a less effective democratic centralism than in the U.S.S.R., and naturally far more limited resources of every kind. Its higher educational problems are, however, very much of the same kind as those touched upon in discussing the Soviets. Both Zagreb and Ljubljana the capital of Slovenia are cultural centres with an extremely long history of Latin, and later Austrian tradition: and in both there is, as it seemed to me as a visitor, much of the best academic inheritance preserved with pride, despite an almost desperate overcrowding in some departments. Though, as in the U.S.S.R., the higher administrative posts are commonly held by those chosen for their value to the Communist Party, there is much encouragement of good scholarship, especially in the fields of local history and antiquities and of all types of linguistics.

The relative lack of effective contacts with Western European and American scholars and higher institutions was due mostly, as it seemed, to sheer lack of financial resources; for the visitor could exchange ideas on all subjects with marked ease and freedom. That academic contacts are eagerly desired, by official as well as unofficial bodies, is demonstrated by the efforts from Britain, and far more from the U.S.A., to provide facilities from their own resources for such contacts. For these are almost always warmly welcomed and utilized, though they cannot be reciprocated.

There is no need here to say anything of the more closely integrated "satellite" states, Czechoslovakia, Hungary, Rumania and Bulgaria, which reflect Soviet higher education as closely as they can. It is only in such fields as the study of the native languages, the making of grammars and dictionaries, that work of a creative character in the humanities is effectively carried on: or in scientific technology in accordance with Soviet requirements.

BIBLIOGRAPHICAL NOTE

In Nicholas DeWitt's large work *Education and Professional Employment in the U.S.S.R.*, noticed at the beginning of this chapter, there is a full and careful bibliography of relevant works, both in English and Russian. This covers the ground up to 1961. In 1959 Unesco published a very thorough and fully descriptive *Technical and Vocational Education in the U.S.S.R., a Bibliographical Survey*, by M. I. Movšovič, from the Unesco Workshops, Place de Fontenoy, Paris 7-e. There is a useful "Selective Bibliography" in Alexander Korol's *Soviet Education for Science and Technology*, already mentioned. All of these, excellent as they are, tend to concentrate on the "scientific" aspects of higher education, though by no means exclusively. On universities there is a very helpful list of books treating historically of the individual institutions in *Universitetskoe Obrazovaniye v S.S.S.R.* already referred to.

There are innumerable educational periodicals covering every aspect of the field, many of them listed in the above-noted bibliographies.

The all-important day-to-day work of the Ministry of Higher Education and its directives appear in the monthly *Vestnik Vysshey Shkoly*. This is the official organ for higher and middle specialist education: *Organ Ministerstva Vysshego i Srednego Spetsial'nogo Obrazovaniya SSSR*. Of particular importance for the present study are the issues for July and August 1961 (Nos. 7 and 8), in which the aims of the education laws of 1958 and the newest plans for implementing these reforms are fully discussed and explained.

Events in the vast complex machine of Soviet higher education move too fast for any work of reference to be entirely up-to-date: but all agencies who can supply the latest information on every aspect of the field are carefully listed in the pamphlet published by Unesco at their Paris Workshops entitled *Information Services in the U.S.S.R.* as Vol. X No. I in the series *Educational Abstracts*, Jan. 1958.

The Ministries of Culture and their agencies in all the communist states provide books and pamphlets on education of all kinds, especially for the instruction of foreigners. But inevitably this kind of "cultural" material will not serve the seriously objective student adequately, save for those works that are listed in the reference-books cited above.

CHAPTER 9

East Germany — Distinctive Features

In the chapter which follows the educational system of East Germany is described and to some extent evaluated. The reader, whether interested in systems of education or in more general aspects of life, is warned of the absolute necessity to separate the social and even the political aspects of the East German educational system from the common picture offered in the West of a repressive police state from which citizens aspire to escape. It may very well be axiomatic that anyone studying the educational system of a country of the communist *bloc* should be willing to ascribe, as generously as possible, the highest professional integrity to all engaged in the service of education. The commitment to communism, which results in a higher proportion of party membership in the profession than in the population generally, seldom if ever leads to a greater distortion of professional honesty than is to be found in different educational systems which condone and encourage other kinds of indoctrination.

Moreover, in looking at Eastern Germany it is well to assume some stability in order to appreciate the devotion of a very high proportion of those working at different levels as teachers and educational administrators. The movement of refugees cannot of course be ignored; but an educational system has been constructed, and is being serviced and maintained, on the assumption that there is continuity of life for individuals and for their state and its system of education, and that at some time there will be settlement of the political and economic conditions which lead to migration. The unsettling effects of existence in a political vortex can be seen in the lives, utterances and work of the mainly young men and women engaged in education. In some ways the extreme social tensions seem to encourage generalizations by professional visitors; *the pressures* certainly make possible the presentation of views about a system of education which the reader, remote from the conflicts, may be tempted to qualify daily as he reads of new developments in Eastern Germany.

EAST GERMANY – DISTINCTIVE FEATURES

A nation's decisions on educational policy result from a series of external and internal pressures. Clearly all governments in the Eastern *bloc* subscribe to fundamental theories about, and evolve functions for, education which differ substantially from those of the West. If one detaches oneself from major contemporary issues it is possible to detect that all countries, east and west, north and south, use their educational systems to preserve and further certain aspects of national character and heritage. Thus Eastern Germany (more properly the German Democratic Republic) has an educational system characterized at once by themes common to all communist educational arrangements and by features that are distinctively German.

The broad common elements of communist education have been introduced in previous chapters and will be referred to later, on occasions, in this chapter. Here may be elaborated some of the features described as distinctively German. In the first place education, like all social services in the G.D.R., has been developed since 1948 to bridge a wide gap in time. It is still frequently pointed out that the gulf between 1933 and 1948 created a special problem. The educational ideals of Nazism in the period of preparation for war between 1933 and 1939 have had to be completely eradicated. The teachers who succumbed to, because they failed to resist, Nazism were disqualified from service in the new socialist school system. Pupils and students, who were indoctrinated in this period, and those who failed to receive adequate education, offered a special challenge in the immediate post-war years. The war period, 1939–45, saw for many a continued indoctrination, for some a complete disillusionment, and for others death and destruction. Education in every sense was, in Germany as elsewhere, a casualty of war; schools were razed, children orphaned and teachers, Nazi, non-Nazi and anti-Nazi, indiscriminately slain by the sustained bombardments from plane and tank. The three years from 1945 to 1948, when the occupied areas or sectors became two separate sovereign or near-sovereign states, now appear in retrospect either as a period of achievement or an epoch of machination. Certainly the Control Commissions in the different areas of Germany as a whole and the Four Power Administration in Berlin Sectors helped in various ways to lay foundations for subsequent educational progress. In the area that was to become the German Democratic Republic co-operation between Russian and German authorities led to some slight school building programmes, teacher screening and emergency training schemes, and the provision of a modicum of equipment and stock for a service that had to be thought of as starting in conditions of considerable improvization.

In the minds of many thoughtful Germans, not simply in the East, 1933 was a date to return to for another reason. This was the year, it was argued, in which the greatest mistake was made – a mistake which was brought about by economic, political, and social forces, both national and international. But it was also urged that there must have been something wrong with an educational system which resulted in a whole nation being misled so disastrously. For this reason pre-1933 education was arraigned. This was why in Eastern Germany when the opportunity was offered in 1948 for nearly complete redevelopment, scepticism about the system of education of the social democrats gradually found a full embodiment in theory and practice for what was, and is, thought to be the superior system of education resting on Leninist principles of communism.

The years between 1948 and 1959 in the main represent a growth towards the full development of the system now in being. This may be described as a centralized common-school offering an undifferentiated curriculum and a ten-year "standard" system. The schools are co-educational and pupils in effect are required to make the grade each year from their starting point at the age of six. Woven into the curriculum, often only as illustrative in the first class but developing in the tenth class into a full "subject", is a treatment of life as it is lived in a modern industrialized socialist community; this is not obviously propagandist at the early stages, although it is thought of as an essential part of "polytechnical" education. In the last four years polytechnical education takes a more demanding and more formal and very interesting form. After the ten-year school every pupil has the obligation to continue part-time education, in some cases, indeed, full-time; and in theory universities, and the different kinds of *Hochschule*, are open to all who have the normal or modified entrance requirements. Great importance is attached to the provision of courses in the Workers' and Peasants' Faculties, adult schools leading to University entrance.

The programme of the new law of 1959 represents a gradual transition from a system of eight years or classes followed by three years of vocational training to a ten-year, or class, system followed as a rule by two or three years of vocational training. Something between 10 per cent and 15 per cent of the pupils in the former eight-year school continued their education in the twelve-year school in order to secure their *Abitur* with its right to enter a university. The transition to the system to be created as a result of the new law means that by 1964 all pupils will be in attendance at a ten-year school. At the end of 1960, the last year for which statistics have been released – though, it must be added, there is nothing sinister in being twelve months behind with national statistics – 35 per cent of the pupils in the existing eight-year schools were leaving to go to work. The remaining 65 per cent were staying on at school to complete the ninth and tenth classes of the ten-year school. In practice this 65 per cent could be further subdivided into 12 per cent who were attending twelve-year schools, which meant a commitment to continue to the completion of the *Abitur*, and 53 per cent who were in the Ten-Class Polytechnical High Schools, the new kind of institution which was created by the 1959 law. The pupil who chooses to complete the twelve-year curriculum must follow his school course with one year in industry. It is confidently expected that the proportion of an age-group gaining the *Abitur* will increase to 15 per cent in 1963, 20 per cent in 1965 and will reach 30 per cent at some foreseeable date.

The nature of the educational provision to follow the Polytechnical High School course has been worked out as a result of an analysis of the needs of the planned economy of the G.D.R. It has been represented to the administration of the service of education that up to 1975 the annual output of students in the G.D.R. should result in 23 per cent graduates, 45 per cent qualified in the *Fachschule* and 32 per cent highly skilled workers.

To satisfy these demands in the field of technical education the new law requires that the school leaver must continue in further part-time education for two or three years. Provision is made for this in *Berufsschulen* attended by some 100,000 pupils; this is a reduction to about half of the former provision, as the 1959 law has lengthened school life by about two years and the curriculum now contains some elementary treatment of technical matters. The option to attend *Berufsschule* for two or three years depends on the decision of a child or his parents to stay on at a *Berufsschule* to complete the *Abitur*. If the child has not attended a twelve-class school his chance of catching up with those who have is provided by the special three-year *Berufsschule* course ending with the *Abitur*. This will bring him to the end of the thirteenth year of education. This is in time exactly the position of the product of the twelve-class high school on the completion of his year's work in industry.

The products of the two- or three-year *Berufsschule* courses may continue their education in the *Ingenieur-* and *Fachschule* for further technical courses. Those with *Abitur* may proceed to a university. A system of evening, as opposed to day-release, study can also qualify for entry to *Fachschule* courses. The products of the *Fachschule* may achieve qualifications which will admit them to university courses; in most cases their qualifications will lead them to *Hochschule* or to courses for technical institution teachers in the *Berufspädagogische Institut* in Humboldt University or in the *Pädagogische Facultät* in the *Technische Hochschule* in Dresden.

When the claim is rightly made that there is a direct route for all to the university it must be pointed out that university and *Hochschule* education is available for day students, for correspondence students and for evening part-time students.

Additional to this main provision the G.D.R. provides well-planned facilities for handicapped, including educationally sub-normal, children, and also offers educational pre-school facilities through local, quasi-"voluntary", or industrial, provision. Particularly useful services were developed after the war for the care of orphans or deserted children; these services have been sustained in children's homes where deprived children of various kinds are well cared for.

Well bedded into the 1959 law is the "democratic" obligation to treat all children as equals. This means that testing to differentiate between children is technically illegal. It also means that streaming according to ability is condemned as a reactionary educational device. This application to the technical processes of education within the classroom of the principle of equality before the law has led to the appreciation of techniques found in Russia. Frequently the effect in practice of this apparently fair law is to discourage more adventurous teaching and apparently to concentrate on rote-learning. This tragically is also in keeping with earlier German practices. There has been some stultifying of techniques in the name of democratic principles but there has also been some valuable examination of co-operative emulation as one of the sources of energy in the complex teacher-learner situation.

An interesting situation arises when children fail to make the grade. If by assessment of the general progress of a class the work of an individual child is not up to a required standard the child must repeat the year's work (as is common on the continent). Technically the resources of co-operative emulation are used throughout the year by the whole class to ensure that no children in the class are kept down. To have to repeat a class is therefore an implied criticism not simply of the child who has failed but also of the class as a whole as well as of the teacher. There is obviously a limit to the effectiveness of any drive based on class co-operation, and children are therefore required in some cases to repeat classes. It is, however, extremely difficult for teachers from systems other than those based on Leninist educational theories to appreciate the display of slogans on the approach drive to a school declaring, "It is our resolve to have no one repeating classes in this school".

Here it must be clearly stated that there is a considerable amount of scholarly preoccupation with educational theory, philosophy, history and sociology in the G.D.R. While Western critics may destroy the premises on which this scholarship rests they would be foolish to deny that intellectual activity and sustained application are everywhere apparent. This scholarship is matched by the organization of a good social and professional research unit and by the activity of a corporative Scientific Research Council, at once informing the *Ministerium für Volksbildung* and implementing its policies.

This Scientific Council[1] is required to meet at least once a year to consider education, particularly as it contributes to the development of scientific knowledge, and to advise the Minister on all scientific matters. This council of 100 members meets under the chairmanship of a former professor and Dean of Students of Humboldt University.

A courageous attempt can be detected to provide a solid "democratic" foundation for the educational system: debates, or more properly, reasoned and sustained declarations of educational policies are important business of the *Volkskammer*. The speech by Herr Grotewohl in the *Volkskammer* on Wednesday, December 2nd 1959 was given nationwide broadcast coverage; and the national press, admittedly all controlled, carried the speech describing the new education law in full. While the Research Council consists of 100 members and is divided into four sections viz. (I) pedagogy, (II) applied and natural sciences, (III) social sciences, (IV) technical education, there is also within the

---

[1] In 1962 this Scientific Council has developed into a smaller Educational National Advisory Committee.

ministerial framework a *Kollegium* of twenty-five members. These include leading experts of the Ministry of Education and of other ministries who meet once per month in different districts within the G.D.R. In addition to the Minister of Education there is also a secretariat for Further Education and for Special Schools,[1] having its own Advisory Committees and one member on the Research Council.

A most important central theme, easily detected by Western observers, is that of German guilt, which appears to be quite deliberately inculcated and used as the foundation of informed political attack on Western Germany, and of the underlying communist proletarian philosophy of the G.D.R. The last Fascist or Nazi attempt to destroy the world was almost entirely German in origin and in power; no pupil or student, teacher or lecturer, professor or politician is allowed to forget the attack on "the socialist people's democracy". This is seen in many ways but probably none more clearly than in the use made of the symbol of the concentration camp. Buchenwald, so near to Weimar – and so to the richly sentimental associations of Goethe and Schiller – has become a national shrine. Ernst Taelmann is the great hero of the F.D.J. (the Pioneers of the G.D.R.); his grave in Buchenwald is a most impressive monument visited by young and old from all parts of the G.D.R., and from many Eastern countries. It would be easy to assume that the decision had been taken simply to prevent a chance of recollections of Nazi butchery ever dimming; it is probably truer to adapt the phoenix legend and believe that the struggle is not against an evil but for something good. In this sense the inculcation of a sense of German guilt as part of the educational purpose of East Germany is a wholly admirable catharsis.

One of the attractive aspects of this doctrine of guilt may be, if it proves genuine and permanent, the positive recruitment of East German youth for peace. The danger may very well exist, it is admitted, that this doctrine may induce an excessive partisanship for the new socialism. The attitude to West German youth cannot fail to impress the observer of the East German education system. The ordinary tourist, if he existed in this torn world, is certainly most impressed by the contrast in ethos between East and West Germany. Too frequently critics of East Germany have simply emphasized the Spartan rigour of life and have dilated on the lack of consumer goods and services.

Below the surface there appear to be two profoundly different sets

---

[1] This ministerial dichotomy has also been modified during 1962.

of values. The one we can most easily understand because it is so like our own is that found in the youth of West Berlin. It is extremely difficult to describe fully the totally different attitudes and values of East German and so East Berlin youth. Some have until recently been in a condition almost ready for absorption of Western, i.e. West Berlin values. Others have been so inured to Western propaganda seen through Eastern eyes that they have never looked like succumbing to the pulp magazines on sale in West Berlin but have rather gone over to a militancy for socialism and in defence of class loyalties with which they have been indoctrinated. In short, the mental differences almost exactly parallel the differences between Kurfurstendam and Karl Marx Allee. This is a little hard on the humanity of the young people on both sides and probably particularly unfair to the East German youth for whom Karl Marx Allee is nearly as foreign as Kurfurstendam.

The remainder of this chapter will deal more or less exclusively with specific institutes within the educational system as a whole. It has been thought desirable to deal with Physical Education, the Educational Publishing Industry, the use of Audio-Visual Aids, Technical Education and Teacher Training among others.

Deutsche Hochschule für Körperkultur

Countries in the Eastern *bloc* are frequently criticized because they have appeared to exploit for purposes of political and national prestige the advantages resulting from carefully co-ordinated policies in physical education, sport and games. They are also sometimes accused of over-cultivating the time and energies of enthusiasts who are encouraged in their enthusiasm for physical prowess which, if not satisfied, might lead them to express disaffection. The developments in international competition in Olympiads, Test Matches, and World Cups, all seem to underline the national prestige which may be won in international sport.

Few of these critics would deny, however, that the wise cultivation of physical prowess makes some contribution to national health. If facilities, with a non-military organization of coaching, are spread evenly throughout the community there may very well be a general improvement in the people's health.

The G.D.R. is very conscious of the connexion between physical education and public health. It is quite edifying to note how senior officers of the Ministry of Education will at the appointed time each day perform the day's exercises in their offices. This is done regularly without ostentation but with an invitation to chance foreign visitors to join in.

The key to the G.D.R. understanding of the importance of physical education may be seen in the story of the *Deutsche Hochschule für Körperkultur*. This is one of the most remarkable institutions in the whole of the G.D.R. It is certainly unique in its treatment of physical culture. There is probably no college, or, more literally, no university in the whole world that may stand comparison with it. At a time when very considerable sacrifices were being made to try to secure the economy of this most assailed community the people were persuaded or compelled to make sacrifices for two among many most spectacular possibilities. One, consuming national resources and investment capital with gargantuan appetite, was the brown coal power-Combinat at Schwarzepump; the other, needing EDM 40,000,000, was the *Deutsche Hochschule für Körperkultur*.

The title *Hochschule* most deliberately retains its full German connotation in the G.D.R. The title is used to describe institutions of University status; today it is used, in particular, to show the status of a kind of teacher training and educational research in the *Potsdammer Pädagogische Hochschule*, the achievements of the highest level of technical education in the *Dresdener Technische Hochschule*, and the academic and cultural equivalent of university studies in the Leipzig *Hochschule für Körperkultur*.

The close connexion with the Karl Marx University at Leipzig is seen in the participation by some *D.H.f.K.* students in university classes. These students and their teachers are in every sense on equal terms with their opposite numbers in the university. The nature of the courses offered at the *D.H.f.K.*, the quality of the staff, the range of individual and group research undertaken, the eminent suitability and excellence of the buildings, equipment and amenities all underline the university character of the institution.

The generosity of the policy of equipping the *D.H.f.K.* and the scientific, analytical and objective mode of study and research are both illustrated by the way in which the use of the ciné-camera is planned as a normal aid to the study and presentation of the dynamics of movement. The commitment to the view that physical fitness contributes to public health may be seen from the way future organizers of physical education in factories, youth service or in regions are trained alongside future teachers. The idea of a continuous process of education has been clearly worked out in the case of physical education. The conviction of the original planners and the scope of their vision for physical culture may be seen in the very highly specialized gymnasia that have been provided. That there are separate gymnasia, of different sizes and shapes, for fencing, judo, indoor hockey, basketball, boxing, wrestling and so on makes the *D.H.f.K.* a truly well endowed institution.

In almost every sport engaged in internationally, from team games to individual spectacular events like canoe slalom, the newspaper readers of the world have heard of the achievements of East Germany. Educational theorists may like to learn that much of the inspiration for this success is to be found in the hard and systematic theoretical and practical work undertaken in Leipzig. They may also discover with interest that *D.H.f.K.* is a co-educational institution, where the visitor may only if singularly obtuse fail to sense a remarkable wholesomeness of mutual respect and regard on the part of men and women students.

Volk und Wissen Verlag

In a centralized educational system a very important task faces those in charge of educational publishing. In the G.D.R. some quite remarkable achievements have to be reported. In general the whole arrangement of this kind of publishing succeeds in combining principles of security as interpreted by the administration with typical and traditional painstaking German thoroughness. The *V.W.V.* has the responsibility of editing, and so authorizing, all textbooks for use in schools, and some textbooks and journals for training colleges.

A centralized system with a common programme for all children in each grade raises its own publishing problems. These are particularly accentuated when there are major changes in the curriculum and when educational reform leads to a large proportion of children staying on longer at school. In addition the publishing industry serving a centralized system must at all times be more directly aware of the exact demands of the curriculum than a similar industry needs to be either in a decentralized system or where curriculum options exist.

The common curriculum of the *zehnklassige allgemeinbildende polytechnische Oberschule* (ten-year general education and polytechnical secondary school) has stimulated fundamental discussions both in the central *V.W.V.* and in the directorates of the various publishing contractors, many of whom are not nationalized in the G.D.R.

A most important educational corollary of a common curriculum is that the textbook is required to confirm, and conform to, the declared and implied curricular concepts laid down by the central administration. All educational publications, thus, tend to toe the line, even although no directive may ever be given for them to do so. This explains the earlier reference to principles of security which our G.D.R. colleagues would in good faith hasten to assure us does not arise in a matter as simple as textbook production. Indeed they could produce as evidence some of the very best textbooks for pupils or students of different ages dealing with a range of subjects.

The way in which a textbook is produced for use in school may illustrate how quality is achieved and how the book may be guaranteed to conform. An author may be selected, or volunteer, to contribute a particular new text. All the initial responsibility is his and the whole central responsibility remains his. However, his first draft of contents and his suggestions for their pedagogical presentation are submitted to an Editorial Council empanelled by the *V.W.V.* for the purpose. The Council will include the author, an editor on the staff of the *V.W.V.*, and a number of teachers experienced in teaching syllabuses most closely connected with the new text.

A preliminary discussion of the outline and of the treatment of the subject is held; and when modifications have been agreed the author begins to write. This second draft may not cover the whole ground, but it is treated as a clearer indication than the first treatment of the direction in which the author is moving. This incomplete draft is now considered by the Editorial Council and its bearings and technical resourcefulness checked. For this reason the Editorial Council must include experts and if the textbook is planned to cover a wide field it may include as many as 100 members.

At this second meeting the Editorial Council, as a result of full discussion, gives the final directive to the author to get on with the job. When the MS is completed, the editor (the professional member of the Editorial Council employed by the *V.W.V.*) customarily completes all the rest of the work on the text without further reference to the Editorial Council.

In a country where production figures for every kind of activity have a wide official circulation it is usual to concede that book production is unnecessarily slow, probably solely because of the procedure of using Editorial Councils. It is estimated that the *V.W.V.* receives an annual production of not more than 400–500 printed pages per editor. This is only about one-fifth of the production rate of some other scientific publishing houses.

The MS is sent to the Central Publishing Council and eventually to the Scientific Research Council for Education. These two bodies consider the suitability of the book from the point of view of its contents and of the pedagogical methods underlying it. When they express their satisfaction the MS is at last put into the hands of the printer. Textbook contracts are highly valued by printing concerns and the *V.W.V.* appears to co-operate with about half of the printers in the G.D.R.

Readers of educational works in the West will probably have heard of the high quality of *Geschichte der Erziehung* (History of Education), a history of education produced by an editorial team including Professor Koenig. This work introduced the series "A Library for Teachers", and belonged to a section offering an examination of the fundamental questions of socialist educational theory. Dr Lamprecht's *Grammatik der englishen Sprache* is a most valuable presentation of the grammar of English for foreign, notably German, students. In the same way a periodical "Speak German" designed to enable English speakers to acquire facility in German is an excellent topical treatment of fundamental difficulties. Dr Claus and Dr Hibsch combined to produce *Kinder-Psychologie*, which deserves quite wide study by colleagues in East and West. In addition the range of textbooks produced for use in the schools are interesting in terms both of their quality and of their pedagogical approaches.

In the same way an immense range of interest is covered by the journals published by the *V.W.V.* The following list shows how subject areas and professional interests are dealt with in this wide spread of publication:

Berufsbildung (Vocational education)
Biologie in der Schule
Chemie in der Schule
Deutsche Lehrerzeitung (Teachers' Journal)
Deutschunterricht
Elternhaus und Schule (Home and School)
Fremdsprachenunterricht (Foreign languages)

Geschichtunterricht und Staatsburgerkunde (History and Civics)
Körpererziehung (Physical education)
Kunsterziehung (Art education)
Mathematik und Physik in der Schule
Musik in der Schule
Neue Erziehung im Kindergarten (New infant education)
Pädagogik (Education review)
Polytechnische Bildung und Erziehung (Polytechnical training and instruction)
Die Sonderschule (Special school)
Sozialistische Erziehung
Die Unterstufe (Elementary school)
Zeitschrift für den Erdkundeunterricht (Geographical Journal)

Deutsches Zentralinstitut für Lehrmittel (Central German Institute for Teaching Aids)

This Institute is symptomatic of the new educational ideas to be found in the German Democratic Republic. It also represents interesting developments in educational techniques and controls; the techniques may be universally disseminated and the controls carefully tightened as circumstances demand.

An analysis, thoroughly detailed and Germanic, has been made of the basic professional demands underlying the development of teaching aids. In Professor Hortzschansky's translation, "The teaching aids:

(a) according to their kind, shape, character, and quality, have to be adapted to the new tasks of the socialist school as well as to support the polytechnical character of all educational work;

(b) have to be designed in such way as to give emotional impact and serve the aims of education;

(c) as an image of reality, have to make the characteristics and details so plain that from the numerous impressions an abstract survey and understanding is made possible by their help;

(d) have to influence the pupil in a conscious and methodical way and support the process of learning, instruction, and education;

(e) have to correspond to really up-to-date knowledge of research and its results in science, technique, economy, and culture;

(f) have to help to achieve in education scientific results beyond doubt, and to serve social progress;

(g) have to illustrate fundamental knowledge of objective and general law, and the development of nature and society, as well as helping to form a scientific ideology;

(h) have to give, by their design, an incentive to deal with them and to arouse interest;

(i) have to represent the substantial features; to avoid needless accessories; to be economical, durable, time-saving, and aesthetically unobjectionable in their quality."

A preliminary glance at these claims will reveal that placed first is the recognition of the existence of a school function in a socialist society which may not exist in other societies, in addition to a declaration supporting the development throughout the educational system of what is called polytechnical education.

The second clause describes the aesthetic significance of audio-visual material; and the products of the *D.Z.L.* in the form of films, slides and tape-recordings demonstrate unequivocally the great progress made in this direction. (d) Shows the educational role of the audio-visual material in relation to the classroom practices of the teacher and to the currently fashionable theory of learning. This as well as (e) would be supported by protagonists of audio-visual aids in every country; (f) and (g) go far towards supporting the aim of a socialist educational system and the alignment of scientific truth with Marxist-Leninist ideology; (h) and (i) are intensely practical and will be supported by teachers everywhere, but more especially by those who feel that all kinds of audio-visual aids have a role to perform in the teaching situation as important as that of earlier aids to learning and teaching.

A very important part is played by county and rural district sub-committees in an effort to decentralize the distribution and availability of the very extensive range of audio-visual materials produced at the centre. In the teaching of modern languages, notably Russian, English and to a lesser extent French, recordings of a variety of most interesting topics – including conversations, anecdotes and folksongs – are available universally throughout the G.D.R. A particular virtue of these tapes is that they have through the exigencies of occupation on the one hand and summer courses on the other been made by native speakers of the languages in all cases. While in other countries the development towards a language laboratory has led to the rationalizing of the tape-recorder in a classroom situation offering simultaneous recording facilities to every member of a class of, say, thirty-two pupils, the *D.Z.L.* developed earlier a technique for the reproduction of twelve tapes simultaneously from a single master, so securing wide distribution of the primary material already referred to. This method of tape production is one of the most remarkable engineering achievements of the laboratories in *D.Z.L.*

A further development of the work of *D.Z.L.* is in the production of a 16mm. film projector which is available as an essential unit with additional components, so that an individual school can build up to a full 16mm. sound projector. The main core of the projector includes an excellent motor and a reliable optical system with gates designed to take 16mm. silent films. A school may next wish to add a sound unit including a scanning lamp, amplifier and speaker. Finally, a magnetic head can be added to enable striping and commentary as a refinement.

Technische Hochschule, Dresden

The whole system of technical education rests securely on the long established German apprenticeship system. The apprenticeship system has been continued in the G.D.R. and is supported by the foundation of general awareness of technical processes laid in the polytechnical programme. The arrangement of the *Berufsschule* is very similar to the pattern of part-time education available in Germany in the past: it is, however, the special concern of the *Institut für Berufsausbildung* in Berlin.

At the top of the whole system is the *Technische Hochschule* at Dresden, which has 10,000 full-time students enrolled, and imposes upon its teaching staff the preparation and conduct of correspondence courses for an additional 5,000 students. All the practical work, however, of all the students is completed under the supervision of the teaching staff at Dresden.

The staff consists of about 150 teachers, most of whom (as heads of departments) are deservedly styled professors. A shortage of skilled teaching personnel with technical qualifications is felt almost as acutely as it is in England. The professors are each helped by one assistant professor and by an ingenious and economic use of the equivalent of postgraduate students, who are paid in the fourth and fifth years of these courses for work which they undertake as part-time teachers in their departments. There is considerable optimism that the policies now being implemented to recruit, train and qualify additional staff will lead to a solution of the staffing problem at this level of education in about three years.

The budget for the activities of the *Technische Hochschule* is accepted as nearly adequate for the work it is now attempting; but as industry develops and stabilizes in the G.D.R. it is confidently assumed that even greater sums will be made available. At the moment, despite the political and commercial difficulties of the G.D.R. as a whole, the professors generally are very pleased with arrangements which enable them to get the most recent works of scholarship in their different fields published in Russia, the United States of America and the United Kingdom. This represents a very serious decision to make use of the available sterling and dollars.

Every department contrives to include both initial instruction of students correctly qualified on admission and also sustained research in the main fields covered by the department. An allocation of funds from the *Technische Hochschule* budget is supplemented by the government planning authority's contribution in marks for specific research work undertaken for it by the *Technische Hochschule*, and also by payments from industry both in return for achievements and as endowments for further research.

Every Diploma student (and the Diploma is the main qualification offered), is required at some time in his course to devote a considerable part of his energies to individual general work of a research kind, or to the work of a team engaged on a major research project. In this way students reading for the Diploma in Engineering must do six weeks' research, those reading for the Diploma in Physics two weeks', and the Diploma in Architecture six to eight weeks'.

Students receive varying sums as grants, although it seems to the visitor that grants in the G.D.R. are more nearly treated as wages for the services returned by the student than as grants payable by a beneficent central government. About 25 per cent of all students in Dresden have free places and receive an additional payment of 180 East marks per month. If a student's marks are consistently over 2.5 out of 5 (an almost universal system of scoring in communist countries) he will get an additional incentive payment of 40 East marks. For the work of assisting in the teaching or demonstrating in his fourth or fifth year a student receives a further 100 East marks per month.

After two years of study comes the first examination, related to the whole course in much the same way that an Intermediate degree examination used to be held in English universities. Three years later comes the written examination on which his first major award rests. Like most engineering examinations, this in the G.D.R. seems to attempt to cover a tremendously wide field of subjects. Some students and professors spoke of papers in thirty different but related subjects being taken at this stage. To complete his Diploma the student must now apply for permission to do his stint of research. On the satisfactory submission of the record of his researches the student becomes a Diploma Engineer. He then faces two alternatives: the first is to seek employment in industry and then, if he feels it necessary, return later for a further three years to complete his doctorate. The second is to proceed at once with the research necessary for his doctorate and then enter industry.

The doctor who is anxious to teach in the *Technische Hochschule* or at any technical institute of near-university status must prepare for a further qualification, somewhat akin to the D.Sc in British universities. For this degree, in addition to his own further research, the candidate must show his familiarity with the works of other researches in that field and in related fields in other countries as well as in the G.D.R. He must also normally have a formidable list of publications to his credit.

After three years experience of teaching as a D.Sc. he may then be ready for consideration for appointment to a Professorship.

For the teacher in a technical college it is normally necessary to have followed a full-time course for about eleven semesters, or five and a half years, and to have varied and relevant experience in practical work.

In the pattern of technical education at this high level mention must be made of the *Berufspädagogische Hochschule* contained within the Humboldt University in Berlin. Here, indeed, as in the *Pädagogische Facultät* at the *Technische Hochschule* at Dresden a very high level of professional training is offered in a stimulating environment to those who wish to become teachers in technical institutions.

Teacher training

At the heart of every educational system, giving it thrust and purpose, is the process of preparing its supply of teachers. There have been for historical reasons very special difficulties to be overcome in securing a supply of teachers for the schools and educational institutions of the G.D.R. In the early days, the destruction and loss of records and credentials in the catastrophe of war led to a limited amount of infiltration by those with false claims to earlier training. Political screening excluded those who had been members of the Nazi party. The economic and political compulsions of the régime also added to the loss of both old and newly trained teachers who helped to swell the tide of refugees to the West. An emergency training scheme was instituted in 1947 and continued in 1948, designed to recruit to the schools men and women who would, after an initial twelve- or eighteen-month course, be required to pursue further studies in their spare time and at properly organized vacation courses.

A relatively small number of older anti-Nazi teachers returned to the service of the schools, technical institutions and universities. They had been on the run for varying periods from 1933. Some had been in obscure posts in education, some had survived precariously and heroically in an underground movement where they had worked as propagandists in heavily bombed cities like Cologne, and some had suffered fearful physical hardships in concentration camps. In addition, although it is not widely realized in the West, a handful of quite young scholars, driven by anti-Semitic fury from Germany as children, chose to return to Eastern Germany to make their contribution to the education system of the new anti-Nazi Germany almost immediately after the end of hostilities. Some of these former refugees returned from England, France and Switzerland; many more came back from asylum in Russia.

The teaching profession as a whole retains the traditional continental and German distinction between those serving in lower classes as general practitioners and those working as specialists or quasi-specialists with older children. As a result, however, of the clearly understood mutual interdependence of the professional interests of these two kinds of teachers in a socialist community the worst effects of the traditional distinction have been somewhat mitigated. Moreover, recruitment to training courses now tends to come from pupils who have had a common educational experience at school. There is not as formerly a separate progress from gymnasium to university for the specialist and another progress from elementary school to normal school for the non-specialist. Another most interesting feature of current recruitment to teacher training courses is the large number of applications received from those who have achieved qualifications in, and practised successfully for some time, a completely different occupation. Theorists explaining the polytechnical educational system attribute this keenness to change from a variety of jobs to teaching to an interest in education as a whole, and to the discovery of talents for teaching resulting from the experiences of workers with groups of children in their day's practical work in production in different factories and institutions.[1]

Courses of training for teaching children in the first four classes are provided in co-educational colleges (called *Institut für Lehrerbildung*). Students must have completed the 8th to 10th class programme; and in the interim period before the general provision of the Ten Class Polytechnical High School some of the candidates will have been recruited from special courses following the completion of the 8th class. Arrangements are made in the *Lehrerbildung* institutes for the completion of the 9th and 10th class programmes in some cases. The training period thus extends over a minimum of three years; but for some students who have courses to complete it is a four years course.

The training programme is obviously rather more formal in any country where the curriculum of the school is centrally conceived and universally applied. In *Lehrerbildung* institutes the staff are obviously recruited from experienced and skilled practitioners who, in many cases, have developed an appreciable breadth of outlook not simply about their subjects but also about modern theories of child development. Students, sustained on grants, live in the main in up-to-date hostels and tend to be somewhat over-timetabled. A compromise between study bedrooms and communal dormitories has been evolved so that students spend much of their free time in rooms arranged to accommodate seven or eight students in groups of three intercommu-

---

[1] It is necessary to emphasise that the day's work in production does not last a whole day and opportunites are not confined to factories and farms. It is interesting to note that the City of Dresden Water Works is linked to a school, as is the Repair Workshop of the City of Dresden Transport Undertaking. Some of the most exceptionally valuable work was seen in the Repair Workshop. The syllabuses were sensibly interpreted, and children, teachers and foremen were thrilled and delighted with the success of the scheme.

nicating rooms. The addition of polytechnical education to the school curriculum means that the future teachers are required to complete their stint of this new "subject" during their *Lehrerbildung* institute course. This appears to be needed to compensate them for what currently they may have missed of the four-year polytechnical course, as well as to give them the professional view of polytechnical education as a whole.

The students in the *Institut für Lehrerbildung* in Grossenhain complete part of their polytechnical practical work in collaboration with the local tractor station. It is an interesting experience to attend a staff conference held in the education department of the institute to discuss the programme and planning of the tractor work about to be undertaken by a group of thirty girls. Even more interesting is the conference of tractor drivers held at the tractor station to discuss the problems facing the drivers when the girls descend upon them. At the tractor station the foreman driver, not the superintendent of the station, is in the chair; and also in attendance is the polytechnical education expert from the education department of the *Institut für Lehrerbildung*. On a particular occasion the drivers asked how the girls would be dressed; the institute lecturer said that there should be no problem, and indeed asked for information about any of the students who turned up not properly dressed in overalls. One driver wanted to know if these visitors would not interfere with production. This led to a well-informed, valuable, and practical discussion on the purpose of this kind of secondment of institute students. There was even finally a very lengthy discussion on what could be taught and how best it could be taught by tractor drivers who were not professional teachers.

For children in classes 5–10, teachers are trained in a *Pädagogische Institut* or in Universities. Here they are prepared to become specialist teachers. Admission requirements are higher than for an *Institut für Lehrerbildung*. Similar residential facilities are available and, if anything, students appear to include a higher proportion of older entrants. The *Pädagogische Institut* buildings are impressive, well-sited, and obviously treated with great civic pride and interest. That at Dresden has a most ambitious programme of building, with commendable care being lavished on the setting in which the *Institut* stands on the banks of the Elbe. Gardens, with intelligent use of trees and even of lawns, vie as amenities with quite excellent teaching facilities for the staff in charge of their specialist subjects.

Students preparing for this stage in Universities would clearly have themselves completed the *Abitur* or leaving examination at the end of the 12th year. By choice, however, although in pedagogical faculties or departments, they have decided to teach somewhere in classes 5–10.

Children in the 10th–12th classes are taught by teachers trained either in the Universities or in the *Pädagogische Hochschule* at Potsdam. This is the area of teacher-preparation where, structurally in terms of initial qualifications of entrants, academically in terms of the rigours of the course, and professionally if viewed both through the content of the education courses and the opportunity for research, the arrangements in the G.D.R. are most closely related both to the pattern almost indigenous to Germany and to current developments in Russia. The evolution of a pyramid or hierarchy of colleges from the *Institut für Lehrerbildung*, to the *Pädagogische Institut*, and to the *Pädagogische Hochschule* is a clear demonstration of special seriousness and careful forethought on the part of the academic planners advising the central authority.

At each stage in the pyramid the main structure of the course includes theory and practice. Indeed the principle of concurrent training appears to run through the whole arrangement. In the university faculty there is a measure of deferred practical work. Moreover theorists of teacher training are already openly canvassing for the establishment of close interrelationship among the three main types of institutions; they would probably like to move first to a common "Institute" and then to *Hochschule* status for all teacher training.

This can also be seen in the provision made for teachers in the range of highly specialized technical institutions for which German education as a whole has been well known, and which are now found well established in the G.D.R. We must now refer to the teacher training which is completed in the *Pädagogische Facultät* of the *Dresdener Technische Hochschule*.

This has the obvious advantage of training technical teachers for work in *Berufs-* and *Fachschule* in close contact with the high-level work undertaken with diploma students and with the atmosphere of research found in the *Hochschule*. In much the same way the siting of the *Berufspädagogische Institut* at the Humboldt University has obvious advantages. Further, the existence of *Lehrmeister Institute* helps to show the battery or grid of provision of facilities for the preparation of teachers in the widest sense required by a modern industrial community. A *Lehrmeister Institut* provides courses of training for suitably qualified craftsmen to prepare them for the responsibilities of taking over the education in factory or enterprise of the apprentices recruited from *Berufs-* or *Fachschule* courses. Some of the instructional work of the *Lehrmeister* as also some of the work in *Berufs-* and *Fachschule* courses will necessarily have to be adjusted as the full programme of polytechnical education is achieved.

Progress in these and other fields is effectively examined and planned through the research activities of the *Institut für Berufsausbildung* in East Berlin. Courses for *Berufsfortbildung* help to meet the educational problems confronting technical teachers.

Educational administration

It is too commonly assumed that there is very little opportunity for local participation in a completely centralized educational system.

The conditions of life in East Berlin, which is probably the most visited part of the G.D.R., are so different from those in other cities or in the extensive rural areas that it is probably of most interest to concentrate on the pattern of administration in a mixed rural and small town area. In general, too, it is frequently assumed that in a communist society all power is vested in the Communist Party. In the G.D.R. it is difficult to discover where responsibility for the implementation of policy rests with the Party and where it is delegated through the state machine to its central or local committees. The difficulty, in general, arises in Western minds because in many cases the party member who has helped to shape the policy which the Party has adopted is also the local or national officer charged with the job of carrying out the policy. The officer has thus two functions, one within the Party as a member and the other for the state or the local authority as an employee. That this is a real difficulty for a western observer is seldom fully appreciated by a colleague from a communist country trying to explain his job. Membership of the Republican or Democratic Party in U.S.A., or of Conservative or Labour or Liberal or, indeed, even of Communist Party in U.K. does not clearly commit the civil servant or local authority official to uncritical acceptance of government policies. Curiously in some cases it seems that similarly membership of the Party in the G.D.R. does not prevent a civil servant – even when he has helped within the party to devise the policy – from being critical of the policies he is paid to apply. A further complication in the G.D.R. comes from the multi-party front through which the Communist Party operates. This slight excursion into political administration is important, as it is hoped that it will serve to show the complex situation that may exist in a locality where policy may be implemented in such a way as to produce quite vigorously argued differences of outlook between members of the different parties within the front.

The educational policy now being applied nationally and locally in in the G.D.R. was presented to and approved by the *Volkskammer* in the first week of December, 1959. In some ways, as this was an adaptation of existing policies, it was legalizing what had been more or less in practice from the beginning of the academic year in September. Almost every new proposal had, in fact, been in experimental application for a slightly longer period. Thus in addition to the formal legalizing of the Ten-Year Polytechnical High School, the new law also had to deal with the raising of the school-leaving age, the establishment of new schools, and a measure of curricular reform. Because, however, of the experiments then being conducted to prove the value of polytechnical education, and because the consequent legal changes were adaptations of an existing system which was not being swept away, there was no need for extensive rearrangements of the division of responsibilities between centre and locality. In any case discussions within the Party had everywhere prepared the local officials who were party members for the new "tasks" which they would face.

The unit of local administration which includes the administration of Education, Health, Housing and *Kultur* is the *Kreis* (district). The information available about the services in a typical *Kreis* forces comparison with the social work administered by a unit smaller than an English County Council or than many county areas in U.S.A. The whole administration is supervised by a Chairman who is helped by a Deputy-Chairman, and for purposes of administrative convenience the four aspects of the work of the *Kreis* are represented by officers with special responsibilities.

The *Kreis* under consideration had an annual budget of 4,781,500 DM; the population numbered just over 40,000, including 4,481 children and young people of school age and about 2,000 of pre-school age.

Apart from clerical assistants and one full-time administrator, the *Abteilungsleiter*, the remainder of the *Kreis* education staff combined inspection and administration as their normal functions. Their days were spent either in working and meeting centrally in their offices or in visiting schools, singly or in groups, to inspect the ways in which educational policy was being carried out by the teachers.

The *Abteilungsleiter* together with his chief inspector, the *Kreisschulrat*, appeared to keep a fairly tight hold on even quite minute details of educational policy. The *Abteilungsleiter* held a weekly meeting. In attendance were the *Kreisschulrat*, four inspectors with responsibility for various ages of children; one inspector for extra-curricular activities, mainly confined to the "Pioneers"; one inspector for youth work in the *Freie Deutsche Jugend*; four specialist helpers in youth work; one director of adult education activities; one Pioneer director; and one inspector for each of these subjects: physical education, Russian, audio-visual aids, special schools, metal work, electro-technics and agriculture.

These twenty-one inspectors or advisers and administrators meet weekly to assess the achievement in their area. They are all people trained specially for their jobs. Indeed in many cases they hold additional professional qualifications resulting from full- or part-time courses of study taken after courses of initial training for teaching and after valuable and distinguished experience in education. In some cases they hold special qualifications resulting from participation in full-time courses of study in one of the special political schools for administrators run by the party. The structure of the group with seven members concerned with different kinds of work with youth outside the curriculum and with three specially involved in the implementation of the polytechnical programme reflects the pressure required to implement the new educational policies.

Some members of this weekly conference are much involved as party members in further activities within the *Kreis*, meeting the public regularly either in the role of *Kreis* employees or as party leaders or representatives. There appears, as far as it can be assessed, little confusion in the public mind between these two roles. Inside the teaching profession inspectors are highly respected mainly because their status rests on known past achievement; but they are also treated as very powerful forces affecting promotion and career prospects more fundamentally than heads of schools.

In addition to these local obligations, a really capable and distinguished member of the *Kreis* inspectorate or administration may have national responsibilities thrust upon him by invitation to join important regional or national committees or advisory bodies. It seems that regular attendances at council or committee meetings in Berlin may not be used as a reason for failing to complete the quota of work in the locality. In many ways these demands on distinguished and competent officers are very similar to those assailing men and women engaged in education everywhere. Indeed very often, having made allowances for the language and the political setting, the observer of G.D.R. administrators in conference will discover topics being examined in nearly the same terms as at home.

Some outstanding problems

From the foregoing it will be recalled that advice has been offered regularly about the dangers of prejudging G.D.R. education on political grounds. Here again, without arguing for the merits of liberal education, one may point out some of the educational problems as they may be seen arising in the East German system as it is.

The aims of polytechnical education are entirely laudable; but as they are being applied within the fabric of the school system certain oddities may be noted. In the first place, with the relationship to be established between enterprise or farm and school a singular element of luck may be present. Whatever the syllabus, and no matter how rationally it has been constructed, it cannot match the distribution of different kinds of industry and agriculture throughout the G.D.R. In consequence, while all boys and girls cannot get the same chance of access to work for their day's work in production, it is probably more important to note that the quality of their achievement in metal, electro-technics, or animal study may vary widely. Degrees of accuracy and tolerance of good workmanship may vary from pupil to pupil; but they should not be permitted to vary from school to school. It may well be possible for the facilities for polytechnical education to be developed, so that the degree of accuracy achieved in similar work in schools in other countries and in technical institutions in G.D.R. itself will be expected and obtained in factory conditions.

Moreover, while the economic development of a modern community possibly demands some educational reform like the introduction of polytechnical education, and while this may be of great significance to all citizens, including the teachers, one should not lose sight of the simultaneous need for even further development of the professional role of the teacher. Co-operation between teachers and the rest of society is obviously everywhere urgently needed; it is urged that a plea should be heard for a further advance for teaching.

The advantages arising from the economic administration of larger units must not become a force against architectural experiment with new school plans or against adventurous design in school furniture. Physical conditions can influence the learning situation. Uniformly planned schools may not be good educationally; solidly built school furniture firmly fixed for excellent reasons of safety or hygiene may destroy the chance of real educational progress. Textbook production must be speeded up, and even within the common curriculum it might be of great professional stimulus to have varieties of textbook available. A common curriculum with a succession of common syllabuses need not impose a common textbook.

Quite clearly, unstreamed classes following a common curriculum are inclined to behave like a desert caravan and progress at the speed of the slowest camel. Equally clearly there is an acceptable educational condition at the base of the unstreamed undifferentiated treatment of a school system. With special schools for the totally ineducable, and with a grade system encouraging full group responsibility for the whole group, some of the worst of boredom as well as most of the impossibility has been removed for both children and teachers. However it is felt that group techniques and considerably more individual work would add even more to the interest of children and teachers without destroying the main social and cultural integrity of the class within the common school.

The danger behind the reference to these outstanding problems is that on each side of some arbitrarily constructed dividing line the teachers of the world may divide themselves into two camps with almost as much hazard for the children of the world as arises from the division at the political level. All teachers to the east of such a line may rightly or wrongly feel that they have achieved a sufficient understanding of method, materials, and organization of an education service so that they need never look West. Similarly those to the West, still widely diversified in philosophy, sense of purpose, content and methods may be tempted to feel stronger as a group simply because they differ from their colleagues east of some line or other. The truth is that professionally we have much to learn from each other. As far as concerns the theorists and planners of education in the G.D.R. – to whom this analysis of outstanding problems has already been presented – it may be claimed that many have a weekly familiarity with a journal like *The Times Educational Supplement*. It is open to doubt if as many on this side of the now rather more firmly constructed line ever see *Pädagogik*.

CHAPTER 10

Poland — A Statement of Aims and Achievements

Social background and aims of education

Polish educational experiences flow from the characteristic process of human development, which might perhaps be best described as a process of human growing-up to cope with the professional and social duties that confront man, and to take advantage of the opportunity for cultural advancement that is now being offered to the people. It is this same two-sided process of people's growing-up to meet the new living conditions and the new vistas of their further development that is at the heart of our contemporary educational problems.

The social changes now under way in Poland are universally known; but they are usually — and erroneously — held to be of interest for politicians only, and devoid of any importance for educational theory and practice. Quite the opposite. These changes bring millions of citizens into life situations completely new to them, and open up quite new vistas before them and their children.

One should first of all make a point of the whole nation's great effort aimed at an acceleration of economic and technological progress in our country. Before 1939 ours was a country of underdeveloped industry, backward agriculture, and a low standard of living, with numerous people emigrating in the "search for bread". The war and Nazi occupation inflicted severe wounds upon us. They destroyed not only our national monuments, but also the very foundations of everyday life: our towns and cities and our industrial plants. Ever since the liberation we have been mobilizing our resources to advance along the path of economic progress. It is not without sacrifices that we are building up heavy industry, expanding production in light industry, reconstructing our towns and countryside, building roads and bridges, bringing agriculture up-to-date, raising the standard of living of the masses and the level of consumption of basic foodstuffs, harnessing rivers, and electrifying the country. I could quote spectacular but true statistics illustrating this progress. This, however, is not my task. My task is to show the meaning of this process from the point of view of education. For it would be wrong for one to think that the only significance of these processes is their economic importance. These processes contain human meaning, too; let us not be too rash and divorce man from his economy. Economy is not only a matter of machinery, products and prices: economy means also human labour and people's consumption, and so it means their everyday life.

To mobilize our forces for the cause of economic progress means, from the educational point of view, the task of preparing cadres. But not only the few cadres of the highest-skilled specialists. The task is to prepare, first of all, a mass of workers, for industry and agriculture alike, and also for service occupations, so as to enable these workers to work ever better, more efficiently, in an ever more modern way. The culture of work has never ranked high in our country; the problem is how to lift it to a higher level. What are the duties and possibilities of education in this respect in the early stages of children's and youth's development? Technological education has always been fairly primitive in this country. What can be done to make it grow in the public at large, to raise it to a level commensurate with the atomic age?

It is a commonplace truth that education should prepare for life. But this commonplace truth is an actual truth in our situation – one showing unusual difficulties in fulfilling our tasks, for these difficulties indeed spring from the necessity of improving our life. Just consider a country retarded for ages in its socio-economic development, a country unprecedentedly ravaged by war – for such a country it is imperative to quicken its pace, for we cannot afford to wait. We must stride forward faster than countries rich in resources and wealth, having at their disposal an abundance of capital and experience. Consequently, we must bring up a generation prepared to march at the rate required, a generation able to win the strenuous struggle for the acceleration of economic progress, for the attainment of the level already enjoyed by the more fortunate nations of the world.

How often, indeed, people prove unequal to these objective, historic tasks! How strenuous were the efforts expended for launching industrial ventures never before existing in Poland, for instance the shipbuilding and chemical industries! In many cases it was not merely a matter of organizing vocational training alone. What is involved here is the matter of new human attitudes. If a peasant from a back-of-beyond village is to discard his traditional working tools – the horse and the plough – and engage in work employing modern agricultural machinery he has to transform deeply his entire attitude, all his occupational habits; he has to develop a new style of work and new skills of co-operation in work.

The great problem of technological progress in a technologically backward country is not expressed only in terms of investments, patents and licences; it is, first of all, a great problem of the education of people, the education of a tremendous army of workers at all levels, a problem of technological culture in society at large, and a problem of developing a truly modern attitude in society. There is no doubt about our economic demands growing faster than our capacity of meeting them: the demand for adequately prepared people still exceeds the "productivity" of the educational system.

This state of affairs prevails not only in the field of productive trades and occupations. A similar situation exists in the field of service occupations. Just as in many underdeveloped countries, so in Poland the network of services was not developed to a satisfactory extent in the past. There were too few physicians, too few teachers, too few employed in commerce. In this respect we have been obliged to accelerate the rate of making up for these shortcomings. While in many countries people look for jobs, here work to be done calls for more people. To this call people have to respond, although some of them do so without being adequately prepared. They have to take up occupational tasks to which they have not been trained and which exceed their skills and powers. Thus it is necessary to increase their competence continually, and to acquire additional and new qualifications. The country is flooded with a multitude of knowledge- and skill-improving courses, which give a characteristic trait to our life.

The human aspect of this widespread action of professional qualification improvement is quite obvious: people want to grow up to cope with the tasks posed to them by the historical development of their country in which they participate. The difficulty of these tasks arises not only from the necessary acceleration of the country's economic development and the ever heavier demand for adequately trained cadres, but also from the fact that these tasks are now confronting social strata which have never faced them before.

In the pre-1939 period the better-off strata had a virtual monopoly of all the higher rungs of the professional ladder. The social revolution in our country is doing away with this bad tradition of monopoly and discrimination. Today, an opportunity is offered to all the citizens of the country to enter all professional posts, including the highest ones. To bring this opportunity to fruition a proper educational policy providing the necessary training is called for, as well as an impressive personal effort by the men and women, some of them no longer young, who have come to fill posts of distinction and responsibility.

Ever increasing in numbers is the group of people filling high and responsible professional posts who come from strata that have for ages been barred from taking up such work. A new professional intelligentsia is being formed. We call it "the people's intelligentsia" to stress this sociological innovation: those men and women got their education under new social conditions, and are a first-generation intelligentsia.

The process of developing people from all social strata for new professional tasks is linked very closely with an over-all maturing of citizens – on the one hand for new situations and social and political duties, and on the other for new opportunities of personal cultural development.

Social and political changes in Poland can be viewed from more than the political standpoint. In this connexion I would like to go back to the idea I have already mentioned when speaking of Poland's economic development, namely that these social changes contain educational implications of great import. The socialist democracy which we are now building in our country is something more than the complex of objective forms and institutions in public life: it is at the same time a way of life for real men and women, their everyday social activity, the atmosphere they create. Socialist democracy calls up masses of ordinary people to participate in the management of social life; it gives them access to cultural values and facilitates their taking advantage of them. But to what an extent these social duties are to be taken up by the people, in what measure the people will be able to use their legitimate opportunities, to what degree they will really and personally avail themselves of the culture opened to them – this is decided and shall be decided by the people themselves. That is to say, in final account, it is decided by their upbringing and self-education.

We are witnessing and participating in a great social surge towards an organization of social life built in an ever greater measure on the principle of self-government. We are expanding the competence of local self-government. We are developing responsible workers' self-government in manufacturing establishments. We are at the same time witnesses of and participants in a great social drive towards the universal dissemination of culture, towards a widening of the scope of cultural participation. These social currents find their expression in the personal experiences and aspirations of men and women, in their hopes and plans, in the context of their everyday life. Great social changes in this way reach deep into the personal lives of the individuals who are ever more clearly committed to adjusting themselves to the social duties and rights now enjoyed by everybody, and to the opening opportunities of personal cultural development.

Such, then, are the fundamental characteristics of social change in Poland which I have tried to present as the basis and background of our educational experiment. It has come to life under the conditions described above, chiefly by placing before people their great professional and social tasks, and opening up to them the full opportunities of social and cultural participation.

The chief features of educational development

What are the features of our educational development under such conditions?

Their first specific trait is an unheard-of expansion in the range of educational activity. It covers not only the children and youth but also adults. It is known that adult education in many countries – as in ours – has a rich tradition; but never before did we witness such a tide of adult education and further education as is surging nowadays. When we say in our country that all Poland is studying we are telling the truth; because in all age-groups, in all social strata, in all professions, in towns and villages thousands of people are improving their professional knowledge, expanding their horizon of general education, and seeking for contact with science and art.

These processes are happening in manifold organizational forms. They are found in full-time schools for adults, with varied levels of instruction; in evening and correspondence courses; in "people's universities"; in "centres of culture" and clubs; in societies for the promotion of knowledge and the arts; through the advisory service for educational self-help; and in museums and theatres which run their own educational schemes.

In many fields of this action new educational problems crop up: they are those of raising and deepening the culture of the masses. I shall not exaggerate if I say that among numerous European educators – in Poland too – the view has hitherto prevailed that the main task of educators is to rear outstandingly bright pupils, and to bring up an élite; while educational and training activity directed towards the masses has seemed rather to be a drudgery for the teacher, which could not rise above the "primary" level. When specialists in the theory and practice of adult education met to discuss their tasks, those among them who advocated a programme of intensive education commanded more respect than those in favour of an extensive education programme. In many countries no success was reached in attempts to overcome the scholastic dualism which consists in providing two separate paths of education: one for the élite, the other for the masses. This situation was reflected in educational theories representing education as a process of protection for the development of outstanding individuals.

We have accumulated our educational experience in carrying out completely different tasks. We are desirous of raising the cultural level of the masses and deepening this culture. To use traditional terminology, we want to achieve intensiveness in our extensive educational activity. What an ambitious and difficult task! But this is no arbitrary conceit of educators. It is indeed in this direction that powerful social forces are at work. Theatres and concert-halls are packed to capacity, crowds patronize museums; in this connexion let me recall that the exhibition of French art organized in the Warsaw National Museum two years ago attracted such crowds that it was necessary to call in the police to control their passage. Books are printed in huge editions, in proportion to the population. This is especially the case with Polish and European classics. We, the educators, must meet these requirements advanced by the masses themselves, and must encourage, foster and cultivate these demands.

How are we to develop and deepen the culture of the masses? How can we reach a point at which a common cultural language links all the social strata of the nation?

The solution of these tasks should serve the great cause of future civilization, free both from the sceptical degeneration of a decadent culture and from the barbarity of the primitive. Certainly this is not exclusively a Polish problem. It is the crisis of our entire European civilization, which is now threatened equally by the cultural decomposition of the old strata and the cultural slackness of younger strata. What course can we steer between the two dangers? The educational experience that we are gleaning along this path in Poland comes not only from the field of adult education but also from the schools for teenagers.

The easy access to all levels of education now offered to young people from all social strata must be joyfully welcomed and recognized by all people struggling for the realization of the democratic ideals of equality. The offer of such access, however, faces educators with an extremely difficult and responsible task. What is to be done is not only the creation of a school system with no blind alleys; it is not only an expansion of services of various types making it possible for the children of not-so-well-off parents to study. The main point is, at the same time, to provide consistent educational care, which (in many important respects) must differ from what educators have been accustomed to extend towards children from the prosperous classes.

The entire educational and didactic traditions of secondary and higher education in Europe developed in social conditions that made them cater for young people from wealthy families. They had already acquired a certain background of general education and social manners in their homes. When the secondary schools and universities become predominantly the haven of young people from worker and peasant families – which is now happening in Poland – there arise completely new educational problems.

Many secondary school teachers and professors in university-type institutions met with criticism and misgiving this new kind of youth, rather raw and simple. These young people had little in the way of general education and social graces. They were not easily aroused intellectually. They showed no scintilating intellects. They formulated abstract sentences only with difficulty. But it was precisely for these professors, greatly senior to their charges and accustomed to working with different students, that contact with this new kind of youth provided a source of unexpected experience. This new youth proved to be diligent and persevering. Young people advanced with dignity and doggedness along the paths towards culture now being opened to them. They learned to go to the theatre, although formerly they knew only the cinema at best. They started to frequent concerts. For the first time in their lives these young people entered museums, and took up reading the classics.

School system and organization

In the pre-1939 period Poland's school system was based on the seven-grade universal school. All children in the seven to fourteen age group were obliged to attend this school and to graduate. In fact, not all the children of this age group were at school – there was a period when almost one million were not attending schools – and not all the pupils reached the seventh grade. Sometimes, because of repeating the grades, they were only halfway in school when already fourteen years old. Sometimes they went to a school with no seventh grade in it. Such incomplete schools existed mostly in the villages. These were so-called one-room schools, i.e. schools in which there was only one teacher. In such schools a slightly expanded syllabus of four grades was covered. The school-leaving certificate of such schools did not give the same rights as the complete seven-grade school graduation certificate. For this reason the great majority of peasant children were barred from further education.

New difficulties bristled at the entrance to the secondary school, made up of a four-grade secondary school and a two-grade lyceum. The secondary school admitted entrants graduated from the sixth class of the universal school. Only the best-prepared, that is the children of well-to-do parents, could gain admission. A six-year course of study called also for large expenses, particularly so since upon graduation one had to take into account further study, because the secondary-school graduation certificate gave no vocational qualification whatsoever. All these combined to bring about a situation such that in higher education – universities and polytechnical schools – the bulk of students were of *bourgeois* extraction. It is useful to recall that in agricultural higher schools students of peasant extraction amounted to a small percentage and it was only in theological schools that they were more numerous.

Thus the pre-1939 school system in Poland failed to embrace all the school-age children and it did not serve all social strata in an equally fair way. This was an exceedingly élite-serving system. It was just this élite-serving aspect that attracted our main attack launched in People's Poland. The attack resulted in an impressive victory. All children of school age came to be really covered by the universal seven-grade school system. Likewise strenuous efforts were made to provide the same level of teaching for all universal primary schools: one-classroom schools were transformed into many-classroom schools with several teachers. An overwhelming majority of peasant children has been since receiving the same education as the children attending schools in towns and cities. The primary school is a universal school indeed and provides for great masses of youth a path towards further scholarship.

Further opportunities are as follows. Graduates from class seven of the seven-year primary school may either enter the four-year general education secondary school or a four- to five-year vocational secondary school. Upon graduation at either of the schools a maturity certificate is issued entitling the graduate to higher education. If neither of these two secondary types is chosen, primary school graduates go on to lower vocational schools – industrial, crafts and trades, or agricultural – or they engage in vocational activity, in the parents' farmstead in most cases. Then they are still able to study in part-time education establishments.

Expansion of the educational system allows for an ever increasing number of young people to be embraced by systematic school. Those in the seven to fourteen year age group all come under the obligation to attend the universal primary school. One hundred per cent attend school. This seems to be a very important accomplishment, all the more so when in many European countries a considerable portion of the seven to fourteen year olds no longer attends school.

Moreover, Poland's teenagers over fourteen years of age are to a large extent studying in full-time schools. At present, up to 80 per cent of all fourteen to sixteen year olds go on studying in full-time schools, while one-half of the number are studying in secondary schools with a four- to five-year curriculum. These are very high percentages since, as is known, in many European countries only a fraction of the fourteen to sixteen year olds go on with full-time education.

Finally, it should be pointed out that secondary and higher education has ceased to cater for the privileged. Pupils of worker-peasant origin make up 60 per cent of those at the secondary school. The repercussions of this situation are easily seen in higher education, where over one-half of the students come from the working class and peasantry.

It might be recalled that higher education in Poland may be reached not only through the general education secondary school but also through a vocational secondary school, in addition to many types of education-completing schools that also lead to higher studies. Consequently, university-level institutions have become more democratic than ever before. A widespread network of scholarships brings higher education within reach of the young people from less well-off families for whom it would otherwise be impossible to study. The body of students in university-type colleges is now many times more numerous than in the pre-1939 period – there are now about fifty such students in every 10,000 inhabitants – and still the needs of the developing economy and culture absorb all the university and college graduates, providing jobs for them. Over one-half of the professional intelligentsia got their diplomas after 1945.

Now, about our difficulties and tasks in the field of educational development. First and foremost we have a crisis of accommodation in schools for all children born after 1945, who are very numerous. This population bulge has reached our schools, and will increase from year to year. In 1960 the seven to fourteen age group accounted for over 15 per cent of the total population. The burden may be gauged by remembering that in many Western countries this age group accounts for only 9–12 per cent of the total population.

Secondly, we have the arduous task of doing away with "repeating" pupils, whom we want to bring on to the seventh grade so that they thus finish full primary school. The task of providing the secondary general education as well as vocational school also bristles with knotty problems. As we have already remarked, only one-half of the youngsters of suitable age are covered by secondary schools; but we are also very much concerned with the lot of the other half, whom we would gladly see attending either a full-time day secondary school or receiving their secondary education while working on a job.

Finally we have to tackle the problem of the secondary-school leavers, a portion of whom cannot be admitted to the university-status schools. They should be directed to short-time qualification courses to get training for professional employment, and that rapidly. An important question confronting us today is what secondary-school teaching should be like to facilitate such rapid vocational or professional training.

Notwithstanding these difficulties we hold our education system to be rightly oriented. Of special importance are our achievements in the way of democratization, which do not come about easily in many European countries. Our education system has proved equal to this task: our secondary school, as we have said, is not a bottle-neck obstructing the progress of young people towards universities, but is increasingly becoming accessible. Thus secondary-school leavers are more numerous than the university level colleges can manage to admit. Still, by this achievement the secondary school serves to enrich the intellectual level of society, a matter of the utmost importance from the point of view of our socialist economy and culture.

We also value highly our achievements in placing secondary and higher education within the reach of children from all sections of society. Many European countries are far behind what we have managed to attain. In the wake of the social revolution that has taken place in our country, our education system has done away with the "for the privileged" drawback which still besets secondary education in many countries. Our country's education system has become a really democratic property owned by everybody.

We feel justified, because of these achievements, in being hopeful about the future. Although there is still a great deal to be done, we believe our path to be correct, and feel that it will necessarily be followed by all nations. For it is through the spreading of education to cover the great possible numbers, and through raising the level of it, that the world is able to progress further.

Precisely for this reason we are today busy reforming Poland's schooling system: the period of compulsory basic education, equal for all, is being extended. Starting from the 1963 school year, the eight-grade primary school will be made compulsory (pupils entering it, as formerly, at their seventh year of age), and serve as a basis for the four-year general education secondary schools, the four- to five-year vocational secondary schools, and the lower vocational schools.

Socialist humanism

Socialist humanism is the prime ideal and the main content of our educational endeavour.

In order to grasp this ideal of humanism, which we desire to make the essence of education for contemporary man in Poland, we must first define explicitly the modern meaning of this humanism, differing greatly from traditional humanism.

Traditional humanism came into being and developed under conditions in which people were only beginning to see the importance and possibility of mastering the forces of nature and the forces of history. To be a true man at that time meant to cut oneself off from the real conditions of the people's social life, thus fleeing from man's social duties. We remember that writers such as Thomas More and philosophers such as Francis Bacon sharply contested such an attitude; but the conception that to be a human meant not only to take interest "in what is human", but also to transform the reality of nature and in particular social reality, and make it become worthy of man – this conception was only in the making.

The problems of traditional humanism were centred on setting the human mind free from the shackles of inhuman notions and images which, imposed from the outside, hampered its determination to think about the world and about man. The problems of modern humanism consist, first and foremost, in setting the people free from the degrading thraldom of an inhuman world of social reality shaped by forces defying human interference, a world denying to millions of people a chance of humane life. The problems of modern humanism are indeed what Comenius described as the "improvement of all things human", and what Marx defined as "the overcoming of alienation through social revolution".

The true meaning of modern humanism is this: to transform social reality to suit the needs of all people, and coping with the tasks laid upon the people by this process of transformation.

This is supplemented by another, very important characteristic of this humanism, namely its forward look. Thus the problems of humanism, which have predominantly been the problems of human *traditions*, under these circumstances come to be the problems of human *intentions*. This, of course, does not signify the abandonment of traditions, but does signify its participation in the mainstream of modern life as marked out by the perspectives of the future. In this way new and baffling problems crop up: how to view in the new way the traditional problems of our living heritage.

The forward look referred to contains another very important facet; for the struggle for the future has long been going on through science and technology. Still, grave doubts are often raised to contest this new thesis. A specific hostility between the different standpoints persists. There are humanists who hold humanism to be an opposition to science and technology. On the other hand, there is no dearth of scientists and technologists who believe that the social meaning and value of their work eliminates the superfluous and outdated remnant of humanism.

It appears, however, that the truly modern problem hinges on victory over this trend to struggle and opposition, by bringing out the profoundly human sense both of humanism and of science and technology. Views expounded by some humanists, saying that there is no room for an alliance between humanism and science and technology, are incorrect. For traditional humanism was the ideology of reason, the ideology of the liberation of man. This ideology today wields the weapon of nothing but science and technology. Not only do the latter contradict humanism's tradition but they strive for the fulfilment of what has always been most important in that tradition. The Promethean traditions of human freedom once took on their shape in the daring philosophy that challenged scholasticism. But these traditions could find their weapons only in science and technology, which set the people free from the bondage and authority of blind forces.

It is clear that both science and technology must be aware of these "humanistic" tasks; yet, under capitalism, they could hardly be aware. Experiences of the social role of technology in nineteenth and twentieth centuries justified – to a great extent – the misgivings harboured by the humanists. But, under new social conditions not everything that has caused such misgivings in the past need inevitably recur. Antihumanistic trends in the use of science and technology must be curbed and are in fact being brought to heel.

Simultaneously, the actual progress of science and technology shows the fallacy of believing that the very nature of such progress is inhumane. It is only an underdeveloped technology that degrades man to the role of a robot slaving for the machine; a well-developed technology liberates human beings from the drudgery of purely manual labour as well as from the monotony of mechanized labour. An especially telling model of rapprochement between man and modern work is automation.

The problems faced by modern humanism are those of combining science and technology with humanism, of surmounting their mutual suspicion and mutual isolation. The problems of a humanism which is aware that modern man lives and is active in a world created and kept going by science and technology are the problems of having science and technology serve mankind. It appears specially important to bring home to modern society these aspects of the matter. There is a tendency to view man as opposed to the science and technology created by him, or to view science and technology as being opposed to man and his life.

If this reasoning is right, then the role of the humanities in the education of modern man must be put on a different footing from what has been the rule till now. In today's school curricula the humanities are represented mainly by instruction in the languages, literature, and the teaching of history in its social and political aspects. In the school curricula now to be worked out one must insist on a fundamental widening and re-shaping of these humanistic values.

It is imperative that we introduce into the curriculum the science of society, together with the science of the motives of human behaviour, and above all the science of the principles of social activity and of man's ability to control himself and to take part in teamwork. It is essential that history be taught in such a way as to make the students grasp the process of social development in civilization and, in particular, the part played by science and technology in the progress of civilization. It must be demanded that the teaching of literature be extended – jointly with the teaching of drawing and music – so as to become for young people a true introduction into the world of art in its various aspects and its manifold idioms.

Humanities interpreted in such a way not only will not be opposed to the natural sciences and technology but will co-operate with them, just as was the case in the great epochs of the past. For we have to bear in mind that Plato put philosophy on an equal footing with philo-technics. Humanities thus interpreted not only will not oppose modern living but will be able to prove that the programme of linking school with life is something more than a mere bond between school and productive work; it is truly the connexion of school with all kinds of human work, with their socio-cultural aspirations and needs.

On moral education

In organizing today our widespread activity in secular education in Poland, we perpetuate the noble traditions of the struggle to make the schools independent of the Church and the monastic orders. We resume the traditions of educational work based on a social keystone and oriented towards social goals, traditions created by the activities of the National Education Committee in the eighteenth century. While taking up this tradition, we are also engaging in the thoroughly modern duties involved in expanding socialist construction in our country. We approach these tasks with modern scientific methods which allow for a correct definition of man and his behaviour. We feel that Marx's philosophy is a turning point in the conception of man and in the understanding of morality. We therefore feel that a truly modern moral education must be based on the concept of man as expounded by Marx.

In pre-Marxian times there were two great theories of man. The one defined man by referring to lasting and absolute values: man's essence consisted in his obedience and loyalty to those values. The other theory defined man on the basis of empirical analysis of his life: man's essence consisted in what he was actually like.

For long centuries a conflict raged between the two concepts, between those who approached man from the point of view of his "essence" and those who approached him from the point of view of "existence". The two adversaries made mutual charges: the former believed their opponents to be degrading man by concerning themselves exclusively with what he was like instead of demanding that he become such as the eternal values required him to be; the latter were of the opinion that their opponents were raving about abstract and fictitious human beings, while failing to view man as he actually was. The "essentialists" alleged that their adversaries played false to "humanity"; on the other hand the latter accused the "essentialists" of abandoning reality.

Signally glaring was the contrast of the two attitudes in the field of moral education: one group of contenders understood such education to be an expression of the actual existence of man, and thus adapted to his psychological or social nature; the other faction understood moral education to be a duty of subservience to absolute values, and were bent upon adapting man to his obligations – ideas about which varied. Again reciprocal charges cast doubts on the validity of both attitudes. Those who – as their opponents saw it – limited morality to an expression of human life as it actually was thus seemed to liquidate morality in general. To their adversaries, however, the opposing view seemed to be artificial and harsh in imposing a morality of obedience to absolute values and, while concerning itself with what man ought to be like, in failing to perceive what he was actually like.

Marx reached beyond these traditional antinomies in the concept of man; he pointed out that man is active, and by his activity creates the reality in which he lives and which develops as the work of man in history. The significance of this standpoint was that man can be defined neither by a metaphysical understanding of his "essence" nor by an empirical description of his "existence". The existence of man is of his own making, and changes under the impact of his actions. Therefore, "existence", as it appears at a given moment, never tells everything about man. What he is or was like does not fully define man, for no account is then taken of what he will be like by following his own actions. Therefore, the definition of man as suggested by the metaphysical point of view is also insufficient. His "essence" is only a generalization of earlier historical experiences. Man is not such as the absolute values are; but it is these very values that are a reflexion of what man was like till this day. Man's "essence" keeps changing and growing as a result of changes in existence created by man himself.

This understanding of man opened up completely new vistas for the moral education of mankind. Moral education was no longer to be the subjection of people to absolute values according to their differing interpretations. On the other hand, moral education was no longer a matter of bringing people up according to their actually existing impulses, inclinations and aspirations, or according to their psychological and sociological content. Moral education was intended to be the realization of this fundamental truth: that man plays an active part in creating a world of his own, that his participation in the work of transforming this world towards the goals set by history is essential – with full mastery of men over the conditions of their life.

Moral education entails not only a breach with the power of the Church and the forces of religious metaphysics, but also the abolition of all that reduced man's role to obeying nature or the existing social order. It requires the end of all that kept him in the snares of alienation, of whatever hamstrung the revolutionary activity that was to abolish the pattern of the existing world of bondage in order to create a new, hitherto non-existent world of human freedom – a world based on human mastery over natural and social life conditions. Moral education is a truly humane education, that is, an education of people who are creating their human world for everyone and who shoulder the responsibility for this world.

In keeping with these theoretical concepts the practical, secularly moral education in the working-class movement under Marxian socialist leadership has always embraced a wide range of problems, from the world outlook to revolutionary social activity. Struggle against religion-mindedness has always been waged in both fields; in both fields foundations of a truly human thinking and action have also been laid.

The socialist revolutions of the twentieth century have by their victories enabled many nations of the world to implement a Marxist social programme. Moral education has therefore become a far-reaching and many-sided endeavour in the upbringing of youth, so as to prepare them for creative participation in the work of building a social order that will be the expression of people emancipated from the demands of nature and from man's own wrong ideas, of people who have mastered the conditions of a life equally accessible to all.

The fact that this activity was aimed at creating a new social reality – without further preparing people for the next world or moulding the abstract beauty of their inner self; the fact that this social reality was intended to be something novel in history, something that could not be built upon existing social and psychological traditions but had to be created in defiance of them – all this is the reason for a spectacular reorientation of perspectives in relation to morality and to moral education.

According to our concept, moral education is concerned with the individual in the context of his social duties. Challenging those traditional beliefs which hold morality to be an internal and private affair, we are of the opinion that morality is an internal matter – but of such a type that it leads to objective actions important for social development. We believe that the basic moral problems of modern man are those concerning his responsibility for the course of social events of the widest possible scope. This definition includes matters both of immediate personal concern and also as remote as those which derive from a feeling of solidarity with all people struggling for their freedom.

In this great epoch of historical changes which, of necessity, is a great epoch of individual choice involving taking one's stand on this or that side of the barricade, moral problems are the problems of this choice and the responsibility flowing therefrom. Questions of so-called "small-scale moral practice" – everyday good deeds towards people in our immediate environment – have an unbreakable link with those great moral problems of the epoch in which human aspirations, fears, hopes and efforts find their deepest reflexion. Never before was the human individual so much involved in these matters; never before were moral problems those of people building their own future. Therefore all actions are subject today to an assessment from the moral point of view – not only the individual's actions immediately concerning some other person, but also the individual's actions which promote or retard definite social processes. They thus serve objective forms, activities or institutions, and so directly concern people at large. Man-to-man relations are realized today not only in the sphere of direct personal contacts but also through the objective world being created by people who carry the responsibility for it. Moral education, without challenging the importance of matters of concern in its earlier concepts, is now focusing its attention upon the problems of man's responsibility for the world he creates. The more complicated this world becomes, the more universal the participation of people in creating it, and the stronger the links and bonds between every country and region of the world – the heavier is the responsibility shouldered by the people.

The ethics of man's responsibility for the world he makes does not challenge the value of man's efforts at self-improvement. It only orients them in a different direction and applies more exacting criteria to them. Nor does it deny the importance of impulses and desires as motives for moral action; but, in requiring actions to be put to an objective test, it tends to make inner motivation more profound and crystallized. The ethics of man's responsibility for the world he makes does not underestimate the importance of moral directives for direct man-to-man intercourse, either. It only visualizes that in today's world man may be to his fellow-man either friend or foe, even without knowing him at all; for he does either good or evil to him, depending on the working mechanism of the objective world.

The demand for man's responsibility for the world he creates opens up horizons of moral education more widely than ever before. By introducing, in addition to traditional problems, criteria pertaining to responsibility as well, we also raise novel and baffling moral problems of man's objective activity – especially in relation to his work, to his creativeness in science and art, to social activity, &c., and to his co-operation with other men in actions which are invariably collective in their nature.

Within the category of these novel moral problems also inhere those most complex problems which are called, in a most general way, "the overcoming of alienation". This term refers to the problems of critically overcoming illusions and self-deceptions (of manifold kinds and origins) which sap human effort: problems of shaking off dead tradition while preserving the living one; problems of that struggle with dogmatism which petrifies definite stages of human activity in the field of ideas or institutions, investing them with absolute and unassailable reality; problems of courage to counteract the inertia and smugness of an environment reluctant to show resource in improving reality, or courage to be free from the lures of luxuries, conformism, and the false fascinations of Don-Quixotry; the problem of capacity to break through the customary inner inhibitions hindering the adoption of the novel and the future, so as to abandon the old ways of looking at things and to meet the nascent half-way; problems of wrenching oneself free from *bourgeois* habits of viewing oneself in the categories of the "world for myself", and of placing oneself instead in solidarity with all those who are transforming the unyielding and hostile world into a reality obeying the will of mankind.

This extensive horizon of moral duties implicit in the modern world and its challenges to human enterprise represent the main content of secular moral education as understood today in our country.

Teaching aims

Our teaching aims are based on the propositions just discussed. In teaching we consistently drive at imparting to our pupils the knowledge of scientific facts which enable them to grasp the fundamental laws governing society and nature. Thus, the basis for a scientific world outlook are laid in the minds of the students who consequently are better equipped to participate more consciously in the work of transforming nature and in social development.

In shaping the fundamentals of a scientific world outlook, we take practical steps towards the education of a brave and conscientious citizen of People's Poland. His work and social activity will be facilitated by his correct understanding of the real world. We do not struggle with religion. Religious instruction in state schools is not in any way impeded.[1] Being strict about respect for the individual's

[1] Since this chapter was written, the Polish Sejm (Parliament) has decreed that religious education be discontinued in State schools, and the authorities are gradually closing convent schools. (October, 1962).—Ed.

convictions, we do not prohibit religious practices to children whose parents wish them to attend to religious duties; but we do not force all pupils of our schools to practise religion, either.

We are firm about socialist morality being based, and necessarily so, on a secular world outlook, but all people who, while embracing a religious faith, at the same time discharge their civic obligations are subject to no discrimination whatsoever. Consequently, we are desirous of educating our young people to be convinced that the only instrument for learning about and transforming the world is science; yet at the same time, we also want our youth basically to respect other individuals' personal religious experiences, even without understanding or sharing such experiences.

In process of developing the elements of a scientific world outlook as a mainspring of the process of learning about reality and its guiding principles, and, at the same time, as a starting point for conscious and planned activities aimed at shaping reality so as to conform with the requirements of man, we are placing an ever greater emphasis on education in technology. It is our belief that the traditional concept of a so-called general education linked traditionally to the humanistic disciplines – classical linguistics in particular – should be transformed by introducing the elements which are becoming ever more important in the modern man's life. Today Poland has already become a huge building site; millions of our youths are taking up their posts in industrial plants, in mining enterprises and steel-mills, at the controls of technical equipment. Spectacular tasks are being undertaken to mechanize our backward agriculture and to develop agricultural sciences. Large-scale electrification of our country is proceeding apace, work on harnessing rivers and the construction of waterways is continuing, hundreds of towns and settlements are being built. We have to prepare numerous and efficient cadres of workers in all these fields. We must weed out the remnants of lingering superstition left over from the past, connected with the exclusively rural character of our economy which employed primitive methods of work. We must make a leap forward in the technological education of our society. It is obvious that the young people lead the enthusiasm for technology employed for the benefit of man. It is in every way essential to help our young people in this respect by organizing what we call polytechnical training.

A heated discussion is now taking place in our country as to its content and ways of organizing our polytechnical education. But we all agree on certain basic principles. We want polytechnical training to infuse knowledge about the scientific fundamentals of various branches of production. It follows from this that we do not mean it to be vocational training, which is intended to prepare for work in a definite trade or vocation. Polytechnization of training is based on the teaching of mathematics, physics, chemistry, biology. We try to organize instruction in such a way as to make the students realize the practical consequences of scientific laws. Without wrecking the organization of the school's teaching job, we attempt to link theoretical instruction with practical training in school laboratory rooms and even – if that is practicable – have the pupils participate in socially useful productive pursuits. Schools in rural areas are well placed to organize this sort of activity, which, without overburdening the pupils and without dragging them away from study, is a valuable share in the work of the neighbourhood. While building up the elements of polytechnical training in the general education schools, we gain confidence that by so doing we are better preparing the young generation for further vocational training and for subsequent vocational activity. We feel sure that we are thus going to strengthen the understanding of the scientific basis of production, to develop self-reliance and independent mental creativeness in the field of technology, and make the choice of vocation easier. Also, to a certain extent, we shall facilitate transfer from one vocation to another, which often proves imperative under the conditions of our rapidly expanding industry.

Stress on the polytechnical character of education does not undermine its humanistic elements at all. Quite the contrary, as is obvious, for our technology is built up for the benefit of man. Special care is given to bring to general notice and to consolidate knowledge of the progressive traditions in European civilization from antiquity onwards, while special attention is paid to our national culture. Never before in our history were the great writings of poets and writers of the Renaissance, Enlightenment and Romantic periods so close to the hearts of the mass of readers. Not until our time was such stress placed on the dissemination of our noble traditions of struggle for social justice, for freedom of conscience, for independence and for scientific truth. We want our youth to acquire from our schools a pride in everything that was noble in our history, in all the lasting achievements contributed by our scientists and men of art, of all those great examples of self-sacrifice and daring in the struggle for progress. As we work to strengthen the links joining the young generation to our progressive traditions we are equipped, in this field too, with profuse aids advanced by life itself. With meticulous care and love People's Poland preserves from destruction all her most precious monuments, making them accessible and reviving them from wartime destruction. The old cities of Warsaw and Gdańsk have been raised from the ruin to which the last war reduced them; hundreds of monumental churches are being reconstructed; thousands of ancient houses are being rebuilt in the Silesian and Pomeranian regions; gorgeous castles and palaces are being restored to their former splendour. All this reconstruction and preservation work does not create artificial sanctuaries: in the old town-houses people who build the new, socialist Poland make their homes. The splendid edifices of the Renaissance or Classical periods serve the new culture, the culture of the popular masses set free from the shackles of oppression.

Of course, this element of tradition does not make up the whole content of our humanistic education. When teaching history, we strive to make our students understand that the course it has traversed was not a zigzag of random events, nor was it shaped by any whimsical feats of outstanding individuals. The goal we set ourselves is to impart to our pupils the faculty of discerning the firm trends in historical development revealed by the progress of productive forces and the development of social relationships. We do not deny the political character of our schools in the sense that we want them to bring up people with an understanding of the present historical situation, with an awareness of the historical paths of capitalist development, and with a grasp of the laws governing socialist construction. We do not conceal our desire to infuse our young people with a conviction, based upon scientific knowledge, that the capitalist system is entering the stage of its final decay; that the world's future belongs to free nations who, after shaking off the yoke of oppression and imperialist ideology, will easily find ways of mutual conciliation. We cherish also a desire that our teaching shall contribute to political education by facilitating creative vocational work done with the full realization of social consequences, by making for conscious and active participation in social activity, and for co-operation with the public administration. The People's State is the common boon of all its citizens; no one is exempted from reasonable and responsible care for its development within an individual's immediate reach. We desire our schools' work to prepare the masses of people to participate, with an ever-increasing scope, in the running of their own country; we desire our pupils and students to be able, through the education acquired, fully to discharge their duties in a vocation they have chosen and, moreover, guided by a clear-cut political consciousness, to take part in social and cultural life, and to participate in ideological and fieldwork organizations.

Educational methods

What methods are employed to fulfil our great and difficult tasks? We feel that goals and methods are inseparably linked to each other, and depend mutually on each other. Therefore, what has already been said about the situation in Poland and about our most urgent educational tasks serves to define, to a certain extent, our methods as well.

In teaching we are intent on transmitting systematic knowledge, on developing fundamental mental competence, on evoking the interest and self-reliance in thinking. In pursuing these goals do we use the "creative activity" methods, so keenly prescribed by *bourgeois* pedagogy? We do not employ these methods, deeming them neither right nor efficacious. They appear, we feel, to be based on mistaken psychological views which envisage an individual's development as preordained by its own inner forces, by its innate and unchangeable lines of interest. Our opinion is that an individual's mental development is closely related to its activities and to the teaching process it undergoes. That is why we do not attempt to follow the prescription "adapt school to pupil". We believe it to lead to upsetting the organization of the school's activity, and towards a harmful nursing of the accidental, whimsical and erratic lines of interest that are taken up by a child freed from the systematic and purpose-conscious care of the teacher. What we try to follow is the less easily implemented watchword of "adapting child to school"; that is to organize teaching work in such a fashion as to awaken pupils' interests along lines which are important and valuable.

This can be effected only because the school teaching process has been arranged in a proper sequence of increasing difficulties as regards the material taught, while the teaching is done systematically, and is meticulously controlled and tested. Only under such conditions can the pupil's mind develop, absorb knowledge, train its proficiency, and attain a certain degree of self-reliance. Minds, even those of great scholars, do not operate in a vacuum; they do not develop *per se*, but are cultivated according to the iron-handed discipline imposed by research work in science that opens up new vistas for the student and stimulates his inventive urge. Thus, and even more so, a child's mind is in even greater need of such care.

One might ask, however, whether by so doing we do not destroy a child's individuality, its specific talents and interests. Are we not imposing a mechanical uniformity? Are we not going back to the faults of former schools guilty of teaching everyone in the same way? We answer all these queries in the negative, and calmly so. While preserving a systematic and uniform course of teaching, we still provide outlets for individual likes and talents during classroom lessons, in extra-curricular activities, and in out-of-school activities alike. Our People's State attaches great importance to the adequate organization of such activities. It earmarks huge expenditure for the construction and equipment of "houses of culture" for youth, in which many kinds of workshops and laboratories bring forth and develop individual interests.

In keeping with our principles of didactics, we proceed to implement our aim, the child's adaptation to school, by drawing upon the educational discoveries of the past: the principle of the use of visual methods, and the principle of the pupil's active participation in school work. Developing and transforming these principles in line with the present level of psychological knowledge and practical possibility, we are now in the process of elaborating a didactic system which, though not brilliant with spectacular recommendations and not pursuing the vagaries of educational fashion – a phenomenon so typical of *bourgeois* educational theories – is based on a solid scientific foundation and is applicable to mass teaching by an army of teachers many thousands strong.

What are our educational methods? In the domain of personal education we do not follow the prescriptions of *bourgeois* pedagogy, most of them based to a great extent on the fallacious precepts of psycho-analysis, individual psychology or sociometry. We adopt unsophisticated but correct starting principles: we stress the role of consciousness and will in the process of training, we emphasize the creative role of the collective. We oppose the methods of educational breaking-in as adopted frequently by the old-type school. We also oppose modern methods that depend on resignation from moral education in favour of the sublimation of instincts, which is supposed to take place spontaneously and subconsciously without engaging the will and effort on the part of education itself. Of special importance in the process of education is the active participation of the pupil himself, with a clear-cut consciousness of the goals, the nature of duty, and a strong decision for positive activity. What we are driving at is the fostering of conscious discipline in our pupils, shaping in them the attitudes of personal commitment and responsibility.

Moral upbringing cannot proceed outside a collective. No man lives on his own. In our country, in particular, teamwork tends to become the dominant form in all fields. As educators, we could not possibly afford to ignore the significance of the collective, whose role is noticed by our young people everywhere. Teamwork has become the main system of working in productive enterprises; it is realized as indispensable for mechanized agricultural production; it enables scholars to plan for and tackle complex and difficult scientific problems; equally it is the motive force of both secondary and higher education. The educational influence of Makarenko and his books, of which progressive Western pedagogy is aware, has dispelled certain reservations raised against this method, such as the one charging it with nullifying or limiting the rights of the individual. In fact, it is the team context that offers most scope for individual development free from egoistic aberrations, away from the psychopathic complexes that bear so heavily upon *bourgeois* young people. Individuals thus trained are lively, anxious to work and act, optimistic, hard upon themselves but friendly towards others.

Education and instruction – as we have already remarked – do not stand in conflict in our country. We feel that only a sound character-training is able to shape an attitude towards the outside world and one's fellow men which calls for clear and critical thinking as a supplementing factor. A scientific world outlook derives in equal measure from theoretical teaching and from experiences gained by young people in practical life and collective activity. The attitude of the builder of socialism in our country is in an equal measure the result of both character-training and the inculcation of definite knowledge and abilities. Our pedagogy thus combines the teaching process and personal training in a closer coherence than ever before.

The problem of personality

Our experiments in education, resulting from our bringing instruction to everyone's front door, from the abolition of barriers blocking the access of certain groups of people to the higher rungs of the professional ladder, and from the opening up of cultural values and cultural participation to all – all these experiences serve us not only for the evolution of practical directives and more effective education activity, but also contain, at the same time, certain premises for more theoretical thinking.

First of all they are related to personality. The concept of personality has become the central conception of twentieth-century educational theory. Should generally accepted personality theories be unreservedly embraced by us in the light of our educational experiences? Is human personality really built as a specific form of superstructure, based on instincts and impulses developed or inhibited? Is it really an adaptation to the environment, or an imitation in one's life of the personal examples held out in an environment that is the main factor in personality-building – a concept advocated by others? Or, according to another view, is the shaping of personality a process of the individual choice of cultural values, and their thorough digestion in solitude?

When we follow attentively the development of our young people, when we watch in individuals the processes of progress and inhibition – the conclusions we arrive at differ in many respects from those just listed. Of course, I am not going to say that we fail to notice the explanatory importance of such concepts as inferiority complex, frustration, adaptation, the hierarchy of values, and so forth. But I feel that the heart of the problem of personality lies elsewhere.

Our experiences tend to show that personality is shaped in a process influenced primarily by factors that mark out in the historical and social environment the everyday situations of the people, and provide definite possibilities of further development. Numerous theories of personality have interpreted its development almost as if personality were something detached from historical and social actualities in which real people live and act – as if it were a product of inner psychomachia or a fruit of cultural spiritualization. Sociological theories have now, in point of fact, emphasized the role of environment; but in so doing they have virtually confined themselves to concern with adaptation to existing situations.

Our understanding of the problem is incomparably more dynamic. The motive force of personality transformations is, in our view, the social changes that are taking place in our country. These changes alter not only the situations and duties of the people but their developmental possibilities as well. I have tried to show how deeply political and economic developments, as they are commonly called, penetrate the lives of people; yet they are often thought to have little bearing, if any, on the problems of personality. I have attempted to make it clear that changes in the country's economic structure are not confined to questions of the ownership of the means of production or markets or merchandise, but also affect man the worker, man the producer, man the consumer; they have a bearing on his everyday life. What I have striven to point out is that changes in a country's social structure are not confined to alterations in public laws and institutions, or a rearrangement of social patterns. They also create for the people completely new situations which make them live a new way of life, offering them novel perspectives for personal development and the planning of personal futures.

It follows inevitably from our experience that the decisive role for personality transformation – for its progress or decay – is played by people's everyday life as shaped by the historical development of the world and of their own country in particular, and by the requirements and perspectives implicit in this development. And – as it appears to me – this holds for everyone as well as for our countrymen. For have not the events of the last world war, the occupation, concentration camps, and resistance movement given a proof that human personality is not spun in an isolated world of private experiences and desires but stems from a dramatic dialogue between man and history?

When we discuss personality, we are touching upon a matter which seems to be one of the most essential problems of modern education, that is to say, the problem of modern man's attitude in relation to life. We are worried, as educators, by the swelling wave of pessimism and frustration engulfing the world and young people in particular, by mounting moods of restlessness and uncertainty, by a fading of enjoyment in life. Educators cannot banish the thought that their vocation is concerned with their pupils' finding in their lives a happy path worthy of man, so that they can see the charms of life even when – especially when – it involves hardship and sacrifice.

Our young people – like young people in many other countries –

are not easy to handle. In our country, too, we are anxious about disturbances of personal balance, a lowering of the standards by which one's conduct is measured, an aggravation of aggressiveness against one's family, school, environment. At the same time, though, there are young people who toil and persevere, who deeply cherish the inspiring perspectives of social tasks now facing the whole country, young people who are selfless and enthusiastic.

I am not concerned here with the numerical proportions of the various youth groups. What I would like to point to is the essential mechanism shaping attitudes towards life. Of the utmost importance are two factors which may seem at the first sight to be contradictory. An individual cannot realize and experience the meaning and value of life if he or she feels there are no hopeful perspectives for the future. Without such hopes life is degraded to a grim nightmare, a day-to-day existence lacking all sense and full of man's craving only for the journey's end, the famous *fin de partie*. And yet, before we can experience the sense and value of life, it is also necessary for it here and now to live up to human expectation. When the present time is but a road towards the future, and when man fails to find sense and enjoyment in what is "here and now", his life becomes insipid and gloomy.

Our young people are well aware of the humanistic perspectives of the socialist revolution; they see the future as abounding in hope. But precisely because of this future vista young people notice all too clearly the shortcomings and imperfections of the present day. This is sometimes a source of disappointment, disillusionment, and frustration. I dare say it is not only Polish youth who cannot answer the question why there is still such a vast amount of evil in the world even though people already have such clear knowledge of the ways of doing away with it. This contrast between the present day and the vision of the future, however, more often than not is the springboard for a decision to live and work for the complete implementation of the world's improvement.

When people come to assume the responsibility for the social reality they live in, they cannot but persist in fighting the evil; for to give up the fight would wreck the whole essence of their lives. As we enter upon an epoch in which people are to be masters of the forces of nature and the forces of society, the sense and value of living can and must be found in such mastery – over a civilization of man's making so as to make it a civilization worthy of man.

This is the very core of modern experiences as met by our youth vacillating between hope and doubt, between action and resignation. Contemporary man realizes well that neither God nor his past history can explain or justify the evil existing in the present world. Therefore the only choices are either to feel an intruder in this world and wait for the judgement and verdict of one's fellow men, or to take up responsibility for the human value of man's world.

Perspectives

In Poland the great task of raising the young generation is not only the concern of schools and teachers. The young people themselves and the parents also co-operate. Parents' councils are set up in each school, and many works enterprises assume patronage over individual schools. Youth organizations co-operate with teachers in the struggle for better academic and educational progress.

The key post in the work of education is, of course, held by the teacher. This is self-evident, since we do not identify the educational process solely with the process of spontaneous psycho-biological development in the individual, or with his process of adaptation to the environment. As soon as we emphasize the important part played in personality building by purposeful work in education, we attach special importance to the teacher's activity. This is the driving force of our entire pedagogy, geared to its optimism and its belief in the practicability of transforming the world and re-educating mankind.

This short account of education in Poland would not be comprehensive if we failed to conclude with a mention of the difficulties we are struggling against, and the shortcomings and errors in our work. Of course, not everything is plain sailing for us. Far-reaching social changes have released boundless cultural forces in our country. But they have, at the same time, put very great tasks in the way of education and upbringing. We have to train in the shortest possible time numerous cadres of experts for all fields. The question is how to perform it rapidly, efficiently and without any lowering of standards. We must constantly raise the standard of elementary school, because all subsequent education hinges on the performance of the primary school. We find it difficult to cope with the training of skilful teachers for these schools. We are anxious to overcome the age-old handicap of the rural areas in terms of access to education while driving, at the same time, at the universalization of secondary education, which is a task easier to achieve in the towns. A network of clubs is being expanded to cover the whole of the country; but the path bristles with the baffling problems of adequately staffing them with trained personnel.

Rural youth is drifting to town in great numbers, particularly to the newly built or expanded industrial cities, where no satisfactory education or cultural care is provided for them. The newcomers do not always manage to organize their new lives properly or make reasonable use of the opportunities now open to them. The performance of our schools at all levels of the system renders fair results on the whole; but we are still grappling with difficulties of method, and are seeking ways of teaching which would train self-reliance in thinking better than we are able to do at present. Currently we are taking in hand a reform of secondary-school curricula and textbooks, our aim being to so arrange and time the teaching material as to allow for consolidating the pupils' brainwork. We are striving to build institutions of higher education for student populations several times greater than before 1939, while raising the training of research abilities and the techniques of scholarship to a higher level. To proceed successfully along this path it is necessary for us to analyse many points of principle in the realms of epistemology, psychology and didactics.

The difficulties we encounter stimulate our will for further work; for we staunchly believe in the rightness of the road we follow. In continuation of the great educational traditions which, since the times of Comenius and Pestalozzi, have formulated the social duties of teaching and education and pointed to the responsible part played by the teacher, we are now drawing up the fundamental principles of our work; these are principles embodying our optimistic confidence in man who is himself developing and growing while building a system of social justice. Our pedagogy teaches us to love children but to make stern and serious demands on the pupils. We shrink from ruining the joy of children's play, but we wish to prepare our pupils to lead a life of struggle for righteous values, for social justice and peace among nations, and for the further progress of culture in our own country. We are raising our youth to be selfless patriots, while simultaneously teaching them to love the great international tradition of campaigning for freedom and justice, to establish bonds of friendship and alliance with all the progressive youth of the world – above all with the youth of peoples still oppressed and in the midst of the struggle for their liberation.

In June, after passing their final examinations, hundreds of thousands of our young people leave the school buildings to meet the new, laborious life for which we have tried to prepare them to the best of our abilities. Our good wishes and hopes – the familiar good wishes and hopes of all educators – accompany them in this hour of their launching into life. We may fear whether they will prove equal to the tasks given them to discharge; but we know – and we deeply rejoice over this – that they are not going into life as people with feelings of redundancy or lacking a sense of self. They are embarking on their lives to cooperate in the noble and great things they help to translate into reality. We may fear whether they will cope with the duties they will have to fulfil, but we rest assured that these duties and tasks will mobilize them to redouble their efforts, which will go into the making of a new world and new people.

CHAPTER 11

China

The old system

The roots of the Chinese educational tradition can be traced back, through written works, for nearly four thousand years. For most of the time the dominant philosophy was, of course, Confucianism, itself a refined expression of the primitive traditions of the Chinese people. The aim was the formation, by exercises of an ethical, intellectual and musical sort as well as by rigorous physical training, of a man able to rule himself and others.

Paramount importance was ascribed to the influence of the parents and of the family. "Sons must be educated from the very earliest age. They must be taught to move, to behave, to speak properly, to display good manners, to distinguish between what is due to the old and to the young. When they are four or five years old, show them how to add and count; at six start teaching the written characters. While they are young, they should not get used to dainty food nor to fine clothing: as long as they are neither cold nor hungry, all is well.... After a few years, set them to serious study and let them take examinations... or else, once they know how to read and understand a contract or a tax-form set them to work in office or field..."

After the overthrow of the hereditary and warlike aristocracy (from about B.C. 200) and its replacement by the scholarly mandarinate, education became continually more bookish and formal. By the seventh century A.D. universities had been established as well as a formal examination system, itself the model from which modern examination systems in the West have been copied. From then to the beginning of the twentieth century, changes were relatively few and unimportant.

The chief of every well-to-do joint family engaged a tutor to teach the children living under his care – especially his own sons. The tutor might himself be a learned man, but more frequently was simply a young candidate for the most elementary examination. His place in the household was intermediate between that of adult members of the family and the servants or serfs. Classes were held in a room specially set aside, where the chief article of furniture and the most essential was the Tablet of Confucius, "the very holy, very perfect teacher of ten thousand generations". On entering, the children prostrated themselves before the tablet, and laid down an offering of rice and of incense on feast days.

The primary course, if it can be called a course, aimed at familiarizing the pupils with the shape of the characters. The tutor would show a scroll and then read the logographia aloud – without attempting to explain their meaning. Quite often, an explanation would in any case have been useless, since the scroll might show no more than a list of names. Later would come simple vocabularies, then archaic texts of a moral nature. So the children spent years learning a written language which was no longer spoken and which they did not understand: an excellent way of developing the memory, especially its visual aspect, and of causing complete atrophy of powers of observation and reasoning!

At the secondary level, provided the tutor was himself sufficiently educated, stress was laid on written composition, both in prose and verse. In addition, classical texts were studied in great detail, most attention being paid to the formal elements of grammar and expression. After seven or eight years of concentrated work, the young man was equipped with a thesaurus of ready-made conventional ideas and of apt quotations suited to every occasion. In addition, he had mastered the use of the brush and had probably developed an exquisite appreciation of calligraphy.

In addition to the private schools, provided and maintained by the joint-families, there were also independent public schools in many of the larger towns. Wealthy patrons sometimes clubbed together to buy land, provide a building, pay teachers. No fees were charged to the pupils, who were usually given food and clothing. Admission was by nomination: the governing committee, composed of the heirs of the founders, decided who should be allowed entry. The criteria applied were family connexions and unusual ability.

The most interesting feature of traditional Chinese education was the examination system already referred to, a system well established by the fourth century A.D. There were three grades, corresponding roughly to the bachelor's, the master's and the doctoral degrees of the west. All were official and organized by the State – we have here, in fact, a curious example of a civilized nation where the authorities ran examinations while making no effort to organize public education.

Any Chinese subject of the Empire – though not of any vassal state or people – had the right to present himself for the first examinations, held in the smaller towns once each year. There were three series of papers, set and supervised by the sub-prefects, the Prefects and the Rector respectively. The candidates were asked to write essays on extracts from the Classics (e.g. Discuss: – "The wise man notes three things: the will of Heaven, the orders of his superiors, the words of the wise") and to write verse (e.g. Set in verse: – "The waters of the stream announce by their colours the coming of autumn; the wild geese take their flight." Use the word *tsheiou* (autumn) as setting the rhyme.) The whole of the tests lasted several days. Competition was intense: about one in two hundred candidates was successful and was granted a minor post in the Civil Service. As for the Master's degrees, these were held once every three years in the provincial capitals: during the second half of the nineteenth century, the number of Master's degrees awarded was restricted to 1,500 out of 200,000 candidates. Things were almost as bad at the doctoral level: 320 passes and 6,000 competitors. This last examination was held with great pomp: the candidates were led to their individual cells to the sound of guns and drums, after being paraded before the highest officials of the Empire and after being searched carefully.

The impact of Europe

The influence of Christian missionaries was much weaker in China than in many other countries. The Chinese themselves are a proud people and thought their culture superior to any other. They were not unwilling to learn about the ideas of Westerners, but when they found that Christianity was an exclusive religion – in the sense that if you declared yourself a Christian you could not at the same time accept, say, Buddhism – they concluded that it would be a disruptive, divisive, influence and should be proscribed. Nevertheless, a few Catholic missions were established in the seventeenth and eighteenth centuries and an attempt was made to train priests of Chinese birth. In the nineteenth century, Protestant missions followed suit: schools and colleges were started in all the Treaty Ports. By the year 1900, there were thus both Protestant and Catholic primary and secondary schools as well as a few colleges. Mathematics, geography, science were being taught, in a western style, in English, French, German, Russian and Japanese. The total number of pupils was small, but the force of their example prodigious.

The first attempt at the modernization of China was associated with the so called T'ai P'ing peasant revolt, led by enlightened Christians of a Protestant sect. It was crushed in the 1850's by an unholy alliance of Chinese reactionaries and European imperialists – with it passed the chance of converting the Empire to Christianity. Social and political reform was postponed for fifty years; it looked as if the dynasty had consolidated its power. Nevertheless, there was industrial and technological change. New classes appeared in Chinese society: the capitalists and the industrial workers. Their support of a group of young patriots recruited mainly from students who had been sent abroad added weight to the proposals put forward by the "Revive China Society", founded in 1894 by a young radical, Dr Sun Yat-Sen. At about this same date a reformist, non-revolutionary group, led by the scholar Kang Yu-Wei, came into prominence. They differed from the Sun Yat-Sen group because they had no idea of driving out the imperial dynasty, and from the "westernizing feudalists" who wanted only to adopt modern technology without permitting a redistribution of power and wealth. Their model, in fact, was that of the Meiji restoration in Japan, and they fully appreciated the importance of educational reform. Under their influence, the young Emperor Kwang Hsu "issued a series of unprecedented decrees, actually drafted by Kang Yu-Wei. Among other measures, he ordered the abolition of the classical Confucian tests for civil servants and the establishment of modern public education, including a university ... The result was not reform, but a reactionary *coup d'état* ... The young Emperor was put under detention by the court clique and remained under arrest until his death in 1908 ..."[1] Nevertheless, a good deal was salvaged. Reforms were undertaken, though they were less ambitious in their scope than Kang Yu-Wei had wanted. Peking University was founded and started by offering courses in Western medicine and in six modern languages. In 1904, there were four faculties: morals and philosophy; languages; law and political science; history and literature. In 1901, decrees were issued, according to which there should be one university in each

[1] Epstein, *From Opium War to Liberation*, Peking, 1956.

province and at least one college in each prefecture. Encouragement was given to the establishment of secondary schools, by both private persons and municipalities. The teaching should follow European models, as regards both content and method. A Ministry of Education was created in 1902 – the centralized system of administration being a copy of the French. Provincial offices, under a Rector, had charge of primary and secondary schools. The latter were organized into three levels: primary, free but not compulsory; secondary and higher. The subjects taught included Chinese literature and language; science; history; geography; a modern foreign language; gymnastics; etc. In addition, a good number of technical schools, of teacher training colleges, of girls' schools were started. Needless to say, the total number of teachers and of schools available, say by 1914, was grossly inadequate to provide schooling, at any level, for the great masses. The percentage of illiteracy among young adults was certainly at least 80 per cent and probably nearer to 90 per cent.

The popular movement that found its outlet in the "Boxer" riots (1899–1901) interfered somewhat with the establishment of a modern educational system. In some ways, perhaps the most important outcome of these troubles was a wise and far-sighted gesture on the part of the Americans. After the crushing of the "Boxers" the Western Powers, including Russia, exacted from China a huge indemnity, amounting perhaps to $500 millions. The government of the U.S.A. decided to use its share of this money mainly for the encouragement of education in China. This gesture had a two-fold effect. On the one hand, it served to strengthen the already very lively interest of Americans in China. Largely through the agency of the Protestant missions, money for education and hospitals poured in. Together with the Boxer money this made possible the building of numerous hospitals, schools and colleges in many parts of the country. Many American teachers and educators – John Dewey, for example – travelled to China for months or years. On the other hand, the generosity of the Americans led many educated young Chinese to look with favour upon the ideas they brought with them. In any case, the bustling energy, the drive, the speed of change and of economic development in the U.S.A. raised its prestige and attractiveness. The period from the overthrow of the Empire in 1912 to the victory of the communists in 1949 is largely dominated in China by an attempt to adopt American educational theories and practices.

CHINA

Modernization under the Kuomintang

Sun Yat-Sen became provisional President in 1912 and found the country in chaos. For nearly twenty years, that is until the Japanese invasion of Manchuria in 1931, there were strikes, riots, small-scale civil wars, famines in many districts. All one can say about this period is that, at any rate, it was somewhat better than what followed between 1931 and 1949! Of course, there was order and peace in large areas of the country, particularly in the Treaty Ports. The Kuomintang, whether led by Sun Yat-Sen or Chiang Kai-Shek, had little chance of forming and educating efficient and honest administrative cadres. Nor could they establish and maintain the vast number of schools, still less train the armies of teachers, needed to educate the (about) 20 million children born each year. The Kuomintang was nationalist, paternalistic, socialist in theory, pure and idealistic in its intention, and contained many intelligent, honest, devoted men. A good deal was done for education – less than was needed, of course, but perhaps as much as could be expected. An excellent account of the state of affairs in 1930 is given by the League of Nations Report on The Reorganization of Education in China.[1] The number of pupils in primary schools, it was then noted, had been increasing fast: from 4 millions in 1915 to $6\frac{1}{2}$ millions in 1922 and to 9 millions in 1929, a rate of increase of between 5 and 7 per cent. This meant that between 80 and 90 per cent of children never went to school at all. And of those who went, not all stayed for four years – the minimum period required to establish minimum literacy. It appeared, however, that many of the schools and far too many of the classes were unduly small. One- or two-teacher schools were common and the pupil/staff ratio was usually below twenty. The reason was probably poverty: few parents could afford to send their children to school. They relied on the miserable contribution which their labour could make to the family. But it should be noted that such conditions make possible an extremely rapid increase in the school population when conditions are more prosperous.

The Mission noted that "the organization of secondary education in China has been much influenced by the example of the Universities...

---

[1] The members of the Mission were: C. H. Becker, formerly Minister of Education in Prussia; M. Falski, Director of Primary Education in Poland; Paul Langevin, Paris; R. H. Tawney, London. The Report was published in Paris by the Institute of Intellectual Co-operation 1932.

it is intended to cover a period of six years, lasting from twelve to eighteen, which is divided into two halves, that of the junior middle school from twelve to fifteen and that of the senior middle school from fifteen to eighteen. In practice, the number of pupils diminishes sharply when the junior stage is passed, and a considerable number of pupils appear to begin their secondary education at the age of fourteen, or even later.... Admission to secondary schools is by examination, partly written and partly oral, and as with the primary schools, the number of candidates appears in most cases greatly to exceed the number which can be admitted...."

The general picture which emerges from the Report is that of an inadequate system of schools, in which underpaid and badly trained staff teach docile pupils in a formal and bookish manner, supervised by far too many administrators and inspectors. In a sample of fifty-six higher schools, there were 25,000 pupils, 5,600 teachers, and 2,600 administrators!

One interesting feature of the Report deserves notice. Several pages were devoted to criticizing the adoption of American ideas. "... it is necessary to lay particular stress on the remarkable, not to say alarming, consequences of the excessive influence of the American model on Chinese education ... (it is necessary) to warn Chinese educators against superficial Americanization. Let them rather borrow that spirit of originality with which Americans have succeeded in adapting the culture of Europe to American conditions ... The four members of the Mission, representing four different springs of European culture, came to the conclusion that the cultural conditions of Europe are more suitable than American conditions for adaptation to Chinese requirements ... (But) New China must mobilize its forces, and, from its own history, from its own literature, from all that is truly indigenous, extract the materials for a new civilization that will be neither American nor European but Chinese."

The years that followed the publication of this Report were exceedingly unfavourable for the development of education. Japanese armies marched up and down the land, causing enormous destruction. The public wealth was exhausted in equipping armies intended to wage a double campaign – against the invader and against the communists, whose strength grew constantly. Inevitably, education suffered. Schools fell into decay, equipment was worn out or stolen, books disappeared, paper was not available, teachers left for other forms of employment. Direct observation by the present writer in 1947, including visits to schools and colleges of all kinds, gave evidence of the decay. It would be wrong and foolish to blame the Kuomintang or the officials for this state of affairs, still less the Chinese people as a whole. Most of the officials of the Ministry of Education and nearly all the teachers were undoubtedly decent, honourable, honest, intelligent and hard-working men. Their sense of devotion to the welfare of the coming generation was splendid and inspiring. So was the faith of the common people in the power of education. One remembers, with emotion, the hot, stuffy, crowded halls in Shanghai where adults were learning to read tiny print by the light of dim oil-lamps and the humble hut in a village where a miserable and emaciated old man was struggling to teach the characters to small children, ill-dressed and underfed. But the material conditions, the appalling poverty and the dreadful shortages, were really too bad; while the prevailing sense of frustration and insecurity sapped both will and courage. By 1949, when the communist victory on the mainland was completed, the social machine had almost run down.

The coming of the communists

Let us take stock briefly of the situation in education when the communists established their régime in 1949:

1. Buildings which were badly maintained, with leaky roofs and dirty walls – moreover, too few of them. Very little apparatus or equipment for science teaching. Few textbooks, and those which were available mostly torn and worn. Not much paper and a shortage of writing materials. Desks, tables, &c. which needed replacing.

Just a few, very few, good and well equipped private schools in large towns attended by the children of the wealthy and privileged.

2. Too few teachers, and those mostly lacking modern training. They were used to the formal and bookish methods. For the most part, these teachers, however, were not unfavourable to the communists. They had suffered too much during the long war and had been disgusted by the evidences of corruption all around.

3. At the university and college level: strong American influences and a staff less sympathetic to communism than in the primary and secondary schools. A student body largely drawn from the old

administrative and merchant classes; that is, precisely from those classes which would suffer most from the advent of communism.

4. A considerable number of Christian missionary schools which were, in principle, under foreign influence and hostile to communist doctrines. Here, it may be noted that anti-foreign feeling in China is natural and to be expected. The contacts of China with Europe (including Russia) and America have been unfortunate. True, the old Manchu dynasty was effete, corrupt, inefficient. But it was sustained far too long by the weapons of the West, which defeated attempts at reform. Furthermore, the story of the Western powers in China during the nineteenth century is a dishonourable one: there was far too much raping, looting, burning and massacre.

5. The system of administration, familiar to the Chinese, had been copied from the French and was highly centralized. This was, of course, perfectly acceptable.

6. The organization of the school system was influenced by ideas emanating from the U.S.A. For example, the 6 – 3 – 3 gradation of six years primary school, then three years of junior middle and three years of senior middle school resembles the American plan. It does not quite fit communist doctrine, but could be accepted at least for a number of years.

7. As regards general theoretical direction and ideology: here the American notions were strong, and it was considered they should be re-orientated as soon and as quickly as possible. For instance, there should be less stress on individuality, less praise of differentiated curricula allowing the pupils or their parents to choose or reject subjects. Polytechnization, it was thought, should replace Deweyan progressivism.

Here then are a few of the factors to be taken into account. The conditions for developing the education of the people of China in the direction desired by the communists could be created only by securing immense resources of men and materials. Now, whatever one may think of the Marxists and their socio-political views, one can admit that they have immense, unbounded faith in education – their own version of it, of course – and that they are prepared to make prodigious efforts to develop it quantitatively.

In addition, for the first time in a century, there was peace in China, together with firm leadership. Direct observation by the present writer on a second visit in 1957 gave abundant evidence that there had, indeed, been a spectacular improvement in the material condition of the people. They were still poor, very poor, but there was no evidence of any food shortage; people were decently though drably dressed; there were no obvious signs of beggars. Everywhere one was deeply impressed by the energy with which men and women worked and, in particular, by the enormous amount of construction which was going on in all cities. The numbers of buildings being erected in Peking, Sian, or Chungking left far behind anything that could be seen in Germany, or, for that matter, in Britain. This applied above all to the buildings of schools and colleges. The new ones were plain, overcrowded, but at least solid. And not unpleasing to look at.

Problems of policy

In every country of the world, there are fundamental problems arising from natural, demographic, technological, historical factors. They have to be considered and tackled by the authorities, no matter what government is in power. The ideology professed by those in charge of public affairs affects their attitude towards these problems and determines the nature of the solutions proposed.

As seen by the leaders of the Party, the primary purpose of education is two-fold. First, to mobilize and train the population in order to increase the production of material goods. Secondly, to maintain social unity and cohesion by fostering loyalty to the government and régime. To mobilize the human resources of China is a tremendous task. The population is huge – over 600 million – and it is increasing at the rate of 10 or 12 millions every year. Furthermore, in 1947 fewer than a quarter of the children attended any kind of school. Consider the meaning of the figures. About 120 million children are between the ages of six and fourteen. Thus, in order to enforce universal, compulsory elementary education it would be necessary to keep up an army of at least four million teachers – accepting a staffing ratio of thirty to one. This, in turn, would involve an annual output from training colleges and universities of at least 200,000 teachers. To put the matter in another way, think of the difficulties caused in Britain by the so-called bulge, which arises from an increase in our school population of fewer than a quarter of a million children a year. To the Chinese, this would seem not a bulge but a ripple. Theirs is forty or fifty times larger.

The attitude of the Mao Tse-Tung government towards this demographic problem oscillates between two extremes. At times, it is urged that the socialist organization of society provides a flexible framework which permits the adequate solution of all problems. If the population increases at the rate of 3 per cent, 4 per cent, even 5 per cent a year, that is splendid. The disciplined efforts of the embattled proletariat, led by the scientifically trained communist intelligentsia, will so increase production as to make it easy to feed and bring up the large number of children. And increasing population strengthens the communist state. Then come a series of bad harvests and difficulties in the industrial field. Dialectical switchover. It is seen that the effort needed to cope with an annual increase of population of 12 millions sets too great a strain on the economy and greatly harms the prospect of rapid advance in the industrial field. In consequence, official propaganda rather suddenly shifts to the recommendation of birth control, abortion and sterilization. In the villages, traditional Chinese methods including acupuncture are made freely available, but they are probably ineffective. In the cities, Western contraceptives are made available, but their cost is high. In addition, an increasing number of men submit themselves voluntarily to surgical sterilization.

To an outside observer, it seems obvious that it will be difficult to establish rapidly a modern and efficient educational system of a modern kind unless the rate of increase of the population is diminished very significantly. But, in any case, a painful policy decision will have to be made. Should one attempt to develop immediately universal mass primary education? Or should one concentrate the available resources upon the secondary stage, upon teacher training, upon technical education? In point of fact, the appetite for education of any kind is vast and insatiable. The people's faith in the power and value of schooling is tremendous and growing. There is a popular demand for the establishment of a school in every village and hamlet. Yet this is a demand for consumer goods; and wisdom would counsel concentration upon *producer* goods – that is, upon the higher stages of education. It is, in fact, the latter policy which is being applied, as far as this is possible.

The energy displayed in tackling the problem of quantity is altogether admirable and exemplary. The Ministry of Education's statistics claim that three times as many students are now receiving instruction as in 1947, and one can well believe it. But even then, for the country as a whole, fewer than 60 per cent of the children between the ages of seven and fourteen are at school, though the proportion is larger in cities like Peking or Shanghai, where attendance rises to well above 90 per cent.

Yet another aspect of the mobilization of human resources for industrial development involves the re-orientation of the traditional curriculum. As was pointed out earlier, the old Chinese school was attached to the study of the classics and of literature. Those subjects had high reputation, and they may have had some value in developing the skill in language, written or spoken, which is necessary to old-fashioned administration. The new government realizes, however, that progress can come only from a re-orientation of this traditional curriculum towards the sciences and technology. How can this be done? Teachers have to be trained in new ways and they will have to learn new subjects. Furthermore, sciences and technology require expensive apparatus, laboratories, and workshops. Here again wisdom would counsel slow rather than quick advance since the danger exists that by too rapidly increasing the size of scholastic institutions one might produce far too many teachers of subjects with no industrial value – such as the classics – and thereby create a vested interest in the teaching of obsolescent subjects.

Over and above these problems there are two major issues which have not only educational but also social and political importance. Any government and particularly a communist one is concerned with the maintenance of national unity. In China this has two important aspects: the problem of national minorities, and the problem of language.

The minorities

As seen from afar the Chinese people seem to be uniform and cohesive. It is true that there are differences in the appearance of the tall northerners and the short southerners as well as in their food habits, and even their dress. Nevertheless, they all read the same language and they have all been formed by that compound of Confucian, Buddhist, and Taoist thought which we call Chinese culture. Important exceptions must, however, be noted. In the first place, there is an important Muslim minority, numbering perhaps 40 millions. These present no problem whatever since they are fully assimilated into the dominant culture of the Hans. All they retain is a ritual and a system of food taboos which causes them to avoid eating that favourite Chinese food, pork. Apart from this religious minority, there are in certain regions considerable groups such as the Li, the Miao, and the Chaungs, who wear a different dress, speak a different language, and think of themselves as a separate group possessing their own individuality and their own nationality. Communist doctrine, particularly as expressed by Stalin in the nationalities policy, lays emphasis on the need to give these national minorities full national rights. This policy has been pursued in China. There are special Ministries, Institutes in all the major cities, in which the problems of their economic and social development are studied. In the regions themselves great efforts are being made to provide schools and colleges of national pride as well as of loyalty to the Central Government. It is said that at the moment 80 per cent of the children and young people of Inner Mongolia and 100 per cent of the Koreans are now at school.

Language

The Chinese written language is the same in all parts of the Chinese culture area. Each symbol stands for an idea and the connexion between idea and symbol is the same in Japan, Korea, or Canton, just as the connexion between our number signs and the ideas they represent is the same in all parts of Europe. But when these symbols are read the spoken translation differs very much; that is, the spoken languages of Peking, Chungking, Shanghai and Canton differ from one another quite as much as, say, the spoken languages of Stockholm, Berlin and Amsterdam.

The Chinese symbols are beautiful to look at and calligraphy, an art much prized by all, has played an important part in the development of Chinese aesthetic sensibility. A proposal to latinize the writing system arouses the same kind of feelings among the educated as would be caused by a proposal made to the Classical Association or the Headmasters' Conference to replace the teaching of Greek and Latin by the teaching of Basic English.

Mao Tse-Tung himself is a noted calligraphist and an exceedingly able and gifted writer of verse in the style of the thirteenth and fourteenth centuries.

On the other hand, the ideographic system is little suited to the necessities of modern life. First, it is difficult to teach it. Chinese children work hard, but it takes about four years to teach them 1,200 characters. At the end of the junior middle school, say at fifteen, the average pupil probably knows about two or three thousand characters. A university graduate may know between 5,000 and 8,000 characters. But even at that level he will still need to go on learning to read his own language. Often one sees intelligent and industrious youths of eighteen or twenty (inevitably wearing spectacles) learning lists of words. And often one encounters university teachers unable to read words they come across in their reading. Think, too, of the difficulty in sending telegrams. As for using a typewriter, that is obviously out of the question. As a curiosity, typewriters with 2,000 keys have been constructed; but they are clearly useless in commerce.

It must be admitted that there are real difficulties in latinizing the Chinese language. As spoken, it consists of about 500 monosyllables, which are, however, pronounced in four different tones or, to be more precise, in five different tones of pitch combined with five different tones of intensity. Philologists say they could probably deal with this point fairly satisfactorily by the use of accents. Indeed, some urge that the difficulty of latinizing the script has been exaggerated.

But a fatal obstacle remains. The whole point of latinizing the script would be to establish direct relations between written symbolism and spoken language. Unless there is a certain degree of phonetic connexion between the two, the gain would be small. But suppose one latinized the spoken language of Canton; it would then cease to convey any meaning to the people of Shanghai. In other words, latinization of the writing system would involve sacrificing the cultural unity of China, a unity largely based upon the possession of a writing system which is the same for all parts of the area. There would be a gain in efficiency but a loss of unity. That this danger does exist is proved by the painful experience of India, the national cohesion of which is being gravely threatened by the centrifugal force of intransigent linguistic loyalty. In this dilemma, the policy adopted is again wise. Through the schools, the attempt is being made to secure the adoption of the Mandarin dialect of the Peking area as a spoken language throughout the whole of China. Within a measurable future, say ten or twenty years, it will be understood and spoken everywhere. Then and only then will the Latin script be adopted and taught. Meanwhile in schools, especially in the north, experiments are being tried. To sum up, therefore, one may say that there exist in China problems of policy which any government, communist or not, would have to consider. What distinguishes the new régime from others is the energy and decisiveness with which these problems are being tackled.

In addition, of course, communist doctrine shows its effects by the faith which it displays in science, by the resolution with which leadership is given and enforced, and by the degree to which the policy of equalization is pursued – equalization as between national groups and equalization as between social classes. Most significant of all, perhaps, is the way in which popular demand, understandable but short sighted and ill advised, can be moderated and controlled through the political apparatus.

The school system

As in every other communist country, the monopoly of education in China is vested in the state. Private schools cannot exist unless they accept control and inspection, nor unless they follow the curricula prescribed by the authorities. Eighty per cent of the total costs are provided by the Central Government in Peking, the remaining twenty being found by the Provincial Governments or the municipalities. Such centralization has marked advantages in an underdeveloped country which is expanding quickly. Speed and relative efficiency are obtained at the cost of freedom and experimentation by teachers. It should not be thought, however, that only a public authority establishes and runs the schools. In many cases, a trade union, or, to be more precise, a union of workers in a particular factory or village, may decide to allocate part of the funds at its disposal to running a school. At the moment 50,000 schools have been built by such unions, and they have $3\frac{1}{2}$ million pupils. In many cases prosperous enterprises making industrial goods have pursued this course of action in order to make sure that their own children have access to a good general schooling. The Central Government welcomes such initiative, since it is beset by grave problems of finance.

Three ministries are concerned with the educational effort: the Ministry of Culture, which looks after museums, broadcasting, the theatre, and so on; the Ministry of Higher Education, which is in charge of all higher technical institutions, research institutes, universities and colleges; and the Ministry of Education itself. This controls all elementary and middle schools, all teacher training, and all the general education provided in part-time schools; in addition, it runs special schools for handicapped children, of which there are at present sixty-two with 65,000 pupils and 960 teachers. The Ministry of Education is also in charge of the rapidly growing system of nursery schools and kindergartens. The policy of the state is to encourage the development of these, since they make it possible to absorb female labour into factories. It might be added that other ministries, such as Agriculture, provide technical colleges for pupils older than 18, and run Research Institutes.

The Minister of Education is assisted by six vice-ministers and six directors, the latter being permanent full time, non-political, civil servants. There are also more than 100 general inspectors who are sent out by the Ministry to collect information, statistics, and so forth. The whole body of these people forms a unified corps, of which the minister is the voice representing their interest in the Council of State.

Money comes from the general budget of the state. The principal sources of revenue are excise taxes on commodities, such as tobacco or spirits; the profits made by state enterprises; and the taxes on collective farms and collective enterprises. Income tax is virtually non-existent. It is rightly thought silly to keep one lot of clerks busy paying out wages and salaries and another to take back a part of those same wages and salaries.

The chief source of educational expenditure, as everywhere else, is the cost of teachers. There are, in all, eleven different salary scales, which vary according to the location and nature of the school. The position of any particular teacher upon the appropriate salary scale is determined by three factors. First, the number of years he has taught. Secondly, his professional competence. Thirdly, his moral quality. These last two somewhat imponderable factors are evaluated by general agreement at a School Staff Meeting. Such meetings are held regularly at least once a week, the principal taking the chair. The teachers discuss one another's work, the principal gives his own view, and in the end, agreement is reached as to the quality of the teacher. In the evaluation of his "moral quality" attention is paid to his behaviour and conduct both in and out of school, to the way he corrects pupils' work, how well he gets on with the other teachers, how his pupils behave in school and out. It is asserted very strongly that political views play no part in the evaluation of this moral factor. I had long discussions as to whether it would really be possible to give a mark, either for the quality of a teacher or for the excellence of his moral standard, at a staff meeting. I argued that this was liable to create jealousies and conflicts, but I was assured that such doubts would come only to a European, and particularly to an Englishman. In China – so it was said – the procedure worked excellently, since all teachers were absolutely united in their devotion to the welfare of their country and its children.

The actual salaries paid vary between about 50 Yuan a month up to as much as 150 Yuan for principals of large schools. The exchange value of the Yuan is about 3 shillings or 40 cents – but to attempt calculations on this basis leads to wrong conclusions. There is no income tax for teachers and rents are never more than 5 per cent of salary. It should be remembered, however, that the accommodation provided is always very cramped and austere. Few city families have more than two rooms, and exceedingly few enjoy the luxury of a private bathroom or lavatory or even water tap. Food and cigarettes are cheap – relatively to income these cost about the same as in England. But clothes and all manufactured goods are expensive; a bicycle, for example, costs about 150 Yuan. For purposes of comparison, it is interesting to note that a skilled worker earns about 80 Yuan a month and a labourer about 50. It should be added that inequalities of income are moderated by public opinion, which is strongly opposed to ostentation of any kind, and by the need to subscribe heavily to the State Loans.

The general educational system comprises, firstly, nurseries and kindergartens, which some children attend up to the age of seven. Then come five-year primary schools. These, naturally enough, vary very much both as regards buildings and equipment, as well as in the quality of their teachers. In many villages they are little better than mud huts. In the towns they may be either old-fashioned places or well proportioned new buildings put up since the advent of the new régime. In Peking there are two experimental schools in which the work done is of the kind which would be expected in any good progressive primary school in Europe.

One of these has about 1,000 pupils and thirty-three teachers, most of whom are women. One third of these teachers have had four years of post-secondary education; the rest are two-year training college graduates. The school day begins at 8.30 in the morning and goes on till 2.30 in the afternoon, with an interval for lunch – which is provided in the school, and is quite good and substantial. That is paid for by the parents. The pupils may remain in the school if they like until 5 p.m.

During this free time they will either do their homework or undertake group activities. Most of them are Young Pioneers, the activities pursued by the latter being analogous to those of the boy scouts, although a leader of the Young Pioneers adversely critized our own Scouts system on two counts: (*a*) that it was too authoritarian, laying too much emphasis upon obedience and too little on the freedom and needs of the child, and (*b*) that too little was done to encourage pupils to concentrate upon their school work, particularly in mathematics and science.

The subjects taught in primary schools are not unlike those that would be taught in primary schools over here, except that more attention is paid to calligraphy and that "arithmetic" includes a great deal of practical work with the abacus. Of a total of 5,000 periods, 2,200 are devoted to Chinese, 1,200 to arithmetic, 190 to history and 190 to geography, 170 to nature study, 400 to physical training, 300 to singing, 200 each to drawing and to handwork. After the five years, the pupil may move on to a three-year junior high school, and then to a three-year senior high school. If the number of applications for admission to such schools is larger than the number of vacancies, the "best" pupils are selected by sitting an old-fashioned examination, doubtful ones being decided by an interview. At this secondary stage, the curriculum broadens: increasing stress is laid upon mathematics and science; and gradually "political education" is introduced, though it never plays a large role. It is felt that the teaching of doctrine is not necessarily the best way of forming good citizens; the whole curriculum and the general atmosphere of the school should lead to the acceptance of communist ideals and to an understanding of socialist philosophy.

By the side of these "general" secondary schools there are, especially in the large towns, a number of vocational middle schools, and trade schools. A difficult point of policy, at present unsolved, is whether it would be wise at the moment to encourage the increase in number of the "general" schools or to concentrate resources upon the vocational schools. Public opinion among parents favours the former; economic needs, the latter.

And, lastly, by the side of the whole system and relatively independent of it, there is a great and growing system of short-term worker and peasant primary and middle schools for adults who did not have the opportunity of going to school when children. Here exceedingly interesting experiments are going on. It must not be thought that the government, the Party or the people are happy and satisfied with the educational system as it is. As in every country of the world, there is much talk about reform of structure and reform of curriculum. There is dissatisfaction with the shortage of schools and of teachers (after all only 60 per cent of the children over the nation as a whole get any schooling at all), criticism of the methods of teacher training, concern at the shortage of scientists and technicians, and sharp argument about the work done in universities.

Quantitative data

This sketch of the educational system should be amplified by referring to a few figures, though of necessity the statistics available are not completely reliable. Nor are they up to date – inevitably so with a very large, diversified state still lacking effective public services. First – the population was stated to be 670 millions in 1958, and increasing at the rate of 2 per cent or 3 per cent a year. But the margin of error may well be over 100 million. It seems probable that the population is somewhere betweeen 550 and 700 millions. Little is known for sure about the age-distribution, though the proportion of young people is certainly very high.

In 1955–6,[1] the total pupil enrolment (60 millions) was about 10 per cent of the population. Of these 1 per cent were enrolled in kindergartens; 87 per cent in primary schools; 6 per cent in secondary schools; 1 per cent in vocational and teacher training schools; 4 per cent in institutions of higher education. There were nearly 2 million teachers. Pupil/teacher ratios: thirty-three in primary schools; twenty-six in secondary schools; nine in universities. In the two previous years, total enrolment was increasing by nearly 2 per cent a year in primary schools; 15 per cent in secondary schools; and 40 per cent a year in universities – evidence of the stress being laid on "producer-education" i.e. on education intended to produce educators and experts.

On the assumption that these trends have persisted, very rough estimates – rough guesses – may be hazarded. It seems possible that in 1962–3 the total pupil enrolment is of the order of 75 millions. Of these

[1] These figures are based in part upon documents supplied by the Ministry of Education in Peking and in part upon those provided by the Unesco *World Survey of Education* Volume III (Secondary Education). 1961.

about 65 millions may be in primary schools, representing say 50 to 60 per cent of children between the ages of six and thirteen. If this figure is even approximately correct, it would mean that in a period of about fifteen years, illiteracy among young adults in China had been reduced from 80 per cent to 50 per cent – a truly stupendous achievement.

At the other end of the educational scale, there were $2\frac{1}{2}$ million students in post-secondary institutions in 1955–6: the third largest higher education population in the world. But, of course, very many of these are part-time or short-course students. Only 400,000 were full-time students duly enrolled in one of the 194 institutions of university rank.

The curriculum of the general secondary schools includes all the subjects to be expected. Music and drawing are dropped after the first three years (one period a week). Chinese language and literature are taught throughout the six years, average six periods a week. Mathematics, six for six years. History, socialist education: two periods a week each for the whole six years. Biology, physics, chemistry: average of a total six periods throughout for the three subjects. Productive work and physical education: two periods each. Foreign language (usually Russian or English): four periods during each of the last three years. Thus the direct propaganda content is relatively small. Reliance is placed chiefly on the Young Pioneer groupings, the extra-curricular activities and the influence of out-of-school groupings, mass demonstrations, etc.

Achievements of the Communist Authorities

From the point of view of quantity the achievements of the present Chinese government are most impressive. More than three times as many children are in school, and this improvement applies not only to China itself but to the minority areas. For example, when the University of Inner Mongolia was set up in 1957, teachers from Peking University and from twelve other colleges were assigned there. In the pastoral areas of the region, where families still follow the herds, tent schools travel with them. For the whole of Mongolia, the increase compared with 1951 is 3.5 times as many pupils in primary and 8.8 times as many in middle schools and 10 times as many at college level.

In addition, before 1949 the fees charged at schools and colleges everywhere tended to keep away many children of the working classes in town and country. Tuition fees today in some primary and most middle schools are very low, while colleges and technical schools are free. The children of poor parents may get grants towards their food and board. As a result, 75 per cent of the pupils in secondary schools and 48 per cent in colleges and universities are now the sons and daughters of workers and farmers. Equality of educational opportunity has certainly been promoted. At the level of the university the same thing is true, although here the authorities still find it difficult to recruit as many children of the poorer parents as they would like. Secondly, there has been very considerable success in increasing the amount of training provided for young technicians. The Chinese themselves claim to have provided a working force of nearly two million young people with college or other special technical education. This development is of great significance for the industrialization of China. Thirdly, a not altogether unsuccessful attempt has been made to modernize the curriculum.

Adult education campaigns aiming at literacy and improving technical skills – particularly in agriculture – have been undertaken in most parts of the country. The degree to which such campaigns have been successful evidently varies widely. Nevertheless, one may accept the notion that at least in some areas considerable success has been achieved and that farmers and industrial workers in consequence have been sensitized to the idea that education can help them. The popular slogan that "Socialism is a paradise but you cannot get there without culture" may well have had some effect. It should be added that tremendous efforts have also been made to encourage education for girls, much neglected before 1949. To communists, women represent a potential source of labour; and for this reason, as well as their belief in the equality of the sexes, genuine attempts are made to open the doors of schools to them. Their sincerity in this area need not be questioned.

All these are undoubted successes. There are, however, failures and partial failures. First, there have been attempts at reforming the actual structure of the school system. Partly for ideological reasons, communist doctrine holds that a 6-3-3 system, is *bourgeois* and to be regretted. The preference is for an undivided seven, eight or ten-year school. So far, however, it has not proved possible to move far in this direction.

More important perhaps is that only partial success has been achieved in a matter which appears fundamentally important to all good

Marxists, namely the re-valuation of manual work. In a speech which has often been quoted Mao Tse-Tsung expressed his views on this matter. He began by confessing with shame that when he was a student, he thought that even carrying one's luggage was disgraceful, and that he was convinced that only intellectuals were clean. "I would, therefore," he said, "readily borrow clothes from an intellectual but never from a worker, peasant or soldier, because I thought that their clothes would be unclean." He then goes on to say how his views were altered by his experiences and concludes "The cleanest people in the world are the workers and peasants. Even though their hands may be soiled and their feet smeared with cow-dung nevertheless they are cleaner than the *bourgeoisie* and *petty bourgeoisie*. That is what I mean by the re-valuation of a sentiment – a change from one class to another".[1]

This change in the attitude to manual work is to be achieved through two measures. On the one hand it means "Arming the peasants and workers with cultural and scientific knowledge". On the other hand, it means "giving intellectuals the opportunity to acquire practical experiences of productive work, and feeling akin to those workers". The main methods used are "Schools run factories and farms" and "Factories and communes run schools". With students the chief emphasis is still on studies, with workers and peasants, on production.

What is involved in all this, concretely, is sending students as well as school children into factories and farms to work for a few hours a week, and providing courses of lectures as well as tuition in factories and in communes. All this may be valuable; but how far it succeeds in really making people appreciate the value of hard and tiring work is questionable. Schools have been urged to make products which can be sold; but such measures – as the experience of India has shown – are unlikely to be fruitful. Nevertheless, efforts will surely be continued.

Trends of reform

Speeches and declarations of policy by high State and Party officials give indications of the problems perplexing the leadership and of the possible solutions being discussed. In the forefront, of course, are obvious and reputable desiderata . . . "the complete elimination of illiteracy among young adults, workers, and peasants and the provision

[1] Quoted from "Schooling for the Millions" by Chang Chien in *China Reconstructs* October 1959.

of elementary-school facilities for all children during the Second Five-Year Plan (1958–62). During the Third Five-Year Plan a junior middle-school education is to be made available to all, while senior schools and higher institutions are to be extended gradually".[1]

In addition to such unexceptionable statements, one finds others which display a certain anxiety and uncertainty. The Minister of Education in Peking spoke (1960) about the need "to reduce appropriately the age limit, to raise appropriately the academic standards, to control appropriately the duration of study, and to increase appropriately the productive labour". In other words, the problem is how to reduce the total number of years spent by young people in schools, so as to set them free to work in factory or on the fields, while maintaining quality by improving methods of teaching and making everyone work harder. The suggestion is that by amalgamating the elementary and junior middle schools into a single common school and then adding one year the total length of general education could be reduced by two years. The 6 – 3 – 3 system would yield place to the ten-year school, though this might be reduced to an eight-year school. Some even consider that a universal seven-year school might suffice, at any rate as a first step. In the words of Vice-Premier Lu, "We plan beginning now to carry out a large scale experimentation on reducing the number of years spent in education, raising the standards, controlling the study hours, and increasing physical labour to a suitable extent in our full-time middle and elementary schools. We plan to carry out a reform programme on the schooling system step by step. . . . To carry out the education of our people properly will require a prolonged trial-and-error process. . . . Marxism, Leninism and Mao Tse-Tung ideology are our guiding philosophy".[2]

Regarding curriculum, the dominant view is that languages and mathematics should be the central focus, since progress elsewhere depends upon real mastery of these two. "If languages and mathematics are properly mastered, it becomes relatively easy to master physics, chemistry, biology, history and geography . . . one-half the (present) effort will yield twice the results". But success will be reached only if the "*bourgeois* slogan" of "education for education's sake" is rejected as cant, and only if it is perceived that when policy is

---

[1] Quoted from Stewart Fraser's exellent article: "Recent Educational Reforms in Communist China" in *The School Review*, University of Chicago Press, Autumn 1961.
[2] Quoted by Stewart Fraser.

directed by professional educators education becomes a device to insure the hegemony of the *bourgeoisie* over the workers. "While we hold that education should be co-ordinated with productive labour, the *bourgeois* holds that education should be separated from productive labour ... education should be led by the Party and be carried out according to the mass line. The *bourgeois* holds that schools must be directed by professional experts and be carried out according to the expert line." But communists reject the latter alternative as mere trickery of the proletariat.

The future

Dare we guess about the future of education in China? What might things be like, say, about 1985–90? Can we assume that there will then still be a communist régime ruling the immense areas once claimed by the Empire, and including Tibet, Inner Mongolia, Manchuria and parts of Indo-China? Evidently everything depends upon whether major nuclear war can be avoided. Assuming that it can, the continuance of the régime is likely only if two further conditions can be fulfilled: (i) the success of the communes; i.e. the socialization and modernization of food production, involving a break-up of the joint-family system and the abandonment of the idea of private ownership of land, while maintaining and even increasing the amount of food produced; and (ii) successful development of modern industry based upon scientific technology in the towns, so that they will have commodities that can be exchanged for food. The U.S.S.R. has solved the second of these problems, but not the first. China seems better placed to tackle them, since the notion of communal life is rooted even more deeply in Chinese than in Russian traditions, and since Western liberal traditions of respect for the individual were never as widely accepted. Even then, success is far from certain.

Assuming, however, that things go not too badly for the communist plans, there would be reason to think that in another thirty or forty years the masses of China would have reached a standard of material prosperity corresponding to that of the masses of Southern Europe today – scarcely more. It would be altogether foolish to think that by then they would have "caught up" with the agriculturists of England and America.

Some types of industry, however, and particularly those concerned with the waging of war, may develop fast. China is already a formidable military power and it is not impossible that she may manufacture atomic and nuclear weapons within the next five or ten years. A totalitarian state can divert to such purposes any fraction of the national production it chooses. But if China does so choose, her prospects of making solid progress in improving the well-being of her people will be gravely prejudiced. In any case, we can suppose that by the end of the century the competitive power of her industries will be at least as great as those of Hong Kong today. All this, of course, pre-supposes the establishment of an efficient and modernized educational system – and this brings us back to the questions asked at the beginning of this section.

Let us speculate, and itemize our forecast. A population of 800 or 900 millions, by then increasing more slowly than now. A total school and college population of, say, 160 millions with 8 million teachers. In the countryside a vast number of six-year or eight-year communal agricultural schools. Perhaps full-time up to twelve; then half-time work, half-time study. Central schools, providing general education for the able village children, between the ages of twelve and seventeen – sending some to higher agricultural colleges, to be trained as agronomists or managers, and others to technological colleges and to universities. A steady drift from country to town facilitated by the kind of education provided in the schools.

In the towns, universal eight-year schools, with a technical bias, followed by two-year special courses leading to technical colleges and universities – the general orientation being similar to that of Russian schools today.

At the tertiary level, a total of say 10 million registered students, half of them part-time or correspondence students; the others studying full-time in universities, teachers' colleges or technological colleges.

Throughout the whole system, complete acceptance of the ideal of polytechnicization. And, of course, general replacement of the old characters by the romanized script.

In some ways this all presents a grim, daunting and cheerless prospect when contrasted with the increasingly diversified and joyous systems of the democratic West, which are attached to the notion of the development of the personality and to the free expression of individuality. Yet when we take note of the unhappy and miserable history of China during the last hundred and fifty years, clearly all this is advance and progress. There is no freedom, little human dignity; social, not individual, values prevail certainly. But there is an immense improvement in security, in health, in well-being, in physical condition. Is all this to be regretted?

The people of China are an immense reservoir of courage, strength and genius. In native gifts of intelligence, ingenuity, percipience, artistic feeling, and wisdom they stand second to no race on earth. Their contributions to culture and civilization have enriched the common patrimony of mankind. The régime that now rules is in many ways tyrannous and harsh. It denies human values rightly prized not only in the West but by the sages of old China. Who can doubt that time will soften the rigours? It will not be long before "a hundred flowers" once again bloom in the antique soil. Then the Chinese will enter again into the community of nations, which can learn so much from them.

Are such hopes too optimistic, too naïve? Perhaps. Yet a study of history shows that time and again the kindly genius of the Chinese has embraced and transformed barbarian conquerors. The descendants of the brutal Mongols, the heirs of Genghiz Khan, became the patrons of the arts and the protectors of culture. So, too, may those who follow the ruthless and rigid communists of today be succeeded by lovers of freedom and defenders of peace and beauty.

CHAPTER 12

Common Ground between Communist and Western Education

Societies, whatever their form, whether large or small, ancient or modern, primitive or advanced, are social aggregates made up of individual human beings bound together by common interests, needs, and goals. In all societies men seek to control the physical forces of nature, to perpetuate themselves and their way of life, and to improve upon the mode and manner of their living through engaging in various forms of economic and political activity. Furthermore, men everywhere have their images and aspirations, their beliefs and superstitions, their fears and foibles, all of these more or less consistent with their history and traditions, and their place in the space and time of man's evolution.

Communist and Western societies are alike in that their growth and development follow similar social principles. The paradoxical aspect of this development is that these societies follow identical processes of socialization despite differences in ideology. Both types of society are concerned with controlling natural forces and materials; which accounts for the fact that in each society dams are built, atomic power is developed, electricity is distributed, jet propulsion is adopted, mines are opened, and medical experiments conducted. Governed by the same motives, both societies experiment with new processes and techniques in the natural and social sciences. Both types of society, too, are confronted with rapidly increasing populations, the consequence of which is that they have similar problems to deal with in matters of increased housing, social services, and productivity in many branches of the economy. Both are concerned with the problems attendant upon the automation of industry, one result of which is to require programmes of retraining and re-education of sectors of the working population. Each society, too, is seeking the widest possible application of scientific principles to industrial processes, a search which must inevitably confront personnel so engaged with more or less similar problems, and which in addition, must breed similar attitudes and conceptions. Still further, both must concern themselves with the political process which involves all participants in establishing some kind of working relationship with individuals and groups, in arriving at some kind of decision affecting internal and external policy, and in conflicts and accommodations respecting modes of procedure relevant to local, regional, or international affairs. This total process of socialization which characterizes every society as it moves from one phase of development to another is perforce evident in both communist and Western societies.

The values men live and work by are everywhere and in all societies established by tradition. These values, however, whether in art or science, in politics or economics, in aspiration or education, are always subject to the stresses and strains of historic and natural forces, not the least of which may be a revolutionary or evolutionary conception of life as it manifests itself in all of the social organizations and institutions in society. The process of socialization, though providing a common denominator for all societies, may nevertheless be interrupted or redirected by cataclysmic alteration in the society's development brought about by revolution and war. The resultant of such cataclysm is a change in the hierarchy of values in the society affected. Thus, communist values emerged after the Revolution of 1917, in the same way that French values underwent a change after 1789, American after 1776, and English after 1688. Nevertheless, the force of tradition continues to exert its influence despite the changes brought about. Though the pre- and post-revolutionary values may be different in each instance, it is the substance rather than the shadow which men live by; it is the values held in common, rather than the ideologies which separate them, that in the end spell out their common humanity, and common destiny. And the values men live by are usually incorporated into their educational programmes and systems.

The place of education in any society is indicative of the value placed on education by that society. In both communist and Western societies, a great deal of value is placed upon education, but the place of this value in the hierarchy of values tends to be different. To some extent this is indicated by the models which the two societies hold up to their youth. These models provide what is considered to be the measure of the successful man. Thus, in the United States, Canada, France, and

Britain, the image of the successful man is the business man, industrialist, or banker, who controls vast corporations and directs the destinies of commercial empires. The successful politician is also accorded pride of place in the social scale and a significant measure of financial reward and prestige. By contrast with the place of the teacher or the professor, or even the researcher in Western society, the businessman and the politician rank high as models for young people. Doctors, lawyers, and engineers, in this society, are accorded prestige; but in the last analysis their place in the hierarchy of images approaches but does not reach that of the successful industrialist or politician. Communist society also provides models of success for its youth; but in this instance it is the engineer, the scientist, and the politician who are accorded pride of place. Western and communist society both place value on education, but this education differs in its emphasis largely as a result of the differences in images held up to the youth as measures of success, and these differences in turn spell out the difference in the place of education in the two societies, and in the aims which they both pursue.

The aims of education in communist society are singular in purpose and cover the physical, intellectual, social and aesthetic dimensions of man. The aims of education in Western society are similar in kind, but the emphasis given to them in Britain, Canada, the United States, in France and in Germany are different. France, for example, aims primarily at an élite possessed of the finest elements in the humanist tradition, despite a changing conception of what this ought to be. Furthermore, Western aims of education differ one from another in several important respects. The first of these is in regard to what constitutes a general education; the second in regard to the place of science in education; and, the third with respect to the place of technology. For communism, these differences have been reconciled in what is called polytechnicization. In both types of society, however, the aims of education are designed to select the best brains in the society for positions of responsibility in the social, economic, and political realms; to develop in the youth of the society those habits, skills, and attitudes which will most likely contribute to the development of the individual and of the society; and, to ensure that school and society are together in agreement as to their point of view and philosophy.

In both communist and Western societies the ultimate object of the elementary and secondary school is, in the first instance, to lay a foundation such that the individual will fit into the society of which he is a part and with which he can be in comfortable communication. In the second instance, the ultimate object is to differentiate the potentialities of the students in line with the needs of society, though here communist and Western societies differ with respect to the means adopted. Because Western individualism has emphasized individual differences throughout its programmes, Western educational practices have tended to leave choice of programme to the student, though exceptions are clear in several Western societies. By contrast, in communist society, egalitarian in its outlook, and stressing the universal possession of abilities, little choice is provided. Nevertheless, secondary education programmes in both types of society serve as a screen whereby the academic, the artist, and the artisan are differentiated. It is significant that in both societies universal secondary education is coming to the fore as a major political question, a development which points up the increasing need for higher education everywhere. Although Western societies have had more advanced secondary education programmes for a longer period than communist societies, rapidly increasing populations and changing needs of industry are forcing both societies to examine this level of education more carefully.

The administrative structure of the communist educational system is centralized with all power stemming from the Council of Ministers at the top; but this is not unlike the centralized structure found in France. For the most part, Western societies have decentralized administrative structures on the premise that education is a matter for local control. Canada, for example, has no Federal office of education; but within each of the Provinces the educational system is highly centralized, a form of administration which is also to be found in many of the states in the United States. Primarily the differences in the administrative structures between Western and communist education are less important than the fact that in both systems the responsibility for the final product of the schools is distributed over superintendents, supervisors, principals, teachers, and parents in a way that is common to both systems.

Western and communist educational systems have much in common in the way in which the educational machinery operates as a whole. Where they differ is in the interpretations of official statements as to policy permitted at different levels of the educational system. In communist society the policies once agreed upon and stated may not be adapted to local conditions and viewpoints except with the express approval of the central authority, a condition which makes for uniformity throughout the system. Western society, even where there are highly centralized systems, as in France and in Canada, are more permissive of adaptation of policy, though even here some sectors of education are considered to be inviolable. Though the administrative structures of Western and communist educational systems are alike in many ways, it is yet necessary to recognize that the functions of each vary directly in proportion to the political involvement to be found in the educational systems of both societies.

Communist society decides what goes into its educational programmes through the joint participation of the Soviet of the Union and the Soviet of Nationalities, the Party Praesidium, Ministry officials, members of the Academy of Pedagogical Sciences of the R.S.F.S.R., the Educational and Scientific Workers' Union, and others, in discussions designed to consider the adequacy of what is offered. The Khrushchev Reforms of 1958, designed to bring the schools closer to life and to give students a practical as well as a theoretical education, resulted from widespread discussions throughout communist society over a period of some two years. By contrast, Western society has also been concerned with the content and organization of secondary education curricula, but here the political involvement is noticeably absent. In the main, political bodies in Western societies appoint independent commissions to examine the schools' programmes, and upon receiving the recommendations act or do not act as the case may be. Thus, communist education is more closely identified with the political ethos of communist society than is Western education with its. Indeed, serious gaps have appeared from time to time in the West between what society has expected of the schools and what the schools have done. Despite the evident discrepancy between communist and Western education in respect of the identity of the school with their respective societies, there is nevertheless common recognition of the role the schools play in shaping future citizens. The means differ, but the end, n each instance, is the same.

The process of education in communist and Western societies is essentially alike. This, of course, stems from the nature of the educative process itself wherein teacher and student are bought into a necessary situation and relationship. All of the accoutrements of learning, all of the paraphernalia of instruction are common to both communist and

Western societies. The buildings, classrooms, equipment, gymnasia, playgrounds and offices may, in Western societies, be architecturally and materially superior, but the learning facilities these provide are identical. Again, the books, blackboards, test tubes, biological specimens, models, maps and technical provisions may differ in respect of their form and content, but the purposes these serve within the educative process itself are the same. This, of course, extends to lesson organization and presentation, reviews and drills, and all of the host of technical details involved in having students acquire information, skills and attitudes which are the object of the process itself. An examination of the exercise books of communist pupils is revealing of the uniformly high standard of performance expected of all, and though in the exercise books of Western pupils there would be a wider range of performance, there still remains the high level of expectancy common to both systems.

Communist education, however, differs in one important respect from Western education. Communist society, following the Revolution of 1917, and Lenin's prescription, embarked upon a programme of polytechnicization, by which means theory and practice would be reconciled within the framework of bringing the school closer to life and at the same time make possible the widest possible application of scientific principles to everything of matter and mind. Western education by contrast had, in line with its long humanist traditions, kept the sciences distinct from the humanities, and engaged in long debates as to whether the schools were a part of life itself or a preparation for life. Despite these differences, however, communist and Western education have come to recognize the integral place of science and technology in their educational systems, and the necessity for the greatest possible integration of these two dimensions of learning in the total educative process. What this in effect means is that the general education concepts of Western and communist societies are at base fundamentally similar despite superficial differences of arrangement and organization of courses and programmes.

From the beginning communist society has emphasized politics, science, and technology in its educational programmes, as these are considered to be the realms of learning which can best shape both the individual and society in the image of the ideal state envisaged by communism. This approach is not out of line with what Western societies have striven for except that the humanist tradition plays a much more significant and determinative role in their educational programmes. Both communist and Western educational systems operate within social systems which are determinative of their role in society. The image of man which constitutes the ideal for the communist is one that characterizes him as selfless, co-operative, and efficient. Communist belief holds that man and woman are together capable of achieving the best that is in them by serving the ideal of the state which is individual man writ large. The West adheres to the democratic ideal wherein the state contributes to the development of the individual and is, more often in theory than in practice, subordinate to him. By contrast with the communist, Western man may be considered to be selfish, competitive, even though he is also expected to be efficient. The significance of these two divergent emphases for their respective educational systems is the form which education takes as a result of the social forces at work in each.

Communist society had early placed great emphasis upon the education of children in crèche and kindergarten. At first this emphasis grew out of the need to release the mother for work in industry or on the farm; but it was soon realized that these programmes provided the state with opportunities for the education of the very young in the habits and attitudes desirable for living in communist society. Western society, particularly since the period of the industrial revolution, also placed a great deal of value on early childhood education. In the West, however, this programme stemmed largely from a charitable rather than a political motive. Both communist and Western education, however, view early childhood education as a process of socialization in the course of which the child will acquire those habits and attitudes deemed necessary for their respective societies. In both societies these early childhood education programmes provide for health habits, physical development, social concepts and attitudes, imaginative play and recreation, development of aesthetic and artistic interests. Love of children, and respect for their individuality is common to both types of society.

The curriculum of the schools in communist society is remarkably similar to what is found in Western society. Thus, in the primary schools of both societies, language, mathematics, drawing, music, physical education are to be found in the first three grades, to which are added literature, history, nature study, geography, and foreign language at a later period. In the main, both societies consider the elementary school as the place where the child lays the foundations for later development, socially and intellectually. It is the place, too, where to some extent he reveals his potentialities. Although the secondary school in communist societies differs somewhat in its place in the system from that found in Western societies, its purposes and practices are similar. Thus, in communist societies the secondary programme provides for studies in literature, mathematics, history, constitution, economic geography, physics, astronomy, chemistry, biology, technical drawing, foreign language, and physical education. Provision is also made for practical work in factory or farm, or for some other form of socially useful work. For the most part, Western societies provide similar curricula for their secondary school students, though here considerable differentiation takes place, as for example in the sixth forms of England where either a classic or science side is provided, or as is the case in France where the curriculum of the *lycée* differs from that of the *collège d'enseignement général*. Again, in the United States and Canada, secondary curricula provide for courses of study designed for students proceeding to the university, or different courses which are terminal in character. In both the latter countries of the West, vocational and technical curricula may be provided for in the secondary school.

Communist education, from the earliest grades, requires the pupil to absorb fact and to memorize information. This stress upon acquiring knowledge, however, is not without its distinct advantages; for, in addition, the student at all levels is expected to be able to apply this information to the solution of problems in the course of which he is also expected to be creative. Western education varies greatly in this regard. Among the best schools of Europe and America, the same balance between facts and ideas will apply. On the other hand, there are those educational systems in the West, particularly in non-university secondary educational programmes found in English secondary modern and in Canadian general programmes, where facts are obscured by broad generalizations, and true learning is sacrificed to the holding power of the school. The uniformity of programme to be found in communist education is absent from Western education. One of the results of this communist uniformity is the relatively high drop-out rate of pupils who, since they are not able to benefit from the educational programme offered, soon find their way into industry or agriculture, though here they still have opportunity to pursue educational programmes in evening or extension courses. Western education, by contrast, has been attempting to design educational programmes which will better suit the wide variety of abilities of pupils than a single academic or technical programme can do. The observation programmes of France and the exploratory programmes of Canada are examples of this type of adaptation. In the main, however, both communist and Western educational programmes are similar in respect of selecting the academically able. And both are alike in seeking ways and means of helping pupils achieve all that they are capable of in their respective systems.

The communist educational system administers examinations at elementary, secondary, and higher institutions in both oral and written forms at critical points for the purpose of testing the pupils' knowledge of the field or programme in which he has been studying. Examinations are considered as important for practical as for theoretical programmes. In general, only senior personnel are permitted to set examinations, though the marking and evaluation of these examinations will be allocated to assistants. Western educational practice, particularly in Europe, has been similar in the matter of examinations to that obtaining in communist education, which indeed took its cue from the rest of Europe in the first instance. American practice – in the United States and Canada – has been to place much more emphasis upon written than upon oral examinations, largely because mass education here precluded any simple administration of oral examinations to large numbers of pupils and students. Communist educators, however, have not made use of standardized tests because of the principle of selection and distribution implicit in these. It is contrary to communist ideology to recognize individual differences in innate ability stemming from inherited characteristics, their educators preferring to subscribe to the belief that all at birth are equally educable. Any differences in performance which result from the pupils' exposure to the social and academic life of the community and the school are ascribed to differences in interaction with the environment. In fact, alter the environment and you alter the individual. Although Western society has for its part long debated the issue of nature versus nurture, it continues to debate the issue until such time as it obtains conclusive evidence for either one side or the other. In the meanwhile, the Western bias is towards inheritance though at the same time recognizing the place and force of environment. Communist thinking, in this regard, however, is entirely on the side of the environmentalists. It is within this context that basic differences exist between communist and Western conceptions of instruction and of examination. Nevertheless, since similar situations demand similar procedures irrespective of differences in belief, the pupil in the communist educational system is submitted to the same examination experiences as his Western counterpart.

Special education constitutes another area in which communist and Western societies are alike with respect to concern though unlike with respect to means. Communist society provides for the training of its physically, mentally, and emotionally handicapped children in special programmes in its regular schools, though special schools are also provided for the extremely handicapped. Handicapped children are required to follow the regular programme, with permissible variations in length of time to allow for specific disabilities. Western society has also its special educational facilities for the handicapped, but here there is wide variation as to the means for providing them. In Britain the handicapped are generally provided for in special schools under community jurisdiction, whereas on the American continent there is a wide variation in practice from community-supported institutions to parent-supported institutions. The educational authorities of both societies have come to recognize the need to educate the handicapped, but in the main, communist society has tended to consider this phase of its educational programme as a regular part of its educational system, whereas Western society still considers special education as something apart. Despite this difference in attitude and approach, the handicapped in both types of society now have opportunities to become useful members of society in a way that was not possible even a few short years ago.

There is a remarkable resemblance between Western and communist conceptions of the role of discipline in education. Discipline in both societies is a matter of self-control, of a sense of inner direction. The communist teacher is enjoined not to punish the child physically, but rather to lead him to understand and identify his place and responsibility to himself and others. From the time the communist child becomes a member of the Octobrists and throughout the period of his membership in Pioneers and Komsomol groups, the young communist is subjected to the social sanctions of the group, and measured by the products of his individual performances in school and out. Character training and ethical behaviour are both involved in all that he does or wishes to do. Western discipline is also a matter of individual and social responsibility, but the formal character of the social sanctions is less obtrusive, since in the West children and youth are less subject to formal social organizations directly linked to the state. Western conceptions of discipline place more emphasis on the individual's responsibility, and less on the social sanctions aspect. Fundamentally, however, both societies recognize that they can only continue if they have disciplined individuals who over time come to accept what is the norm for behaviour. The West, too, relies upon religious education to provide a measure of self-discipline, a measure which is absent from communist education. Religion is not usually taught in any school or university in a communist society,[1] and may be forbidden. There are churches, and there is a priesthood, but neither of these is given official recognition by the State, though they must be licensed. Certainly the education provided Soviet youth is devoid of anything pertaining to religion, as that is to be found in parochial and separate schools (and even in some tax-supported school systems) in the West. At first glance there would appear to be no possible common denominator between communist and Western society in respect to this dimension of learning. Yet closer examination reveals that both systems of education are concerned with inculcating a system of values which may serve as a code of behaviour – a value system which, in fact, operates in both societies as guides to individual and social discipline. In this, both societies are at one.

Higher education in communist society is essentially at one with what is meant by the term in Western society, referring to studies and research in universities, colleges, and technological institutes. One sharp contrast is immediately obvious. Higher education in communist society is economically feasible for all who have the ability, a condition which does not apply in Western societies to anywhere near the same extent – where, in fact, many of the best brains are lost to leadership because of lack of opportunity. Higher education in both societies has to do with the education and training of students in all of the fields of knowledge encompassed by the sciences and the humanities. Mathematics, physics, chemistry, history, literature, and so forth, are all

---

[1] There are notable exceptions to this observation in Hungary, Poland and Czechoslovakia, where religious instruction and the performance of priestly duties have been subsidized from state funds; but even there religious life is discouraged. In 1962 Poland discontinued religious instruction in schools. [Ed.]

studied as pure fields in themselves. However, communist education places much more importance upon the application of findings to social need. Thus, the study of linguistics is directed not only to better understanding of the structure and function of language but the findings of this study are applied to the learning of languages as soon as possible. Western society has its long tradition of university scholarship but this tradition, as is the case in Oxford, emphasizes the study of the humanities for their own sake as a liberalizing education without any necessary application of the needs of society. In addition, Western society has for long restricted admission to universities to those economically able to attend, with the result that quite large segments of intellectually able youth are unable to realize their potentialities in behalf of their society. The "ivory tower" concept of the West's higher educational institutions reflects one of its weaknesses. Only since the Second World War has Western society awakened to the significance of the gap between its higher educational institutions and its society.

In its higher education programmes communist society has placed much more emphasis upon science and technology than has the West. It is from these two areas of study and research that communist society draws its ever increasing cadres of specialists needed for development of its industrial and natural resources. Because both industry and education come directly under government supervision it is possible for communist society to control the number of specialists graduated by its institutions and to ensure their employment upon graduation. It is furthermore possible to have the most recent research findings made available to industry, not only through making available a regular stream of recent graduates to every phase of the developing economy, but to ensure that techniques and processes are up-to-the-minute by requiring every scientist and technologist to concern himself with some one or more practical problems in industry, agriculture, education or some part of the economy where his knowledge would be useful in improving processes. Western higher educational institutions are also concerned with pure and applied studies and research, but here there is not the planning nor the close identification with the needs of the economy. Large corporations may indeed have their own scientific laboratories; government agencies will contract for projects at universities and technical institutes, but again this is done on a more or less occasional basis. In the field of education itself the money available for research in the West is pitifully small when compared with what is available for research in other sectors of the economy. Communist society, being closer to its initial revolutionary impetus than Western society, is extending this impetus in a momentum that encompasses research programmes on an ever-increasing scale into all fields of knowledge. Higher education in communist society is essentially considered as the spearhead of an advancing frontier, and, as the frontier of its society, is handled with the zest and zeal of the pioneer.

The higher educational institutions of both communist and Western societies are structurally and in terms of study and research programmes remarkably alike. This similarity extends even to the place and status of personnel within the systems. Where they differ is in respect of the role academics are called upon to play in the advancement of their respective societies. In the West the academic, scientist, humanist, or technologist is looked upon somewhat as a theorist whose ideas may or may not be realistic and particularly relevant to the current problem or situation. By contrast, communist society, though giving primacy to the politician, nevertheless gives the academician a place in the highest councils in order that no political decision be taken without due consideration of expert knowledge. Sectors of Western society also follow this plan, but the very existence of such terms as "longhair" and "egghead" indicate an all-too-popular version of the place and product of the graduate of higher education in the West.

Teacher-training provisions in communist society are remarkably similar to those found in Western society. Programmes for the training of kindergarten, elementary, secondary, technical, and university personnel, though varying in minor details are essentially similar to the Western pattern in respect of length of training, material and techniques, aims and methods. Secondary school teachers are trained in both the University and in Pedagogical Institutes with differences in programme that are sometimes identical with those found in the West. Communist society, however, provides all of these programmes at the cost of the State, with the result that there is no teacher shortage as is found in Western society. Another aspect of this, of course, is the fact that the status of the teacher in communist society is relatively higher than it is in Western society. The status of education in communist society is such that the incomes of personnel in this field are in the top brackets of the society. The interest and enthusiasm to be found everywhere among this category of workers in communist society reflects the social, economic, and political status enjoyed by them. By contrast, teachers and other educational personnel in Western society, though coming under the aegis of the state in many instances, are still frequently required to stand the expense of their own training (notably in America), and upon graduation are almost certain to find that their incomes, relative to other incomes in the community, are relatively low. Thus, though both communist and Western societies recognize the need for rather equivalent types of training for education personnel for their respective societies, nevertheless the differences in emolument indicate a real and significant difference in attitude towards the place of education.

Although community attitudes towards education in communist and Western societies are different, within the education communities themselves there are similarities of another category. University personnel in communist society are as critical of the methods and professional courses in pedagogical institutes as they are in Western society, with this particular difference, that in communist society university personnel are more and more becoming involved in helping to shape the training programmes for elementary and secondary teachers, in a way that has only begun to emerge in Western society. Essentially, communist society considers education at all levels and of whatever kind to be all of a piece, and an integral part of the fabric of society. Western society, on the other hand, still labours under the tradition whereby education was originally designed for the select few in society who would provide the professional and spiritual leadership and be reserved for them alone. The historical dichotomy which attends the educational planning and direction of Western education is thus seen to be absent from communist education. It was this societal dichotomy, of course, which was attacked by the Revolution of 1917, but which the evolutionary process of Western society has as yet not outgrown. In this regard it is well to note the extent to which in both communist and Western society community attitudes towards education are reflected within educational programmes and personnel.

The extent to which this is manifest is perhaps best illustrated through consideration of the role of professional educational personnel in communist and Western societies. In communist society almost all teachers from all levels of the educational system belong to the Educational and Scientific Trade Union and are encouraged to be politically active. Furthermore, the Praesidium will meet with the executive of that Union to discuss the place of educational problems within the total political picture. In Western society, teachers' organizations tend to be fragmented, and in many instances are discouraged from participating in political life. On the surface this would appear to be a very wide gap indeed between communist and Western conceptions of education, except for the fact that in the latter society the programme of studies calls for much closer discussion of the social sciences and the humanities in the course of which the teacher's interpretation of political events provides the student with an insight into the nature of political problems and of the factors involved in arriving at a responsible decision. Communist education places a great deal of emphasis upon political action, and upon an early commitment to communist ideology to the exclusion of other political views. Western publicly provided education prefers to delay commitment until such time as the individual has arrived at years of discretion and is in a position to arrive at a responsible decision based upon all relevant and available facts. Despite these differences in ideological approach both types of society recognize the value of political education for the continued development and preservation of their respective societies.

Apart from the formal provisions for political education in the educational systems of both types of society, Western and communist societies each have informal organizations by means of which youth are acculturated to the political ethos. Communist society is more systematic than Western society in this respect. The Octobrist, Pioneer and Komsomol groups fostered by a communist society are each of them branches of the party system and differ from formal schooling only in that they are to a degree voluntary and informal. However, good standing in Pioneer and Komsomol activities brings with it recognizable rewards within the school system itself. Western society does have its Boy Scouts and Girl Guides and other organizations like the YWCA, but these are not in any way politically identified, nor is there any necessary relationship between what happens in these programmes and what happens in the schools. From the foregoing it is evident that while communist and Western societies are both concerned with the citizenship qualities of their respective youth, they are at the same time placing widely different interpretations upon political theory and its role in shaping their societies. Political practice, if considered in the context of the process of socialization is seen to be identical in both types of society. So far as children and youth are concerned, to be politic is to be in harmony with peers, and to this extent Western and communist societies are in accord.

Though Pioneer Palaces provide educational programmes of an informal character outside of school hours, there are additional agencies which have as their purpose the education of the youth of the society. Theatres, museums, art galleries, libraries, community groups, even department stores and bookstalls, place great emphasis upon the educational interests of children and youth. In some respects it is possible to say that all of communist society is engaged in a vast educational programme of which only a part is in the schools, and that part directed to the youth mainly. This total commitment of communist society to education manifests itself in theatre programmes, providing scientific films for the populace, in exhibitions displaying charts and graphs of industrial and scientific processes, and in communal organizations devoting large portions of programmes to what is considered educative. Thus, the climate of opinion outside of school is entirely supportive of what goes on in school, and this unity of purpose and practice of education in communist society gives the communist youth a sense of mission. Western society likewise has its informal educative agencies outside of school. It has its museums, theatres, clubs, and the like, but the commercial aspects have not always considered the educational outcomes of their entertainment offerings. By contrast with the place of informal education in communist society that of Western society is ill-defined, particularly in so far as there appears an evident unity of purpose between what goes on in school and out of school in communist society, and a sharp disparity between the two realms in Western society.

Throughout communist society, whether in rural or urban centres, collective farm or factory, provision is made for cultural establishments of some form. In the main these may be looked upon as adult education programmes. Thus there are to be found clubs catering to the interests of journalists, painters, writers, architects, actors, tennis and ping-pong enthusiasts, and certainly to the devotees of chess. Other clubs cater to the occupational interests of groups. For the most part these programmes will be identified with social and political questions of the day, but their broad educative function is kept foremost. Whatever form the club may take, whether as part of a tractor station, or as part of a working men's club, or as part of a city or village reading-room, the central purpose is the same: to provide an atmosphere for leisure pursuits which will be conducive to the broadening of the individual's perspectives in line with what is of value to him as an individual and as a member of the society of which he is a part. The West also has its clubs and its adult education programmes as well as its cultural and political institutions. However, Western society varies widely in respect to the forms of these provisions, and just as widely in the matter of State patronage. There was a day in the West when kings and princes prided themselves as patrons of the arts and sciences, but this day passed with the passing of the principalities. Only in recent times have Western societies become aware of the aesthetic hiatus in the body politic, and of the role of government in contributing to this educational dimension of human life.

All societies have their aspirations, and communist and Western societies have many of these in common. Thus, both types of society pay their tribute to sculpture, music, painting, literature, drama, sports and athletics, and the like accomplishments. Both societies recognize that each of these forms of expression derives from individual talent and genius. Both societies provide honours and emoluments in keeping with the degree of achievement. Both societies recognize the value and significance of a diversity of art forms to the aspirations of their peoples. That communist society has seen fit to have these cultural institutions and programmes closely allied with their educational and political institutions does not take away from the values implicit in these programmes. The West does consider art forms necessary to the all round development of the individual, but their cultural institutions are not as closely identified with their educational systems nor is there any real political identification. Communist society does make use of the puppet theatre and cultural palace stage play for propaganda purposes, but within this society's ideology, these are programmes designed to educate the public. Despite this, however, what both societies have in common is a desire through art to reflect their aspirations, and in this both societies provide for the expression of the individual.

Art, in all its manifestations, whether a ballet at the Bolshoi, or a Shostakovitch symphony at the Leningrad Concert Hall, or a banner bearing a picture of Lenin, is always a part of life. Art, in this sense, is in communist society an integral part of the life of the individual and of the nation. Although art is recognized for its culturally aesthetic contribution to the shaping of the individual there is seen to be no necessary discontinuity between art and any other form of practical or theoretical expression in or out of the realm of education. The special honours and emoluments are the same as in any other social endeavour. Art in Western society is also recognized for its culturally aesthetic value, but the idea that art is a necessary part of life is not as clearly countenanced by the political and economic communities of the society. Western society varies widely in the ways in which art is accepted. France, Italy, and Britain have a considerably more mature approach to this realm of human experience than does either the United States or Canada, and communist society lies closer to the European tradition in this respect than do either of the two latter Western societies.

Status follows success in both communist and Western society, and this is as true of education as of any other endeavour. However, success in communist society is measured by the individual's capacity for social, intellectual, technical, artistic, and physical performance at any task, and not by the measure of money obtained as a result of these performances. Money is accorded its due in communist society as in the West, but this due is identified primarily with the social value of the initial performance or product. Money as a measure of individual success has been removed, and in its place there is to be found status deriving from the individual's capacity for contribution to social as distinct from individual success. Communist educators, whether in school or university may add to their basic salaries by writing for their field, but the primary emphasis is upon the professional value of the writing rather than upon the money given in recognition of this value. Western educators may also add to their basic salaries by writing, but where there is a commercial value it will be paid for, but all too many research efforts of educators in the West go unrecognized, unpublished, unpaid, and unrewarded simply because there is no immediate commercial value attached to the writing or the research. The communist educator, like his Western counterpart, is desirous of the best he can personally obtain in the way of his personal life, but this best may not be obtained at the expense of his personal, social, or professional integrity.

As Article 12 of the Constitution of the U.S.S.R. stated in 1938, "The principle applied in the U.S.S.R. is that of socialism: From each according to his ability, to each according to his work." Despite the fact that "work" has been altered to read "need" in later versions, the basic principle operative in the area of status is that of work. As the same article states, ". . . work is a duty and a matter of honour. . . ."

It follows that no work, no status. The better the work, the more widespread the influence of the result of good work, the more important the status. For the realm of education in communist society, this principle has significance with respect to ability in furthering the bounds of knowledge and its early application to the needs of society. In Western society there is an hiatus between the concept of work as premised in education and that in society at large. Status, in Western society, is too often achieved without work. Despite this hiatus, basically both types of society recognize status as a function of effort.

Communist society has had a long tradition of respect for learning. The U.S.S.R., Poland, China, are countries where learning has been held in the highest esteem for generations. The educational systems of these countries, and others of like political persuasion, have over time made their significant contributions to the world of learning, and have produced scholars of the first rank. The political revolutions which altered their régimes did in no wise change the innate respect for learning. If anything, the communist societies which emerged sought to harness the evident goods of education to sustain and direct their political gains. In this regard communist society is seen to give top priority to education in the hierarchy of values, without at the same time forgetting that the tradition of learning established by Lomonosov, Sklowdowska, Lobachevsky, Mendeleyev, and the like, is to be adhered to. It is evident that the revolution did not eradicate the tradition of learning, but rather pointed up the place of this tradition in the people's image of itself.

Though this tradition was in the main redirected by the revolution from the humanistic to the scientific channel, this was done chiefly because a mainly agriculturally oriented society had, following the revolution, to become a mainly industrially oriented society. With this framework, education was seen to be the means by which the society could best make progress in taking its place in the roster of modern nations. So far as communist society is concerned it would appear from the priority given to education at all levels and in all forms that education is considered the single greatest source for energy and direction in their society.

Western society has also had its long tradition of reverence for learning. The Western tradition, however, developed in a stream apart from that in which politics and economics played their roles, with the result that education never was considered as lying in the main stream of the development of societies. With the coming of the welfare state to Western society, however, it looks as if the tradition will undergo change so that political bodies in Western society, like their counterparts in communist society, will see education as integral to social and political development. Both of these types of society recognize that their political systems depend for their success upon the widest possible participation of people in achieving the objects of their societies. This participation, and this achievement, depend upon an educated citizenry in both societies. And both societies, communist and Western, have recognized that science and technology must play an increasingly important part in their educational systems.

Western and communist societies occupy a great many areas of common ground in education, primarily because the broad expanse of the field of knowledge, like the universe, knows no ideological or political bounds. And the men and women who labour in these fields, whether teacher, professor, or academician, humanist, scientist, or technologist, are everywhere possessed of qualities of mind and heart which predispose them to base their judgements and their decisions on rational rather than emotional grounds, to refrain from broad and unfounded generalizations and conclusions without first ascertaining the facts. The men and women of Western and communist societies are both of them subject to the same human weaknesses, and the same kind of strengths, and like their students, and their peers, have humanity for their measure.

There are other areas of common ground. The family unit, in both communist and Western society, provides education with the bulwark for its work. In both types of society the family unit is looked to for strength and support, for providing an atmosphere and a spirit which will foster learning and aspiration. Communist parents are no different from Western parents in this role. And their ambitions for their children differ not a jot. Common ground is to be found, too, in the nature of the educative process itself wherein teachers and students find themselves in similar surroundings, proceeding through progressive steps which are more or less alike. Communist and Western educational systems alike find it necessary to group and classify students according to interest, though ability and aptitude tend to sort themselves out in the communist system. Again, common ground exists in the realms of knowledge deemed necessary and essential for an adequate education. Here, communist and Western education are at one in subscribing to a general education even though "general" on the one hand prescribes the sciences, and the other the humanities, neither being exclusive in either respect. Even here, though, there is more common ground than at first appears evident, particularly in pursuance of the logic of society. A keen awareness of what science has done and can do for man is prevalent in both types of society. Communist and Western education alike concern themselves with peoples whose aspiration are essentially similar in respect of the goals they seek to achieve. Despite ideological and methodological differences the parents in these two types of society have the same ambitions, the same fears, the same hopes, and the same faith in education.

Index

Abitur, 203
absolutes, 6
Academy of Pedagogical Sciences, 122, 288
Academy of Sciences, 178, 181, 184, 194
activity methods, 79, 249
administration (E. Germany), 221
adult education 231, 278
aesthetic education, 61, 104, 129, 232-3, 248, 299-301 (*see also:* Pioneers, &c.)
Afanasenko, 81, 86
aims of education, 286 (*see also:* ideology, and purpose)
Akademik, 184
Alma Ata, 183
American influences, 262, 264-6 (*see also:* Dewey)
Ananiev, 31, 47
Anderson, C. A., 89
apparatus, 63
archaeology, 190
Arnold, Thomas, 2
Ashby, Sir E., 93
aspirantura, 183
association (psychology), 46

Bacon, 238
bed-time, 68
Bentham, 10
Bereday *et al.* (eds.), 79, 89, 101, 130, 138

Berufsschule, 203-04
Binet, 29
Blonski, 32 and foll., 79
boarding schools, 22, 81-82, 151, 185
Bogoyavlenski, 31 and foll.
Boy Scouts, 18
brigades, 20, 80
Britain, 170
budget, 97
Bulgaria, 166, 168, 172, 173, 198

camps, 68
Catholicism (Roman), 18, 94
centralization, 83-85, 103-05, 287
Chiang Kai-Shek, 263
China, Chapter 11, 302
churches, 4, 26
class-teachers, 74
Classical languages, 190
collective, 22, 59, 75, 90, 93,99-100
Comenius, 238 (*see also:* polytechnical idea)
compulsory work service, 139
conscience, 6
"culture", 81, 195-6, 272, 299
curriculum development, 103, 109
Czechoslovakia, 14, 24, 160, 166, 198

Darwin, 10
DeWitt, 131, 150-51, 180
decentralization, 86, 287
dedication, 21

305

INDEX

delinquency, 55, 75
Descartes, 8
Dewey, 78–79, 124, 262
diary, 102
dialectical process, 3, 9 (see also: ideology)
diary (daybook), 80, 102
differences in ability, 29, 49–50, 89
differentiation in schools, &c., see: selection
discipline, 59, 73, 90, 105
Diploma in Technology (U.K.), 170
docent, 182
Dostoyevski, 91–92

eleven-year school, 81, 114 (see also: reforms)
empiricism, 8
enuresis, 76–77
examinations, 80, 84, 292
examinations in China, 258–60
exemption from work service, &c., 84, 134, 141–2, 150
experimentation, 83, 102, 195, 274

Fachschule, 203–04
factories, 81
family, 55 and foll., 75, 81–82, 90
fees, 132, 144, 277
finance, 97
five-point marking system, 80–81, 149
foreign languages, 102, 148, 181, 188, 213
French revolutionaries, 4
Freud, 10
friendship, 17, 72

Gal, R., 83
Gal'perin, 190
Georgia, 179, 186, 188
Germany, East, 163–4, 166–8, 172–3, Chapter 9

Gestalt psychology, 40
Gorer, G., 57
grandmothers, 56
grants (to students), 187, 215

habit-formation, 22–23, 47
handicapped children, 204, 293
handwork, 66 (see also: polytechnical idea, and Pioneers)
Hans, N., 83, 85
Harvard University, 180
Harvard/Newton programme, 126
Hazard, J. N., 55
Hegel, 5, 9
homework, 87, 102
hospitals, 59, 76
humanism, 237–240, 289
Hungary, 166, 168, 198

ideology, Chapter 1, 93–95
illiteracy, 97, 279
industrialization, 160, 288 and foll., 278, 281–2
"inevitability", 4
Inkeles & Bauer, 125
institutes, 184 and foll.
intelligence quotient (I.Q.), 29
interpretation, 13 and foll.

Jamaica, 126
Jersild, 111

kafedra, 182
Kairov, 22, 146, 165, 173
Kalinin, 87–88
Kandel, I. L., 83
Kandidat Nauk degree, 182
Kant, 8, 9
Kazakhstan, 183
Kerschensteiner, 79 (see also: polytechnical idea)

Khrushchev, 84, 94, 98, 132, 139, 142, 164
kindergartens, 60–68, 290
Kirilov, 87
Komsomol, 16, 20, 87, 139
Kondakov, 116
Korol, 180
Korolev, 85
Kostiuk, 43–44
Krupskaya, 79–80, 87, 99, 156–7
kul'tura, 195 (*see also*: "culture")

labour education, *see*: polytechnical idea, and "production".
labour school, 79–80
languages, 179, 270 (*see also*: foreign languages)
Laurentiev, 142
law, 5
learning stages, 40, 44, 48
Lenin, *passim*, and 4, 18, 30, 88, 98–99, 119, 125, 155
Leningrad University, 192
Leontiev, 28, 38–40
Levin, D., 66
libraries, 14
life, training for, 63 (*see also*: polytechnical idea)
literary criticism, 14, 145
Ljubljana, 197
Lomonosov, 92
Lublin, University of, 197
Lunacharski, 79
Luria, 35, 39, 51, 130–31
Lysenko, 14, 130

Makarenko, *passim*, and 28, 91–94, 251
maladjustment, 76
Mannheim, K., 8, 11
Mao Tse-Tung, 270, 280
marking, 73, 80–81, 142, 149
Marx, *passim*, and 2–4, 11, 78–79, 154

materialism, *passim*, and 14, 26, 188
Mead, M., 90
medals, 84
memory-work, 73, 291
Menchinskaya, 31, 47 (*see also*: Bogoyavlenski)
Ministry of Higher Education, 193
minorities in China, 269, 277
minorities in U.S.S.R., *see*: Georgia, Uzbekistan, &c.
missionaries in China, 260, 262
moral education, 15, 22, 94, 240–44, 251 (*see also*: ideology)
morals, 2, 6, 15, 22; (of teachers), 273
More, Thomas, 238 (*see also*: polytechnical idea)
museums, 191, 232, 248

Natural Law, 5
nurseries, 60, 158
Nove, A., 98
Nazism, 201, 206

objectivity, 7
"objectivity" (Party), 11
obrazovaniye, 195
Octobrists, 16
Olympiads, 19, 135
orderliness, 58
Oriental languages, 190
Orthodoxy, influence of, 13, 22–24, 94–95
Owen, Robt., 79, 153 (*see also*: polytechnical idea)

Pädagogische Hochschule, 220
parent committees, 62, 69, 100
partisanship, 24–25 (see "objectivity")
Party role, *passim*, and 13, 25, 90, 221
Party schools, 144, 152, 191

INDEX

Pasternak, 20, 196
Paul, St., 15
Pavlov, *passim*, and 28, 39 and foll., 46, 51
Pearson, K., 30
Pedagogical Institutes, 194 (*see also* teacher training)
personality development, 252-4
physical education, 207
Piaget, 70
Pinkevitch, 79
Pioneers, 16-18, 80-81
planning, 65-67, 84-85, 245-57
Plato, 25
play, 63 and foll., 158-9, 256
Poland, 197, Chapter 10, 302
polytechnical idea, 22, 83-85, 134, 140, Chapter 7, 286, 289
population problems, 236, 267-8
"positive attitude", 15, 17
pragmatism, 89
principals, 109
"production" study, 85-86, 170-73, 224
professor, 182
psychology, Chapter 2
Public Schools (U.K.), 11, 15, 51
publishing, 14, 209
punishment, 59
purpose, sense of, 12-22, 75, 91-92, 94-95, 121, 191, 196, 245-54 (*see also:* polytechnical idea, and ideology)

reading (learning), 69
reason, 8
reforms (1958 &c.), 84, 98, 114-16, 132, 177, 288
religion, 3, 18, 192, 245, 294 (*see also:* theology)
repeating grades, 132, 205, 236
research, 183-5, 194, 205, 295

rest, 68
rules for school, 71, 101
Rumania, 160, 198
rural problems, 81, 255-6

salaries, 111
Sarajevo, 197
school age, 67, 69
school attendance, 70
"science", meaning of, 178
"scientific understanding", 4, 245-6
selection, 84, 89, 109, 115, Chapter 6
shefstvo, 16
Simon, B., 28
social background, influence of, 126-9, 144, 227, 234, 278
socialization, 17, 62, 72, 290
socially useful labour, *passim*, and 20, 160, 175, 185
Spartakiads, 19
Stalin, 80, 132
starting school, 70, 72
stilyagi, 139
streaming, 42, 74
students (in higher education), 117-19, 181, 185, 215, 233
Suchodolski, 3, 12, and Chapter 10
Sun Yat-Sen, 263
swaddling, 56

Tashkent, 179
Taylor, G. R., 112
Tbilisi, 179, 183, 188
teacher training, 61, 70, 113, 117-22, 217-21, 296-7
teachers, Chapter 5, 200, 273-4
teachers in universities, 181, 193
teaching, effect of, 37 and foll.
technicum, 115, 133, 150
Technische Hochschule, Dresden, 214
ten-year school, 81, 114, 132; (in Germany), 160-64, 202 and foll.

308

INDEX

testing, 29, 35, 41
textbooks, 21, 24–25, 98, 103–04, 109, 188
theatres, 21, 233
theology, 190
Thorndike, 38
toys, 63, 158–9
unions, 110, 272, 297
universities, 125, Chapter 8, 294

vacation work, 187
Vigotski, 32 and foll., 48

vocational training, 115–17, 133, 235 (*see*: technicum, polytechnical idea)

women (and girls), 112, 145, 174, 219
Yesipov, 59
Youth organizations, *passim*, and 16, 135, 223, 250, 275, 298–9 (*see also*: Komsomol, Pioneers)
Yugoslavia, 197–8

Zagreb, 197
Zaporozhets, 43–44
Zinchenko, 43